D1784775

B.F.

PROSPECTS FOR NATURAL THEOLOGY

**STUDIES IN PHILOSOPHY
AND THE HISTORY OF PHILOSOPHY**

General Editor: Jude P. Dougherty

**Studies in Philosophy
and the History of Philosophy**　　　**Volume 25**

Prospects for
Natural Theology

edited by Eugene Thomas Long

THE CATHOLIC UNIVERSITY OF AMERICA PRESS
Washington, D.C.

The paper in this publication meets the minimum requirements of
American National Standards for Information Sciences—
Permanence of Paper for Printed Library materials,
ANSI Z39.48–1984.
∞

LIBRARY OF CONGRESS CATALOGING-IN-PUBLICATION DATA
Prospects for natural theology / edited by Eugene Thomas Long.
        p.   cm. — (Studies in philosophy and the history of
philosophy ; v. 25)
     Includes index.
     Contents: Theological clearances / Kenneth L. Schmitz—Reason
and reliance / James Ross — On the very strongest arguments /
George I. Mavrodes — Hermeneutic philosophy and natural
theology / Joseph J. Kockelmans — Natural theology and positive
predication / Frederick Ferré — How to avoid speaking of God /
John D. Caputo — Is a natural theology still viable today? /
W. Norris Clarke — In defense of a kind of natural theology /
Bowman Clarke — Soft natural theology / Ninian Smart —
Experience and natural theology / Eugene Thomas Long —
Theodicy / Louis Dupré.
     ISBN 0-8132-0755-X (alk. paper)
     1. Natural theology.   2. Theology—21st century.   I. Long,
Eugene Thomas.   II. Series.
B21.S78   vol. 25
[BL 182]
100 s—dc20
[210]
91-41756

Contents

Preface

Natural theology, which suffered significantly in the eighteenth century as a result of the criticisms of Hume and Kant, appeared to be a terminal patient by the mid-twentieth century as a result of vetoes by both philosophers and theologians. Since the 1960s, however, several developments in philosophy and theology have led to renewed interest in natural theology. The purpose of this volume is to provide a sample of what some philosophers are thinking about the prospects for natural theology in the last decade of the twentieth century. Pluralism in philosophical method is both intended and evident in this volume. Contributors represent Thomistic, Process, Continental, and Anglo-American approaches to philosophy and they differ with regard to both the prospects and the roles of natural theology. Together, however, the essays provide a map of some of the primary routes being traveled along the road of natural theology as we approach the close of the century.

I want to thank several persons for their support in helping to bring this project to a conclusion. The essay by Louis Dupré in chapter 12 is a significantly revised version of "Evil—A Religious Mystery: A Plea for a More Inclusive Model of Theodicy," published in *Faith and Philosophy* 7, no. 3 (July 1990), 261–80, and portions of the earlier essay are reprinted here with permission of the editors. The essay by Norris Clarke in chapter 8 is a significantly revised version of a paper published in *Physics, Philosophy and Theology: A Common Quest for Understanding* (1988), edited by R. J. Russell, W. R. Stoeger, and G. V. Coyne, and portions of that essay appear here with the permission of the Vatican Observatory Foundation.

This book had its beginning with a conference held at the University of South Carolina in the 1988 fall term to celebrate the one-hundred-year anniversary of the Gifford Lectures. Approximately half of the essays in this volume were presented in their original form at that conference and I wish to thank the Franklin J. Matchette Foundation for its support in that venture. I also want to express special appreciation to Jude Dougherty, Editor of the series in which this volume appears. On this as on many other occasions over the years, his wise judgment has been indispensable and his character and support unfailing.

EUGENE THOMAS LONG

Introduction:
Prospects for Natural Theology
EUGENE THOMAS LONG

I

On August 21, 1885, in the garden of his residence on the northern edge of Edinburgh, Adam Lord Gifford, Associate of Scotland's Court of Session, signed his will. The will provided a trust of 80,000 pounds sterling for the purpose of establishing lectureships in natural theology at the then four Scottish universities, Aberdeen, Edinburgh, Glasgow, and St. Andrews. Lord Gifford died on January 20, 1887, and the first lectures were given during the academic year, 1888–89. Since that time, more than 150 lecturers have contributed to the series, most of the lectures have been published, and some are counted among the classics in natural theology.[1]

It is ironic that Lord Gifford is buried in the old Calton Cemetery only a few yards from the tomb of David Hume. At the time that Lord Gifford signed his will, natural theology was still reeling from the blows of Hume and Kant. And by the mid-twentieth century the illness suffered by natural theology appeared to be terminal as a result of increasingly hostile attacks by theologians and philosophers. The 1960s, however, brought forth what John Macquarrie has called a watershed in religious thought, and some of these currents have led to reconsiderations of the prospects for natural theology, albeit often in different and more limited form.

Natural theology is often understood to refer to the traditional arguments for the existence of God developed in detail by the philosophers of the Middle Ages and appearing most prominently in St. Thomas's Five Ways. Historically, however, there have been two primary traditions of natural knowledge of God. Paul Tillich, in his well-

---

1. For a brief history and list of the Gifford Lectures, Lord Gifford's Will, a selection of Lord Gifford's lectures, and his brother's Recollections, see Stanley L. Jaki, *Lord Gifford and His Lectures* (Edinburgh: Scottish Academic Press, 1986).

known essay "Two Types of Philosophy of Religion," distinguishes two ways of approaching God, the ontological and the cosmological. In the ontological tradition, which can be traced in the early church from Augustine through the Franciscan School of the thirteenth century, God is held to be present and immediately knowable to every soul. God is the basis or the presupposition of the question of God itself. In this tradition, says Tillich, "man is immediately aware of something unconditional which is the prius of the separation and interaction of subject and object, theoretically as well as practically."[2] By contrast, knowledge of God in the cosmological tradition is understood to be a way of rational inference from the world to God, or, better, from·God's effects to God.

The cosmological tradition has a long history in the West, particularly among Thomists, and the ontological tradition can also be traced beyond the Franciscans through the Reformers, the philosophers of the seventeenth and eighteenth centuries, the German classical philosophers, and to much recent philosophy of religion. However, one should probably avoid drawing absolute distinctions between these two traditions, because frequently philosophers and theologians appeal to both in their understanding of natural knowledge of God. Tillich himself gives priority to the ontological tradition but argues for a dependent use of the cosmological approach.

Philosophers and theologians often limit the expression *natural theology* in such a way that it refers primarily to the classical arguments for the existence of God. It is clear, however, that natural theology is also used in a broader and more inclusive sense to refer to all natural knowledge of God arrived at without appeal to the authority of revelation and faith as manifested in a particular community of faith. In his Gifford Lectures, *The Modern Predicament,* H. J. Paton argues that fewer questions are begged if we contrast natural theology with dogmatic theology, where the latter, although it proceeds rationally, is nevertheless ultimately based on authority or revelation.

Given the complex history of natural theology in the West, I myself see little point in providing very restrictive definitions of the subject. Natural theology in the broader sense might be understood to refer to all knowledge of God not dependent on appeals to the authority of special or particular revealed traditions. This would not exclude those approaches that talk in some more universal and less particular way about all knowledge of God as in some sense revealed. And natural theology would be able to appeal to any relevant data including that

2. Paul Tillich, *Theology of Culture* (New York: Oxford University Press, 1959), 22.

of religious experience and would be able to use any philosophical method appropriate to its task. The purpose of natural theology in this case would be to provide connections between religious faith and the more general dimensions of our knowledge and experience.

In the earlier stages of the Christian theological and philosophical traditions, the ontological and cosmological styles of natural theology often walked side by side without clear distinctions being drawn. Augustine and the Franciscan School of the thirteenth century, for example, were not unaware of the Aristotelian and Platonic arguments for the existence of God, but they tended to place primary reliance on an intuited or a priori knowledge of God already present universally in the minds of persons. By the thirteenth century, however, the Aristotelian or cosmological type of natural theology had become dominant under Dominican influence and had received classic expression in the work of Thomas Aquinas.

St. Thomas established a clear distinction between natural knowledge of God (knowledge drawn by rational inferences from the observed world) and revealed knowledge of God. In the first case, "man, by the natural light of reason, ascends to a knowledge of God through creatures," and in the second case, "the divine truth—exceeding the human intellect—descends on us in a manner of revelation, not, however, as something made clear to be seen, but as something spoken in words to be believed."[3] Although Aquinas held that we could not through argument or the natural light of reason know God perfectly as he is in his essence, he believed that we could demonstrate the existence of God from his effects that are known to us.

As John Baillie has suggested in *The Idea of Revelation in Recent Thought,* much of the history of western religious thought can be understood in terms of the relation between natural and revealed knowledge of God, with emphasis shifting from one side to the other. In the Protestant Reformation, for example, natural theology played a diminished role in discussions of religious knowledge. Martin Luther did acknowledge a twofold knowledge of God, one general and available to all persons and one particular and available only in the revelation of God in Christ. General or natural knowledge of God was understood to be dependent on God's revelation in creation and included such knowledge as that there is a God and that God created heaven and earth. This general or natural knowledge of God is said, however, to become perverted by sin and to lead persons to idolatry.

3. Thomas Aquinas, *Summa Contra Gentiles,* bk. IV, chap. I (Notre Dame: University of Notre Dame Press, 1975), 37.

In practice, the emphasis in Luther's theology shifts from general knowledge of God to particular knowledge of God as revealed in Jesus Christ, and little role is given to natural theology. In a related way, Calvin begins his *Institutes of the Christian Religion* with a recognition of the sense of the divine implanted in our minds and acknowledges that the world of nature provides us with evidence of God. But he, too, believed that, given our sinful nature, such knowledge amounts to little.

By contrast with the Reformers, some of the Rationalists of the seventeenth and eighteenth centuries shifted emphasis away from revealed theology back to natural theology. Revelation was often thought to be for the benefit of weaker minds. By the end of the eighteenth century, however, natural theology faced significant challenges in the work of David Hume and Immanuel Kant. Aside from references to mathematical and logical truths, Hume argued that matters of fact were to be tested by reference to experience where experience meant essentially sense experience. On these grounds, Hume rejected metaphysical inquiry and in *Dialogues Concerning Natural Religion* mounted an attack on the classical arguments for the existence of God. In a related way, on the Continent Kant argued that metaphysical inquiry attempted to extend knowledge beyond the limits of experience and ultimately into the realm of the unknowable. From this vantage point, he, too, challenged the classical arguments for the existence of God, arguing that knowledge must make way for faith. Kant displayed his Lutheran roots in this move from knowledge to faith but, unlike Luther, faith for Kant was a rational faith based on practical reason.

Efforts to establish some truths of God by rational inferences from the world were widely understood to have suffered significant blows during the late eighteenth and early nineteenth centuries. J. Hutcheson Stirling, the first Edinburgh Gifford Lecturer, devoted most of his lectures, *Philosophy and Theology,* to a history of the traditional arguments for the existence of God and their criticisms. In doing so, however, he admitted that such might be perceived as merely an antiquarian study and that one who takes them up again might be regarded as a fossil.

The first Gifford Lectures came at the end of a century that had witnessed on the Continent an extension of the Kantian view by Schleiermacher and the Romantics. Dissatisfied with both the tendency to identify religious knowledge with authoritatively communicated propositions of revelation and faith and the tendency to identify religious knowledge with propositions of philosophical rationalism, Schleiermacher sought to recover the spirit of religion in an appeal to religious consciousness. Experience, not the authoritatively communicated truths of revelation and not the truths of speculative reason, was understood to provide the foundation of religious knowledge. The propositions of religious belief were understood to be interpretations and explications of religious consciousness, the feeling of absolute dependence. Efforts to prove the existence of God were judged to be superfluous.

Hegel, Schleiermacher's colleague at the University of Berlin, rejected the classical distinction between natural and revealed knowledge of God and located religious knowledge in religious consciousness. Unlike Schleiermacher, however, Hegel sought to translate the images of religious consciousness into metaphysical concepts. Although Hegel's influence had waned on the Continent, his way of thinking was rediscovered in Britain in the late nineteenth century and formed the basis of a number of the early Gifford Lectures. Although J. Hutcheson Stirling, as mentioned above, devoted most of his 1888–89 Gifford Lectures to a study of the history of the arguments for the existence of God, he was in fact recognized by many as the person most responsible for first introducing Hegel into British philosophy. And, in the first section of his Gifford Lectures, Stirling takes up a theme that had been central to his 1865 study, *The Secret of Hegel.* Stirling says he abhors the view that tends to separate understanding and feeling and he goes on to argue for the need to translate the figurative expressions of faith into rational concepts. While ordinary religious persons tend to think of religion in terms of figurative representations arising from religious consciousness, these representations are often distorted by error and prejudice. Thus there is the need to bring the figurative expressions of faith into clearer rational expression and to lay a philosophical foundation for them. Reason, as understood here, is not the merely intellectual reason of the Enlightenment but refers to a speculative effort to bring differences into relation and to think the unconditional and the infinite.

This Hegelian approach to religious knowledge was a dominant force in late-nineteenth- and early-twentieth-century British religious thought. John Caird, one of the leading Scottish Hegelians, argued that when conceived as formal proofs, the traditional arguments for the existence of God were subject to the criticisms of Hume and Kant. These arguments could not serve as proofs for the existence of God. They could, however, serve a purpose if they were understood as expressions of the stages by which a person moves from a limited secular awareness of reality to a religious or philosophical one. In his Gifford Lectures, *The Fundamental Ideas of Christianity,* John Caird called the distinction between natural and revealed theology an arbitrary and untenable one. The impact of this distinction, he argued, was to fence off revealed religion from critical philosophical intelligence. The question whether reason or philosophy could comprehend revealed ideas was held to be distinct from the question of the source of the ideas, whether or not they were communicated by God. Revelation was said not to add to our ordinary knowledge some supernatural level of knowledge but to enable us to penetrate to the moral and spiritual principles of the world in which we live. Caird argued that even if there were a supernatural revelation, it would still have to be appropriated within the experience and intelligence of humankind, and this process of appropriation he understood to be the province of philosophy.

If the classical arguments for the existence of God suffered significant blows in the eighteenth century, natural theology in all forms was placed in a state of crisis in the first half of the twentieth century. The attack on natural theology came from two directions, one philosophical and one theological. The philosophical threat to natural theology and indeed to all claims to cognition in religion was marked by the publication of A. J. Ayer's *Language, Truth and Logic* in 1936. Building on the doctrines of the Vienna Circle and its so-called principle of verification, Ayer constructed a theory of meaning in language based on the distinction between analytic and synthetic propositions that had been drawn by Kant. On Ayer's account an analytic proposition is one whose validity is dependent on the definition of the symbols contained in the proposition, and synthetic propositions are those whose validity is testable by reference to experience. Since analytic propositions are tautologies and say nothing about the world of experience, it is the synthetic proposition that is relevant to the question of natural theology. Synthetic propositions are held to be meaningful only if they are subject to empirical verification, and by that Ayer means the kind of verification that is used in the physical sciences. On these grounds metaphysical and theological propositions were judged to be meaningless.

In the 1950s, a view related to Ayer's position appeared in Antony Flew's contribution to the symposium, "Theology and Falsification," published in *New Essays in Philosophical Theology*. Flew argued that in order for a statement to be meaningful, one must be able to show what would falsify it, what would count against its being true. And since he had in mind the kind of evidence that would count against an empirical assertion, he also excluded religious assertions from the realm of the meaningful. Efforts to defend the meaningfulness of theological statements while responding to Ayer and Flew on their own grounds often resulted in a reduction of metaphysical and religious assertions to the noncognitive. Religious assertions were stripped of factual and metaphysical meaning and were said to express attitudes toward life and world. On R. B. Braithwaite's account, for example, religious statements are expressions of an intent to behave in a certain way, to carry out a certain policy. The Christian's statement, "God is love," should be understood as a declaration of her intention to behave in an agapeistic way that she associates with certain Christian stories. In a related way, R. M. Hare argued that on his own grounds Flew was victorious and that religious utterances should not be thought of as making factual assertions. Rather, religious utterances were said to express *bliks* or attitudes that were neither verifiable nor falsifiable.

The theological attack on natural theology was presented most forcefully in the work of Karl Barth. Indeed, in some ways Barth provided an even more hostile attack on natural theology, albeit on the grounds of religious faith. Barth made it clear in his Gifford Lectures, *The Knowledge and Service of God*, delivered at the University of Aberdeen in 1937–38, that he was an opponent of natural theology. His reaction to natural theology was rooted in part in his objection to the nineteenth-century tendency to overemphasize the continuity between God and man and in his assertion of the complete otherness of God. But it was also rooted in a deep sense of the sinfulness of persons and an inherent distrust of reason as a source of theological truth. So deep was his distrust of human activity and reason that he rejected religion itself, including the Christian religion, on the grounds that all religions represent human attempts to conceive God from human standpoints, efforts closely related to those by means of which persons seek to justify and sanctify themselves. According to Barth, we have to put aside all our efforts to apprehend the truth of God. God's revelation shows us that in the view of God all our activity is in vain. We must no longer seek the truth but only respond to God's Word in obedience.

During the period dominated by the philosophical and theological vetoes of metaphysics and natural theology, existentialist thought provided for many an approach to religious knowledge that did not call for a sacrifice of the intellect. Speculative metaphysics, which sought to extend reason beyond the limits of the empirical world, was suspect. In varying degrees, however, twentieth-century existentialist philosophers and theologians, while distrusting speculative metaphysics, remained open to metaphysics and natural theology of a more limited kind. For many who were studying philosophy of religion and theology during the 1950s, the philosophy of Karl Jaspers and Martin Heidegger and the theology of Rudolf Bultmann and Paul Tillich provided alternatives to the ways of Ayer and Barth. Like Augustine, these thinkers explored the depths of the meaning of human existence, which was believed to point to an inexhaustible transcendence. Natural theology, however, was often limited for the most part to questions of the meaning of human existence. Bultmann, for example, claimed that natural knowledge of God was a negative knowledge of God that at best showed man's inquiry after God. Bultmann's effort to translate theological statements into statements about human existence resulted in a limited ontology and his efforts in dealing with questions concerning the justification of religious belief were far from adequate.[4]

In the mid-twentieth century, then, prospects for natural theology appeared to be rather limited. There were exceptions, of course, but in general neither the theological nor the philosophical climate appeared to promise support for the view that there were standards independent of the authority of revelation and faith by which religious claims could be evaluated. Beginning with the 1960s, however, there were visible signs of change in religious thought, some of which subsequently have led to renewed interest in the question of the place and viability of natural theology.

II

One sign of this change was the emergence of a broader conception of experience. If experience is conceived narrowly, either in terms of science or in terms of subjective or self-authenticating states of consciousness, there is little room for natural theology in either older or newer forms. As the American philosopher John Smith has reminded us on numerous occasions, however, such theories of experience are inadequate. In "The Experiential Foundations of Religion" (1958), Smith distinguishes between two principal theories of experience, the classical British theory in which experience is generally understood to refer to sense experience and a broader theory, sometimes called radical empiricism, that can be found in the work of philosophers as diverse as Hegel, Bradley, James, Dewey, Whitehead, and Heidegger. According to this broader conception of experience, "experience is not a single affair, an identifiable subject matter such as sense, or particulars, or impressions of the mind, but is something initially far

4. Eugene Thomas Long, *Jaspers and Bultmann: A Dialogue Between Philosophy and Theology in the Existentialist Tradition* (Durham: Duke University Press, 1968).

more complex and vague; it is a great mass of contents resulting from the interplay between the self and the world in which it lives."[5] Only if we reconstruct our conception of experience along the lines of this broader view, Smith argues here and in many subsequent publications, will we be able to talk in any significant way of religion as a dimension of human experience. Smith himself holds that direct although not immediate experience is an indispensable ground for belief in God. The long history of rational arguments for the existence of God is said to have no compelling force unless the person understands what is meant by the term "God." And this, he argues, is impossible apart from the kinds of experiences that are generally described as religious.

In Great Britain, there were also signs of the development of a broader conception of experience. In 1959, H. D. Lewis, who describes himself as a realist at home in the British common sense tradition, published *Our Experience of God*. Lewis argued that religion requires definite commitments and must be subject to claims of truth and falsity in some ordinary sense. The solution to the question of the justification of religious belief to be presented in this book, wrote Lewis, "will be in terms of experiences which have this peculiarity, that while they remain in themselves finite throughout, that is have a content appropriate only to finite beings like ourselves, yet they can be seen to have also a reference beyond that; and in their patterns and ramifications in experience as a whole, they afford us the clue we need to the way unconditioned reality on which we are dependent enters into special relations with us and discloses itself, through this communication as a personal being addressing himself to individuals and present to them."[6]

There were also signs of a broader conception of experience and renewed interest in natural theology among British philosophers in other traditions. In 1961, *Prospects for Metaphysics,* edited by Ian Ramsey, was published in England. The book consists of essays read originally at a conference organized by Ramsey at Downside Abbey in 1959. In introducing the volume, Ramsey speaks of the reasons for holding the conference and says, "Thirty-five years ago metaphysics was no more than a topic for abuse and ridicule. But in more recent days there has been evidence of a broader empiricism willing to leave room for the possibility of significant metaphysical discourse." He adds that the contributors to the volume share a sympathy for some of the insights of contemporary empiricism and says, "Common to us

---

5. John Smith, *Reason and God* (New Haven: Yale University Press, 1961), 174.
6. H. D. Lewis, *Our Experience of God* (London: George Allen and Unwin, 1959), 58.

all, for instance, is the position that we can no longer view natural theology as a tight, rigorous, deductive system, taking us to God by a process of unmistakable inference."[7] Nevertheless, the alternative to natural theology conceived as a rigorous deductive system was not judged to be irrationalism by the contributors to that volume.

Howard Root's essay, "Metaphysics and Religious Belief," consists of a critical evaluation of recent theologians and philosophers who have attempted to make Christian faith immune from philosophical inquiry. He concludes his essay with the following remark: "If we continue to say that there are reasons for accepting one set of beliefs rather than another, we are that far committed to something which I should call metaphysics. And it will have to be a metaphysics which can somehow do justice to our desire for a Natural Theology but also to our religiously inspired distrust of Natural Theology. Just what it would look like is very much worth finding out."[8] None of the essays in the volume gives us a fully developed picture of what such a natural theology might be but there are suggestions. Father C. B. Daly, for example, argues that metaphysics begins with the recognition of mystery in being and experience. The aim of the metaphysician is to make sense of the meta-empirical within the empirical. This does not mean that theistic metaphysics claims that everything is clear and all problems have vanished. Rather, the theistic metaphysician "postulates intelligibility only in the minimal sense that being shall not be self-contradictory, or absurd. All proofs for the existence of God are, in one form or another, a *reductio ad absurdum et contradictorium* of the nonexistence of God. They try to show that the non-admission of God is the inadequacy of description which admits to a contradiction: treating part of experience as if it were the whole."[9]

Ninian Smart, who begins his essay with the claim that natural theology is the sick man of Europe, goes on to consider whether or not there is a middle way between traditional natural theology and some simple appeal to revelation or any other authority. He concludes by arguing for a limited kind of natural theology, one that claims that traditional metaphysics "expresses, or even evokes intuitions or disclosures of divine being."[10] And Ian Ramsey, following the suggestion of Whitehead that metaphysics has to do with framing a scheme of ideas and exploring the interpretations of experience in terms of these schemes, says that the broad purpose of metaphysics is "to elaborate

7. Ian Ramsey, ed., *Prospects For Metaphysics* (London: George Allen and Unwin, 1961), 7.

8. Ibid., 79.   9. Ibid., 204.

10. Ibid., 81.

some explicit interpretive scheme, critically suited as far as may be to the whole of experience."[11] By the whole of experience Ramsey has in mind something broader than can be explored by the natural sciences. Just because of this, metaphysical concepts or what he calls integrators must have their grounding in what is more than spatio-temporal. The concept of the self is an example of such a metaphysical concept or integrator, as when in a disclosure situation I realize that I am more than the observable behavior that I display. God is understood to be an even more general integrator term "when we speak about God by qualifying any and all descriptive language—whether of people, human behaviour, or the Universe—in such a way that tells more than a descriptive story, in such a way that it evokes a disclosure, and this I suggest is most generally done either by qualifying descriptive language infinitely or qualifying descriptive language negatively."[12] According to Ramsey, we judge the adequacy of our metaphysics in accordance with the success of the integrator concepts in effecting a unified scheme.

III

A second development that has helped contribute to renewed interest in natural theology is the recognition given to the relation of argument and experience in religious knowledge. If, at some points in the past, the way of religious experience and the way of argument were seen in opposition to each other, resulting in an impasse, this seems to be much less the case in recent thought. This has already been hinted at above but needs to be made more explicit. In *The Justification of Religious Belief* (1973), Basil Mitchell develops more fully some of the suggestions implicit in his earlier response to Flew in the "Theology and Justification" article mentioned above. Mitchell argues that, although it is not possible to prove traditional theism or even to render it probable in any strict sense by means of argument, it is also not possible to show it to be false or logically incoherent. The traditional arguments for the existence of God, which Mitchell regards as failures when treated as attempts at purely deductive or inductive arguments, can be understood as contributing to a cumulative case. "Prima facie the elements of the theistic scheme do tend to reinforce one another in a way that is recognisable both by theists and by opponents. Thus although the cosmological and teleological arguments do not (if our criticism of them was correct) prove that there must be

11. Ibid., 154.   12. Ibid., 173.

a transcendent creator of the world, they do make explicit one way (arguably the best way) in which the existence and nature of the universe can be explained."[13] One may, of course, argue that the universe does not require explanation in this sense and leave it at that. But Mitchell argues that the situation is altered when we add to the theistic explanation the claim of some persons to have experienced the presence of God or to have witnessed the action of God in the world.

William Alston, John Hick, and others have argued that there are similarities between religious experience and perceptual experience and that we find ourselves in somewhat analogous situations in these cases of experience. On Alston's account, Christian epistemic practice has essentially the same epistemic practice as perceptual epistemic practice. Religious experience may be said to provide prima facie justification for religious belief provided that one does not have significant reasons for regarding it as unreliable, for example, internal inconsistency or ineradicable conflicts with other beliefs to which one is more firmly committed.[14] John Hick argues in a related way that religious experience may constitute a good prima facie ground for religious belief. The proper role for natural theology, according to Hick, is not to prove the existence of God or even show it to be probable "but to establish both the possibility of divine existence and the importance (that is, the explanatory power) of this possibility. I believe that reason can ascertain both that there may be a God and that this is a genuinely important possibility. In that case theistic religious experience has to be taken seriously."[15]

Changing conceptions of experience and argument also helped prepare the context within which philosophers would begin the task of reconstructing and understanding anew the classical arguments for the existence of God. In 1969, for example, James Ross in *Philosophical Theology* provided what he referred to as the beginning of an analytic reconstruction of natural theology, a task to which he has given much effort since that time. He rejected the views of some contemporary Protestant theologians who argued not only that one could not prove God's existence but that such efforts were blasphemous. He also rejected, however, the views of some neo-scholastics who claimed that the existence of God could be demonstrated to any intelligent and

13. Basil Mitchell, *The Justification of Religious Belief* (London: Macmillan, 1973), 40–41.

14. William Alston, "Religious Experience and Religious Belief." *Nous* 16 (1982), 3–12.

15. John Hick, *An Interpretation of Religion* (New Haven: Yale University Press, 1989), 219.

unprejudiced person and that such demonstrations were based upon self-evident truths. Ross's aim in this book was to show that the rejection of arguments for the existence of God is based in part at least on a failure to understand what is meant by proof and that constructive natural theology is a purely theoretical inquiry that is not undertaken for the purpose of apologetics. "Believers who are waiting and wanting to ground their faith in the achievements of philosophy are waiting for a train that does not stop here; it is their misfortune that so many of our predecessors apparently promised that it would."[16]

Ten years later, in his study *The Existence of God,* Richard Swinburne, appealing to recent developments in inductive logic, also devoted his attention to reconstructing the arguments for the existence of God. He argues that various phenomena, for example the existence of the universe, are more probable if there is a God than if there is not. Swinburne challenges what he considers to be the narrow boundaries of reason in the work of Hume and Kant and says that "those who believe in the ability of modern science to reach justified (and exciting) conclusions about such things far beyond immediate experience, as subatomic particles and nuclear forces, the 'big bang' and cosmic evolution, ought to be highly sympathetic" to his enterprise.[17] On Swinburne's account, unless it is significantly more probable than not that there is no God, religious experience itself is a good reason for believing in the existence of God, and he argues that the total evidence for theism is more probable than not.

IV

A third development relevant to the renewed interest in natural theology after the mid-twentieth century is the new attention given to the work of Alfred North Whitehead. When Whitehead delivered his Gifford Lectures in 1927–28 at the University of Edinburgh, British Idealism had been in decline for two decades and had all but disappeared. Whitehead and Bertrand Russell had published *Principia Mathematica* during the years 1910–15 and the so-called revolution in philosophy leading to a more realistic and more scientific way of thinking was underway. In his Gifford Lectures, *Process and Reality,* Whitehead reflected the development of the realistic and scientific mode of thinking of his time, but he diverged significantly from the growing anti-metaphysical tendencies. In the Introduction to his lectures, he

16. James Ross, *Philosophical Theology* (New York: Bobbs-Merrill, 1969), 321.
17. Richard Swinburne, *The Existence of God* (Oxford: Oxford University Press, 1979), 2.

reports his indebtedness to the English and American Realists, but also to Bergson, James, and Dewey, and says that while he is often in sharp disagreement with Bradley, the final outcome may not be so greatly different. It is natural, says Whitehead, to ask whether his type of thought be not "a transformation of some main doctrines of absolute idealism onto a realistic basis."[18] Whitehead and Charles Hartshorne, whose own work was much influenced by Whitehead, are responsible for the development of a new form of natural theology known as process theism.

The 1950s and 1960s saw the publication of a number of new studies of Whitehead's philosophy, and several younger philosophers and theologians began to develop their own approaches to natural theology based on the work of Whitehead and Hartshorne. In *The Reality of God,* a collection of essays published in the mid-sixties, Schubert Ogden suggested that in Whitehead's thought all the main themes of metaphysics are given a neoclassical expression that meets and overcomes the criticisms of classical metaphysics. He goes on to say that through Hartshorne and others these same insights have been further developed and applied to problems of natural or philosophical theology. Ogden writes, "It is my belief that the conceptuality provided by this new philosophy enables us so to conceive the reality of God that we may respect all that is legitimate in modern secularity, while also fully respecting the distinctive claims of Christian faith itself."[19]

In 1964, John Cobb published *A Christian Natural Theology,* a book Cobb describes as heavily dependent on Whitehead. Cobb agrees with those who argue that when we think philosophically we cannot avoid thinking within some context and says, "If natural theology means the product of an unhistorical reason, we must reply that there is no such thing."[20] He goes on to argue, however, that responsible theological thinking takes one beyond the boundaries of one's own community of faith and that what is learned there is of relevance to the truth or falsity of religious faith. According to Cobb, either theologians will become increasingly dogmatic, looking only to their own traditions for answers, or they will recognize that they bring presuppositions to their work as theologians that must be submitted to rational evaluation in a more general or universal context. In the latter case, says Cobb, the theologian "must acknowledge the role of something like natural the-

18. Alfred North Whitehead, *Process and Reality* (New York: Harper and Brothers, 1957), VIII.
19. Schubert Ogden, *The Reality of God* (New York: Harper and Row, 1963), 56–57.
20. John B. Cobb, Jr., *A Christian Natural Theology* (Philadelphia: Westminster Press, 1965), 261.

ology in his work."[21] Cobb admits that every natural theology depends upon some fundamental perspective and that no philosophical world view can be judged to be true and absolute for all times. He argues, however, that Whitehead's metaphysics provides a particularly suitable framework for a Christian natural theology that takes seriously the biblical faith.

A year later, Bowman Clarke published *Language and Natural Theology*. Like Ogden and Cobb, Clarke was a student of Hartshorne, albeit one with a somewhat different bent. Clarke begins and ends his book with a quotation from Whitehead that reads as follows: "When in the distant future the subject [Symbolic Logic] has expanded, so as to examine patterns depending on connections other than those of space, number and quantity . . . I suggest that Symbolic Logic . . . will become the foundation of aesthetics. From this stage it will proceed to conquer ethics and theology. The circle will have made its full turn, and we shall be back to the logical attitude of the epoch of St. Thomas Aquinas."[22] This quotation from Whitehead is very suggestive of Clarke's proposals in this volume and in his subsequent work.

Building on Whitehead's conception of metaphysics, Clarke argues for a descriptive as opposed to an emotivist theory of religious language. Using the tools of contemporary logic and linguistic studies, he provides a reconstruction of the traditional arguments for the existence of God with the intent of providing a definite description for the name *God*. In this way, Clarke seeks to counter the claim that metaphysical propositions are either meaningless combinations of words or concealed scientific statements and to show that a definite description of God in the process tradition can be religiously adequate. The purpose of natural theology, says Clarke, "is to connect religion through its general ideas to philosophy, particularly to that area of philosophy which deals with the most general categories of existence— metaphysics."[23] Natural theology, Clarke concludes, is a necessary condition for religion in the Christian tradition but not a sufficient condition. For religion to have significance for the practical life of persons, natural theology must be supplemented by revelation and revealed theology.

The work of Whitehead and Hartshorne has had significant impact on natural theology and the philosophy of religion since the 1960s, particularly in the United States. Indeed, a recent critic has described

---

21. Ibid., 262.

22. Bowman Clarke, *Language and Natural Theology* (The Hague: Mouton, 1966), 168–69.

23. Ibid., 80–81.

process theology as the principal competitor with traditional Christian theism. Only in the United States, perhaps, will one find (or would one expect to find) automobile bumper stickers which read "One more family for Whitehead," but there is also evidence of new interest in process philosophy and theology in Europe.

V

A fourth development relevant to the question of natural theology can be found in the traditions of existentialism and phenomenology. Existentialist philosophy of religion and theology can, with justification, be widely praised for its insights into the experience of what it means to be human and can, in most cases, be defended against the more extreme charges of subjectivism and irrationalism. However, some of the earlier existentialists were criticized for their failure to develop a more adequate ontology, a failure to face squarely the issue of secularization and a failure to deal adequately with questions relating to the justification of religious belief. In the Sixties, however, there began to emerge a number of younger philosophical theologians in this tradition who were attempting to work beyond these problems and lay a more solid foundation for understanding the meaning and truth of religious faith in a secular world, one in which some traditional forms of metaphysical thought seemed no longer acceptable.

Langdon Gilkey and his 1969 book, *Naming the Whirlwind: The Renewal of God-Language,* can help to illustrate this development. Gilkey, writing only a few years after the heyday of the death-of-God theologies, criticizes the radical theologians for having presented inadequate interpretations of both the Christian faith and general human experience. But he believes that these thinkers, more clearly than most, discerned and expressed the anatomy of this period of time. What they have shown us, according to Gilkey, is that the question of religious skepticism is not only a question for the nonreligious. It is also a question within the community of faith where the reality of God itself is in dispute, not just whether we can speak meaningfully of God or prove his existence. Gilkey wants to face up to this situation and to the radically secular context in which the meaning and truth of religious faith is guaranteed neither by the experience of faith nor by a system of metaphysics. Just because the world of religious and metaphysical doubt is also part of the world of the community of faith, any theology, says Gilkey, has to be apologetic as well as kerygmatic, and this means that it has to take some form of natural theology or what Gilkey prefers to call prolegomenon to theological discourse.

At this time, post-Bultmannians such as Heinrich Ott and Gerhard Ebeling, with the aid of the hermeneutical tradition, were attempting to get beyond some of the problems that they found in Bultmann's work. But Gilkey does not believe that we can find here a solution to the problems that he raises, for they begin by assuming that the reality of God is already known in faith. Neither does he believe that speculative philosophy in either the Thomist or the Whiteheadian forms can provide the way forward. Both traditions are said to depend on assumptions concerning the ability of philosophical reasoning to establish the reality of God and the intelligibility of language about God that the secular mind finds difficult to make. Gilkey does believe, however, that it is necessary that one develop a natural theology or prolegomenon to faith that does not presuppose the ultimate rationality of experience or the meaning and truth of revealed faith.

Gilkey's own phenomenological approach shares much in common with his mentor, Paul Tillich, although Gilkey refers to his descriptions of experience as more ontic than ontological in structure. Gilkey's aim is to examine the meaning of religious symbols by examining our experience as beings in the world, uncovering or showing the hidden or forgotten dimensions of ultimacy that are held to appear in our experiences of contingency, relativity, temporality, and autonomy. In this prolegomenon, the emphasis is on describing and interpreting, opening up the possibility of an intuitive recognition of the sense of ultimacy within human experience, not on demonstrating or proving in the stricter sense. In the prolegomenon we are said not to approach directly the existence or character of the divine. Gilkey does seem to recognize an implicit ontology on this interpretation of experience but says that, for a more definite symbolization of this "reality" encountered within the ultimate regions of experience, one needs to turn to a more positive theology, to a definite apprehension of the sacred in a definite tradition of symbolic forms.

In his *Principles of Christian Theology,* published first in 1966, John Macquarrie agrees with those who say that natural theology, defined as proofs for the existence of God, is in disarray. While recognizing that there are those who have sought to reformulate the arguments in ways that would avoid some of the defects of older versions, he observes that even in these cases persons no longer claim for the arguments cogency as proofs in the strict sense. Macquarrie does not, however, deny value to the traditional arguments; he later develops his own anthropological argument for God and, in the 1977 revised edition of *Principles,* he suggests, in agreement with Basil Mitchell, that the classical arguments could contribute to a cumulative case. But for Macquarrie, argument follows experience, and he proposes a new style of natural theology in which one presses back beyond the traditional arguments to the experiences and convictions that are said to lie beyond them.

Macquarrie stands in the existential-ontological tradition of Martin Heidegger and says that his new style of natural theology is phenomenological or descriptive rather than deductive in method. His aim is not to prove God exists but to let us see the phenomenon of faith in the basic human situation in which it is rooted. He also describes his natural theology as existential rather than rationalistic. This does not mean that his approach is anti-rational. He chooses the term *existential* to emphasize that the kind of reasoning in which he is engaged is one that arises out of the whole range of our experience as beings in the world. Natural theology in Macquarrie's sense takes as its starting point a secular description of the structures of existence and Being and then attempts to place distinctively religious concepts such as grace, faith, and God on the ontological map of the Being of human existence. In his Gifford Lectures, *In Search of Deity,* delivered at St. Andrews in 1983, Macquarrie argues that Hume's and Kant's criticisms of the traditional arguments for the existence of God are closely tied to classical theism, and that his own form of natural theology depends on a dialectical conception of God.

VI

A fifth development that has contributed to renewed interest in natural theology, and the final to be developed in this essay, can be found in the emergence of the rich and diversified movements called Neo-Thomism and transcendental Thomism. These movements are usually associated with the Roman Catholic tradition, although there are some Anglican thinkers such as A. M. Farrer and Eric Mascall who are also referred to as Neo-Thomists. Although Neo-Thomists and transcendental Thomists at times have significant disagreements, they are united in their indebtedness to Thomas and Aristotle, their realism and their belief in the possibility of metaphysics.

In 1960, Robert Caponigri published a collection of essays, *Modern Catholic Thinkers,* written by contemporary Roman Catholic thinkers, that was intended to dispel what Caponigri called the myth that Roman Catholic thought is characterized by an uncritical and monolithic uniformity that sets it apart from and makes it an enigma to modern critical intelligence. In his introduction to the soft-cover edition of this collection of essays, Caponigri comments that Catholic thought has classically indicated two ways in which persons come to the knowledge and presence of God, one that sends a person out into the world of nature, thence to ascend to God, and the other that sends one into the depths of one's own being to discover the indwelling of God. Catholic thought, he says, has always considered these two ways to be compatible and mutually sustaining, but in different periods of time emphasis has tended to shift from one to the other. In our age, the emphasis is said to be more on the indwelling presence of God.

Neo-Thomism and transcendental Thomism both have their origins in the nineteenth century, the former with the 1879 encyclical of Pope Leo XIII, commending the study of Thomas Aquinas, and the latter with Joseph Marechal, whose work was little known in his time. Neo-Thomism was well established during the earlier half of the twentieth century by thinkers such as Jacques Maritain and Etienne Gilson, and transcendental Thomism, too, had developed a significant following by the mid-century through the work of such persons as Bernard Lonergan and Karl Rahner. However, both traditions received a new stimulus with the Second Vatican Council. As Lonergan has said, "For over a century theologians have gradually been adapting their thought to the shift from the classicist culture, dominant up to the French Revolution, to the empirical and historical mindedness that constitutes its modern successor. During this long period there has been effected gradually an enormous change of climate. It crystallized, burst into the open, and startled the world at Vatican II."[24]

Jacques Maritain begins his book *Approaches to God* by declaring that, while Kant correctly criticized the ontological proof for the existence of God, he erred in his claim that all demonstrations of God's existence depend on or can be reduced to that proof. Aquinas's Five Ways, according to Maritain, can be shown to be independent of the ontological argument and can be supported in face of philosophical criticisms. These arguments are understood as a development or unfolding of a pre-philosophical knowledge of the existence of God to the level of scientific discussion and attitude. This pre-philosophical knowledge of God is said to depend on the natural intuition of Being and to precede metaphysical or philosophical knowledge in the strict sense.

Maritain does not believe that the Five Ways would be regarded as demonstrations, whatever the presuppositions of those we are trying to convince with the arguments. This does not lead him to hold, however, that the arguments are valid only in the context of Thomistic

24. David Tracy, *The Achievement of Bernard Lonergan* (New York: Herder and Herder, 1970), XI.

philosophy. He argues that those philosophers who do not receive the Five Ways as demonstrations are in error in rejecting from the beginning several primordial truths and original apperceptions that are said to support the noetic structure of knowledge as such. Maritain believes that Thomistic philosophy best justifies these principles, but he also believes that other philosophical traditions in the East and West recognize and cultivate these truths.

The work of such Neo-Thomists as Maritain and Gilson help provide the foundations for many Roman Catholic philosophers and theologians today who are engaged in efforts to converse with other religious and secular philosophical traditions. Others in the Thomist tradition, however, are more likely to turn to the transcendental Thomists for resources. Among the most important transcendental Thomists are certainly Bernard Lonergan, whose work is perhaps more clearly in the Thomist tradition, and Karl Rahner, who brings Thomas and Heidegger into dialogue. Another transcendental Thomist influenced by Thomas and Heidegger is Emerich Coreth.

In his book *Metaphysics,* Coreth provides a brief history of the development of this approach to Thomism. He argues that the method that Kant called the transcendental method, and that Kant worked out in detail, was in fact known about long before Kant. He traces it to Plato's doctrine of the Ideas, and to Augustine's discussion of a divine illumination of the eternal verities present in the human mind, and says that the Augustinians within scholastic philosophy remained faithful to this view. Thomas, who attempted to combine the Aristotelian and Augustinian views, was also aware of the a priori conditions of human knowledge, but after Thomas the Aristotelian tradition came to dominate Scholastic philosophy.

Gilson is critical of the transcendental turn among some Thomists and argues that this approach can only lead to phenomenalism or idealism. But Coreth does not believe this to be the case. The cause for Gilson's concern is located in Kant's turning our attention away from the objects themselves to the a priori conditions of the possibility of our knowing objects. For Kant, the principles and concepts of pure reason are limited to the realm of sense experience, and even these objects are known only as they appear to us. On this account, says Coreth, metaphysics no longer has an objective but only a subjective function, and metaphysics has lost its foundation in being. Coreth shows appreciation for Kant's transcendental turn but argues that metaphysics is impossible without a relation to being. We must proceed beyond Kant, he argues, "to show that our a priori knowledge is metaphysical knowledge of being, which opens for us the absolute horizon of being as such."[25] On this account the primary task of metaphysics is not to demonstrate or discover what is new or unknown but to make explicit what is implicit or latent in our knowing, or better, in our questioning.

The condition of the possibility of questioning is being itself, and the unthematic or implicit knowledge of being is said to underlie all the demonstrations of God's existence and to be made explicit in them. Explicit knowledge of God requires the mediation of the world but it depends on an original and immediate knowledge of the necessary character of being. We come to know the necessary character of absolute being when it is distinguished from finite beings which are shown not to be necessary but to presuppose being beyond themselves. Knowledge of God, then, is not a passage to something totally unknown, but an explication of our knowledge of the necessity of absolute being.

In a related way, Karl Rahner argued in *Foundations of the Christian Faith* that transcendent knowledge or experience of God is a posteriori in that our experience of our subjectivity takes place only in our encounter with other persons and things. Because of this, he says, the Scholastic tradition is correct in emphasizing that our knowledge of God is a posteriori. Nevertheless, the knowledge of God is said to be a transcendental knowledge "because man's basic and original orientation towards absolute mystery which constitutes his fundamental experience of God, is a permanent existential of man as a spiritual subject. This means that the explicit, conceptual and thematic knowledge, which we usually think of when we speak of the knowledge of God or of proofs for God's existence, is a reflection upon man's transcendental orientation towards mystery. . . ."[26] We would misunderstand the a posteriori character of knowledge of God, says Rahner, if we meant by this that we look out onto the world with a neutral faculty of knowledge and then think we can discover God there directly or indirectly, or indirectly prove his existence.

VII

Given these developments during the last three decades, and the one-hundred-year anniversary of the Gifford Lectures, it seems an appropriate time to take some soundings of the current prospects for natural theology. The symptoms of recovery, like the symptoms of

25. Emerich Coreth, *Metaphysics* (New York: Herder and Herder, 1968), 36.
26. Karl Rahner, *Foundations of the Christian Faith* (New York: Crossroad, 1984), 52.

disease, can be found in American and British as well as Continental thought. Yet there is no clear consensus regarding natural theology, even among those who agree that in some form it is a needed and viable enterprise. Even less is there an expectation that there will emerge a single metaphysical scheme capable of taking into account the rich diversity of human experience of ultimate reality, East and West. That several sets of recent Gifford Lectures have been devoted in whole or in part to issues dealing with the relations between different forms of religious faith is testimony to the impact of an emerging global view on natural theology. Here, as elsewhere in recent philosophy and theology, diversity and pluralism rather than consensus and conformity are the order of the day.

The essays in this volume are intended to provide a picture of how some philosophers and theologians are looking at the prospects for natural theology. This book had its beginning with a conference organized at the University of South Carolina during the 1988 fall term to celebrate the one-hundred-year anniversary of the Gifford Lectures. Approximately half of the papers were delivered in their original form at that conference. Since that time, other papers have been invited for inclusion in order to give a broader view of what philosophers interested in natural theology think about its prospects. Pluralism in philosophical method is both evident and intended. The contributors represent Thomistic, Process, Continental, and Anglo-American styles of philosophy. Some are more sanguine than others regarding the need for and viability of natural theology, and some propose more limited or restricted forms of natural theology than others. Together, however, the essays provide a map of some of the key routes that are being traveled along the road of natural theology in the last decade of the twentieth century.

The first three essays are concerned with clearing away obstacles and laying the groundwork for a reconsideration of the arguments for the existence of God. In "Theological Clearances: Foreground to a Rational Recovery of God," Kenneth Schmitz shows how modern conceptions often mislead us in our efforts to understand the classical arguments for the existence of God. He explores the metaphysical grounds of these arguments and seeks to recover the possibility of a rational approach to God. In evaluating Aquinas's Five Ways, Schmitz argues, we have to consider not only whether they are valid arguments but what the arguments intend to prove. The paramount issue is that the arguments are not intended to prove the existence of just any God. They are intended to prove the transcendent God of the biblical religion, and this means both that the arguments assume that God must be somehow present and that the reality of God is always more than the conceptions employed in arguments for the existence of God. Further, the Five Ways do not assume that the world is finite in the sense of excluding radical otherness. Rather, they build upon the principle of limit in all things we experience and seek to show that the finite must harbor within itself the infinite.

James Ross, in "Reason and Reliance: Adjusted Prospects for Natural Theology," argues that prospects for natural theology have significantly brightened since the mid-twentieth century as a result of our improved understanding of rational certainty. Philosophers have come to recognize that demonstration in the strict sense is not a condition for rational certainty in mathematics and is even less so in science and religion. There are, however, degrees of proof available to philosophers in all areas of thinking that provide adequate grounds for rational certainty, for example, beyond a reasonable doubt, clear and convincing evidence, and by a preponderance of the evidence. And faith, or the sense of willing reliance upon others better placed to know and upon regularities we discern, has been rehabilitated as a source of knowledge and a foundation for rational certainty in science as well as theology. Finally, feelings function cognitively as a basis for certainty. Cognition, in other words, is a more corporate, collective state than it was often conceived to be at mid-century, and cognitive voluntarism, Ross argues, has come to be recognized as a basis for rational certainty.

George Mavrodes is also concerned with the question of proof and certainty in his essay, "On the Very Strongest Arguments." Some contemporary philosophers, sympathetic with the aim of providing arguments for the existence of God, have argued that, although some theistic arguments are sound, none can be said to prove or establish its conclusion. As we have seen, Swinburne, for example, argues that, based on the total evidence, it is more probable than not that God exists. But he, Alvin Plantinga, and others step back from a stronger claim about proving that God exists. Mavrodes prefers a stronger claim but in this essay he is concerned to investigate the reasons why some appeal only to the weaker claim. Mavrodes argues that both Swinburne and Plantinga specify the ideal of the strongest arguments in terms of universality, saying that the strongest arguments should have premises that have universal or near universal acceptance. Mavrodes, however, wonders why one should suppose this sort of universality to be the ideal criterion. He formulates several versions of the ideal of universality and argues that, for each of these versions, some arguments that do not meet the criterion confer epistemic benefit greater than any argument that does. Mavrodes concludes that universal compellingness does not identify a genuine virtue of argumentation, and that if, in fact, theistic arguments do compare unfavorably in strength with other arguments, we do not yet have a clear idea why that is.

In "Hermeneutic Philosophy and Natural Theology," Joseph Kockelmans takes a different look at the arguments for the existence of God and argues that, from the perspective of hermeneutic philosophy, natural theology, in the sense of Wolff, Baumgarten, and other authors of the precritical tradition, should be abandoned. Natural theology in this sense is said to depend on at least two assumptions, that persons are capable of proving the existence of God, and that persons are able to know the essence of God. Kant, he argues, has shown that the existence of God cannot be proved. This is not to deny that the arguments may have a place in helping the believer convince himself that it is not unreasonable to believe in God. Nor does Kockelmans deny the possibility of a regional ontology or a description and interpretation of religious phenomena that can provide a basis for critical reflection on religious experience. Regional ontologies, however, have to face the difficulties associated with our ability to know the essence of God. Since we are said not to know what God is in a positive sense, we have no means for knowing the essence of God, for saying how God is as opposed to how God is not.

This issue of not knowing what God is in a positive sense is taken up by Frederick Ferré in "Natural Theology and Positive Predication: Might Maimonides Be a Guide?" Ferré grants that the tendency of negative theology to stress the ontological difference between God and everything else is an important counterforce to the philosophical tendency to relate everything to everything else. If, however, nothing positive can be said about God, and if there are no ordinary ways for arguing to the existence and attributes of God, then natural theology, he says, would appear to be impossible. In this context, Ferré analyzes the thought of Maimonides, a paradigmatic example of negative theology. He argues that even Maimonides finds a foundation for positive affirmations of God in worship and in arguments justifying the radical simplicity of God. If, then, we can discover in the thought of this paradigm of negative theology grounds for theological affirmation, there should be no reason for thinking of the *via negativa* as offering an absolute logical barrier to natural theology. Rather, the *via negativa* should be understood to express a piety grounded in a sense of the inordinate greatness of God, and this, suggests Ferré, could be considered with its own sort of natural theology.

John Caputo is also concerned with the question of negative theology in his essay, "How to Avoid Speaking of God: The Violence of Natural Theology." He argues that one cannot avoid the mediation of language in theology, whether natural or revealed, and that just because of this, the absolutely negative theology proposed by the French theologian Jean-Luc Marion is impossible. Caputo shows appreciation for Marion's critique of the classical metaphysical conception of God but defends Heidegger and Derrida against Marion's claim that their "thinking of Being" represents a second and even more insidious form of idolatry. He then argues that Marion's search for an absolutely unmediated grasp of God in the Scriptures is both illusory and dangerous. It is illusory because the Scriptures, like any other texts, depend on mediation and interpretation, and it is ethically and politically dangerous because it opens up the possibility of authoritarian interpretations and presentations of the texts.

The final essays in this volume may be understood to provide different approaches to doing natural theology. In Norris Clarke's essay, "Is a Natural Theology Still Viable Today?" we have an approach within the Thomistic tradition that provides a reconstruction of the classical arguments for the existence of God and sketches a method by which the positive attributes of God can be reasonably affirmed. Clarke challenges contemporary views of relativism, Kantianism, and empiricism that are hostile to natural theology and argues that each in the end suffers from restrictive epistemological and anti-metaphysical biases or from logical inconsistencies. He also argues that the contemporary scientific view of the universe is compatible with the theistic hypothesis, while warning that this does not mean that one can establish the theistic hypothesis from gaps in the scientific picture of the universe. Clarke does not claim that the arguments for the existence of God are capable of convincing intelligent hearers, whatever their presuppositions. He does believe, however, that the arguments can be understood as explanatory hypotheses that commend themselves as worthy of reasonable affirmation.

Although Bowman Clarke appeals primarily to Whitehead and contemporary logic in developing his approach to natural theology, he maintains that his proposed notion of natural theology has much in common with the natural theology of St. Thomas. Clarke begins his essay, "In Defense of a Kind of Natural Theology," with an analysis of Hume's and Kant's criticisms of natural theology. He argues that both operate with the same principle of universal contingency and the same narrow definition of demonstration and that, if the aim of natural theology is to provide a demonstration of the existence of God in their sense, then natural theology is not viable. Clarke goes on to say, however, that few, if any, natural theologians understand their task in this sense, and he argues for a kind of natural theology that has as its primary task providing a definite description in answer to the question "Who is God?" and in providing that description with a particular philosophical framework. Insofar as a proof for the existence of God is given, it is said to be a demonstration that the philosophical framework requires the individual characterized by the definite description.

In "Soft Natural Theology," Ninian Smart assesses the implications for natural theology of the revolution brought about by the development of a global cross-cultural perspective on the history of religions and argues for a form of natural theology that would be sensitive to conflicting world views while avoiding sheer relativism. Some non-Western views are shown to challenge the whole mainstream of Western thinking about God and religion, indicating that there is nothing necessary about the development of Western philosophy or the tradition of natural theology. Cultural and conceptual assumptions of one philosophical system are said to be challenged by alternative systems. This need not mean, however, that natural theology is without force or that religion is a matter only of the authority of revelation and faith. Smart acknowledges some sort of discernment or insight in the cosmological and teleological arguments for the existence of God but recognizes that they cannot be compelling. On his account, the arguments of classical natural theology merge with arguments about religious experience and practice where we engage in general reflections upon world views, give reasons for the views we hold and recognize that the reasons we give must be in some sense soft or less than compelling. The task of engaging in debate with other world views corresponds, suggests Smart, with what was once known as natural theology.

Eugene Long's essay, "Experience and Natural Theology," is also concerned with the role of experience in natural theology. He proposes an approach that is intended to be empirical in the wider sense of that term without ignoring the role of argument or reducing religious knowledge to a matter of appeals to the authority of self-authenticating experience or tradition. Beginning with descriptions and interpretations of so-called transcendent or ultimate dimensions of experience, he seeks to provide connections between one's general experience and knowledge and one's experience of revelation and faith. He shows that the experiences of contingency, freedom, and commitment can be interpreted in a manner at least consistent with the more distinctive kinds of religious experience. The aim of natural theology in this sense is to show whether the religious interpretation of experience can be judged to be the most satisfying, the most reasonable, and the most illuminating of human experience.

The concluding essay, "Theodicy: The Case for a Theologically Inclusive Model of Philosophy," is at the same time an argument for a more inclusive approach to natural theology and a response to what some consider the most serious challenge to natural theology in this century. Louis Dupré argues for an approach to natural theology that is free from the limitations imposed upon it by the rationalist heritage of the seventeenth and eighteenth centuries. Focusing specifically on the problem of evil, which is usually raised as a challenge to the physico-theological argument for the existence of God, Dupré intends to avoid, as he puts it, reducing a transcendent mystery to a logical problem. Major problems in modern theodicy are said to derive from its rationalist conception of God, which is alien to religious faith, and from its abstract, theologically neutral definitions of good and evil. Dupré argues for an approach that would include religious sources as models and patterns that convey concrete content to philosophical reflections on religion, while denying for philosophical purposes the authority that these sources carry within the religious community. His approach to theodicy rests on a more intimate union of finite with infinite being that, on the one hand, allows the creature greater autonomy and responsibility and, on the other hand, enables the Creator to share in the suffering of his creatures and through this to redeem them.

University of South Carolina

1   Theological Clearances: Foreground to a Rational Recovery of God

KENNETH L. SCHMITZ

Near the beginning of the *Summa theologiae* St. Thomas Aquinas presents the well-known "five ways."[1] The *Quinque Viae* make up a single proof of the existence of God by way of five approaches: from *motion* concluding to the First Mover; from causative *action* concluding to the First Cause or Source; from *contingent* beings to Something that is absolutely necessary; from *degrees* of actual perfections in things to the Original Source of their existence and goodness; and, finally, from the *regularity* of processes in the world to a Creative Intelligence that implants tendencies towards order in things. At the end of each of these ways he remarks laconically, "And everyone understands this to be God"; or, again, everybody "names" or "calls" such Being "God"; and, more intimately, "And we call this, God: *et hoc dicimus Deum.*"

The author of a profound modern treatment of this traditional argument has written of the need to "get God out of the categories."[2] By this he meant that further argument is required: to show that the Prime Mover does not move in any usual sense, to conclude that the action of the First Agent lies beyond ordinary agency, to clarify the absolute nature of Divine Necessity, to arrive at Unmixed Perfection beyond the more and less limited excellences found in the world, and to break beyond the bounds of human intelligence to Creative Intelligence. Of course, St. Thomas sets out to provide such further argument throughout the first part of the *Summa*. But, while we must surely attend to the rigor of this prolonged argument, in order to determine *whether* it proves, we need also to ask about *what* the argument intends to prove. In pursuit of this latter inquiry we need to clear away obstacles to understanding what seems to me the most ambitious intellectual enterprise ever undertaken, namely, the attempt to prove the existence of such a God.

---

1. Pt. I, q. 2, art. 3.
2. Gerard Smith, S.J., *Natural Theology*, New York: Macmillan, 1951, 108–13.

IN CONCLUSION: MYSTERY

For those to whom the reality of the biblical God has been preached, the only God worthy of the highest name is a mysterious living God, a God who reveals and does things unlike anything that has entered into a human head. This is the God who is denied by the biblical "fool," and denied even if he does exist, for the fool is not foolish in any ordinary sense. He is no mere doubter. Rather, he is an atheist who appreciates the importance of God, and who says that such a God cannot, could not, must not be, even if he were. So that, even to the "fool," such a God is the only one worthy of the labor of argument in disproof, if not in proof, of his existence.

For we do not set out to prove or disprove the existence of just any divine being; we do not seek to prove or disprove the existence of Diana or Neptune or Apollo. At best, such gods are mythical interpretations of a people's experience of the numinous. Among the Greeks and Romans, the numinous received celebrated poetic expression. Indeed, its echoes are heard centuries later in the nostalgic effort by various Romantic poets to "revive" the ancient deities.[3] Such numinous presence remains close to human experience, comprising its first exotic fruits. The attractive charm of such *numina* arises from the degree to which they share the human condition, while sharing it in a somewhat strange and larger-than-human way. It is not required to deny the presence of such a *numen,* in order to take seriously the biblical disclosure; nor is it even necessary to claim that these "gods" are purely human fabrications. It is enough to acknowledge that they are no substitute for *the* God, whether or not such a God exists. For they do not even fill out the idea of God. Their ghostly presences remain infinitely far from the high God of whom St. Thomas speaks and to whom the proof is addressed and meant to lead. For many of us, no other God will quite do. It would be better that the throne remain empty than that pretenders receive the title falsely. Better atheism denying the high God than polytheism laying claim to a divinity that is not its own. It is as though, having once tasted a great wine, others may serve lesser purposes without, however, deserving the honor paid to greatness. So, too, once the idea of the high God is noised abroad, other conceptions of divinity pale. The very wording of the question forces the singular nature of the issue: "Whether God exists: *Utrum Deus Sit.*"

Nevertheless, the living God is not sought for only in faith. Believers may seek him by the paths of reason and argument as well, while—

3. For example, Schiller's *Die Götter Griechenlands.*

paradoxically—he is also at issue for non-believers. Indeed, atheism has adopted its most vociferous tone in the denial of the biblical God. It was Nietzsche who cried, "If there were gods, how could I endure not being one? Hence there are none."[4] Now, it is clear that he had in mind the high God and not a lesser pantheon. Nor is his protest merely facetious or petulant. It is a cry that rises in the throat and from the heart of a rebellious creature, for it is rooted in the crux of a being that is but need not, even might not, be; it wells up from a being that exists only on the sufferance of Another. Make no mistake: this God, if such there be, is a creator, and there exists nothing without his constant support. Nietzsche's cry, then, is the cry of contingent being, inasmuch as it struggles against a contingency so radical that it leaves nothing to the creature that is entirely its own, or, conversely, leaves it everything that it is as a gift received.

Radical contingency is—according to the biblical disclosure—the condition of every creature, but it takes human form in the cry for liberty. Haunted by the spectre of such a God, Jean-Paul Sartre may be understood to have defiantly argued, "If there exists an omnipotent God, how can I be free? But I am free, indeed I must be free; hence God cannot be." This will-to-freedom also has its biblical origins, for it was believers who first saw in human freedom the reflection of perfect divine freedom. Indeed, the biblical freedom of the sons and daughters of God is made in the image and likeness of divine freedom, so that, *qua* image, human freedom is contingent upon its relation to God's creative freedom. On the other hand, the freedom that drew Sartre into defiance is a freedom without God but that yet embodies a kind of infinity within itself, in the sense that there is nothing in its own order that can limit it. In Spinoza's words, though not his sense, "infinite after its own kind." At least in his early writings, Sartre postulates, if I may so put it, a finite freedom without limit and without measure.

The roots of such a conception may also be traced back to the late medieval "liberty of indifference," which was given its first mature and influential modern expression by Descartes when he insisted that the human will, unlike the human mind, is infinite. This insistence upon infinitude is not of itself the Promethean dream of power, but it can easily turn into it. In its extreme form it can disclose a drive for total power that has haunted modern political thought in the form of totalitarianism and its opponent, anarchy. The dream of total liberty, of a liberty answerable only to itself, has arisen in modern times as a distorted illusion of a discredited divine omnipotence. Thus the issue

4. *Thus Spake Zarathustra*, pt. II: "Upon the Blessed Isles."

of God, his nature and existence, stands at the center of the issue of human freedom. The issue is whether human freedom is created in the image of a greater liberty or is rather the self-vindicating warrant of human autonomy.

But if the issue of God is the narrow gate through which one passes to one or the other of these conceptions of human freedom, how does one go about proving or disproving the existence of such a Being? One thing is sure: we must not play at the fiction that we simply start thinking and accidentally stumble upon the argument that, step by step, proves the existence of such a God. God is not an accident, nor is the structure of our thought simply arbitrary. Either God is absolutely necessary for us, or he does not exist at all. That is the crisis posed by the conception of such a God. On the other hand, if he is unconditionally necessary, why do we not everywhere and always naturally and inevitably follow out our reasoning to its logical and ontological end? Why does not everyone who thinks arrive at the conclusion that God exists? Why are we able to think of so many things and for so long a time in so many ways other than the thought of God? It was Spinoza, in modern times, who converted "It is necessary that God exist" into "Hence God exists necessarily," turning God into the necessary law of being and of thought, *Deus sive Natura*. In the experience of the believer, however, the biblical God remains more manifest yet more wonderfully hidden and more necessary than the laws of nature. God is at once the ancient glory and the ever new mystery.

Still, if the idea of such a God is neither necessary nor accidental, how does the proof or its denial get started in the first place? For if we do not have any idea of God at all before we begin the proof, how can we know what evidence may be relevant and what may not be? It is in this sense that, unless my memory forsakes me,[5] St. Thomas somewhere remarks that we would not proceed to the demonstration of God's existence unless we first *somehow* knew that he existed. Of course, St. Thomas was a believer, and this seems to be overstating the starting point and begging the outcome—unless, of course, the proof shows us what we already *somehow and necessarily* have been aware of all along. For if such a God exists and exists necessarily, and if we cannot exist without Him—and that is the only adequate and acceptable conclusion other than denial of his existence—then he must *somehow* be present in our sense of things all along, and be hidden in the

5. I must confess that I have not been able to locate the remark in his biblical commentaries.

very identity of our own being. The issue resolves into: *somehow already or never at all.*

But there is more trouble yet. For even if the proof succeeds, this "somehow" will never become fully clear. The intelligibility of the reality reached through the conclusion exceeds the concepts employed in reaching it. For the only God worthy of that high name is a mysterious God, a God of will as well as of nature, a God of freedom as well as of necessity, a God who is more than will and nature, more than freedom and necessity. "My ways are not your ways," says the Lord. For our ways are the categories in which we couch the idea of such a divinity, whereas that very idea bends back upon those categories to find them deficient. It is the purgative force of this idea that propelled St. Thomas to distinguish in this matter between the thing signified (*res significata*) and the manner of signifying it (*modus significandi*).[6] He tells us that the manner of signifying God is inherently human, whereas the reality toward which the idea points lies beyond human signs in the mysterious region of the divine. And so the proof is, for him, a process in which the idea leads the mind beyond its own categories, without thereby ceasing to be intelligible. It can do this insofar as the mind breaks through its concepts into a judgment that lies open to the fullness of existence.

When the Schoolmen spoke of faith seeking understanding, they meant, among other things, that they were led by way of such a concept toward its reality. But if the idea and its reality will never become fully clear, or even as clear as other ideas can become, nevertheless the proof is meant to purchase a conclusion that is to become ever more necessary and convincing. Here is a non-Cartesian divide between clarity and certainty. The proof, then, is a process that is meant to prove a mystery without destroying it. In the words of the poet, its reach is meant to exceed its grasp.

Now, the term *mystery* may mean many things. It can be used offhandedly to indicate a question that puzzles a mind ignorant of its solution: "It's a mystery to me." In midnight horror films, it may name the uncanny that is contrived to lie beyond our ken. Or it may be simply another word for obscurity. On the objective side, it may stand for what is dark and stubbornly unenlightening, and, on the subjective side, for a mind that is left in the shadows of doubt and ignorance. This is the negative meaning of mystery. Among the great Christian doctors, however, one finds a positive meaning to the term. For they celebrate the mystery of a great Light. Here the mind is also in a state

6. See, e.g., *Summa Theologiae*, I, 13, 3c.

of confusion, but it is a kind of delirium brought about by a light too bright for clear sight. The mind is confused, not because there is too little to know, but because there is too much to be known. The mind cannot take it all in. An increase in understanding does not decrease the mystery, for the mystery stems from the inexhaustible abundance of meaning that shines from the mysterious reality. Aristotle tells us that philosophy begins in wonder, but his wonder seems to diminish with an understanding of the causes. At any rate, among Christian philosophers and theologians, the greater the understanding, the greater the wonder. Understanding fuels the wonder.

In reality, what is this great light supposed to be? It is not the light of objectivity. The proof does not conclude to an object set over against the human subject. Ordinary categories of objectivity cannot capture the outcome of this proof, not even in the way in which Plato's *Sophist* may be said to have caught the primary Forms, and certainly not in the way in which Hegel's categories in the *Science of Logic* may be said to have articulated the absolute system. These formal categorial names, if they name anything at all, name too mundane a reality. Eugen Fink used to say, half-facetiously, that at least the ontological argument did prove, but he quickly added that what it proved was the existence of the world. Of course, neither St. Augustine's nor St. Anselm's nor St. Thomas's proofs intended such a cosmology, for they did not seek to prove what they thought needed no proof, but rather the existence of the utterly transcendent biblical God.

It is no thing that is reached by such arguments, if anything is reached at all, not even a vast "Thing" such as the entire universe. The proof proves no thing, not even the "greatest or highest Thing," whatever that might be. A similar recognition had already nurtured the long tradition of negative theology (*via negativa*) that finds in the name "Nothing" (*Nihil, Nada,* etc.) the most appropriate name for the utterly transcendent God.[7] Nevertheless, while St. Thomas also understands the proof to prove no thing, it is not because the proof falls short of rational standards, but, on the contrary, because its subject is filled with a surcharge of intelligibility that in its conclusion challenges our entire understanding of reality.

7. While the *via negativa* is rightly associated with Neo-Platonism, on the one hand, and with mysticism, on the other, the works of Josef Pieper have brought out the negative element resident in St. Thomas's thought as well. In *Scholasticism*, New York: McGraw-Hill, 1964, 53–54, he emphasizes the influence of Dionysius the (Pseudo-)Areopagite by citing several comments of St. Thomas, such as: "God is honored by silence—not because we cannot say or understand anything about Him, but because we know that we are incapable of comprehending Him" (*Commentary on Boethius' De Trinitate,* 2, 1 ad 6). Cf. also *The Silence of St. Thomas*.

AT THE START: LIMIT NOT YET FINITUDE

If the end is mysterious, the beginning is problematic. For at the initial point of the argument we cannot begin with a finitude of such a character that we could never reach the infinite. Thus, for example, by stipulating the self-enclosed and distinct impressions that purportedly make up human experience, David Hume made it impossible in principle to ever reach the actual infinite, permitting us to postulate at most an isomorphic and otiose parallel with the world of impressions. Instead, the proof must begin as far as possible without arbitrary presuppositions and more simply with whatever is, without declaring beforehand that what is is so thoroughly finite that it is inescapably enclosed within itself. In other words, we must not preempt the possibility of proof by defining the starting point in such a way that a transcendent order of reality is excluded from it a priori.

In fact we must not begin with finitude at all. It is enough to acknowledge the principle of limit in the things we directly encounter: as moved, caused, contingent, more or less adequate and more or less regular in behavior. For there are two stages in defining the starting point. First (A), it is required to establish in what sense, and on what evidence, we may conclude that what is limited is indeed finite. Secondly (B), once that is done, to establish the nature of the relation between the finite and the infinite in order to determine in what sense the finite is finite. Neither of these tasks is easy or obvious.

(A) First, if the limit is taken to be atomistic, that is, if we start with an impregnable and irreducible finitude, with a plurality of impervious self-enclosed units—whether they be separate Humean psychic impressions or supposedly real indivisible ultimate particles—then no such argument as St. Thomas has in mind is possible. What is in question here, then, is the nature of unity. If, in accordance with the tendencies of nominalism, unity is identified with simplicity, so that the basic units of reality are defined as ultimate incomplex particles, then there can only be displacement of units within the totality or at most intrusion of an alien and external force after the manner of classical Deism, the so-called "god of the philosophers," that is, a functionary in the service of certain metaphysical systems. Such a God would exist at the borders of time and space, and would sustain the only kind of relation admissible in such a totality, namely, an external relation to it as part to part within a greater totality (pantheism) or as whole to whole (Deism). But such a mechanistic definition of the starting point risks being gratuitous and at best dubious, given the transformative energy of the perceptible universe, in which real transmutation does take place. Even the methodological advantages of such a mechanism seem nowadays to have all but exhausted themselves. Certainly, physics seems to have moved away from this unreal restriction of thought, away from the search for ultimate particles toward larger wholes, toward waves, fields, and holographic structures.

But if the more systemic approach of the physical and chemical sciences, the more organic and ecological approaches of the biological sciences, and the more holistic approach of the social and human disciplines are more adequate to our experience, they do not of themselves translate the limited nature of the data into finitude. And although cosmological thought requires a reversal of perspective from the part to the whole, its theories about the beginning of the present condition of the universe presuppose an antecedent totality of potential forces, so that its explanations (whether the so-called Big Bang or the Bubble) move among the limited categories of thought. They attempt to describe the relative beginning of the present order of things, rather than to give an account of the absolute origin of reality. And so the concern for totality does not lend itself easily to translating our experience of the limited nature of things into a recognition of their finitude. For scientific explanations show how the elements of things pass on into new forms, rather than how the things themselves may cease to be. Nothing short of the explicit concern for being seems able to articulate this radical nothingness.

(B) But even if it can be shown that what is limited is a finite that finishes, where does it finish?[8] Does it finish by passing over into the infinite? And into what infinitude? With Hegel it is the infinitude of the absolute system, so that the finite does not so much transcend itself as it, rather, integrates itself into membership in the totality of being, essence, and spirit. Or does the finite end by passing over into nothing? So that all is mere sound and fury, signifying nothing? Hegel thought that such a fate was senseless, since it led to nothing constructive, but he located the failure of such a negation in a non-dialectical conception of finitude. He called such a negation merely positive, a sterile, simple, negative self-identity that leads nowhere.

(C) Before banishing this nothing, however, we ought to look more closely at it. It may tell us that the finite, considered in itself, does indeed lead nowhere, passes over into nothing, has no issue or result. Still, such a consideration can help us to discern the tension in the finite: it both is and is not. Its *is* teeters on the brink of an *is not* that—far from being Hegel's all-inclusive infinite—is radically ambiguous.

8. The references to Hegel are from *Science of Logic*, pt. I, bk. I, chaps. 1 and 2.

On the one hand, it is sheer nonbeing. Hegel had his own reasons for branding this non-dialectical negation a dead end, since the "where" to which such a dead end does *not* lead is his dialectical absolute system. For it does not lead in Hegelian fashion to the mere indeterminacy of Hegel's primal negative category, *das Nichts*. Instead, the metaphysical conception of negation leads to nonbeing in its emptiest sense, to sheer nihilation, not merely to a relative moral nihilism, but to the most radical metaphysical nihilism. But suppose that, following upon this recognition of metaphysical negation, the proof succeeds, then it will turn out that this radical nothing is the dark harbinger that leads us, on the other hand, to the Nothing who is the high God. This "Nothing and/or nothing" draws out the radical ambiguity of contingency.

Now, if in this root-like darkness we can still raise up the question "Where is this nowhere to which such sheer contingency leads?" then there must be more in that contingency than sheer nonbeing. For questions can arise only from the base of a questioner who, in all his or her fragility, is present there in that darkness. For the darkness is the darkness of contingency, of an *is* that is yet an *is not*. And the questioner asks: What is the value of such an *is*? Does it provide a starting point? What is this *is* that simultaneously simply *is not*? For we must not divide the questioner into half *is* and half *is not*, as though he or she were made of two parts, an *is* that is not negative and a negation that is in no way affirmative. The existence of the questioner is one singular existence, an existence that (taken in itself) is simultaneously a nonexistence. That is the precise character of contingent being: it is an is that simultaneously is not.

Moreover, the simultaneous identification of is and is not is not a convenience of our making; it belongs to the character of contingent being itself. We rightly recognize the distinction between is and is not, for that is the lifeblood of reality and thought. But we are not entitled to make over the distinction between the negative and affirmative character of such a being into a separation. On the contrary, in the contingent being itself, its very being is shot through with the fragility of nihilation. The bearers of that possibility within the being include its merely formal and potential factors. But its existential being is of one texture: a being that in its very being exists in such a way that its nonexistence is always a real and constitutive possibility.

And yet, if the question can be raised by such a being, there is a point of light in its darkness after all. Suppose that the point of light is reflected from an order of being that does not teeter on the brink of annihilation? Suppose that contingent being is an *is* that is in continuous communication with a quite different order of *is*? Of course, this supposition is just what needs to be proven, or disproven. It is not yet proven in the saying of it, though if or when we are entitled to say it, we can also say: Q.E.D. These prolegomena are meant to clear the ground of current and conventional obstacles, so that the true issue of the proof may be laid bare. The genuine difficulty, as distinct from barriers or obstacles due to misunderstanding, is first of all to bring ourselves to see in what lies before us whether there is evidence of such a simultaneous *is/is not*, of the real possibility of annihilation, and only then of a parlous affirmation.

We ought not to assume that we can easily take to heart the annihilation of a being, let alone our own demise. Consider the simplest change. If I eat an apple, I can imagine its elements continuing to exist under new forms; and this continuity is true. But is it not also true that the apple ceases to exist in reality? It may continue to exist in memory and in its effects; but *it* is no longer. And that possibility is a real possibility during its entire existence, and during ours as well. It is a negative possibility that is constitutive of its existence; so that we can characterize its existence, even as it exists, as being really able to cease to exist throughout the duration of its whole existence. Without the recognition of such radical contingency there can be neither proof nor disproof of the high God.

These reflections are meant to chart the course required if the proof is to reach safe harbor or encounter shipwreck. In sum, to say "limit" is not yet to say "finite," for, far from starting obviously with the finite, it must start simply with what is limited. The proof then requires that we establish that what is limited is in truth finite. More clearly than any other philosopher, Hegel has charted the transition from the category of the "limit" (*die Grenze*) to that of the "finite" (*das Endliche*). There is no change in the content of the two categories, but there is a change in emphasis, internal structure, perspective, and ontological status. The difference of meaning arises through a change in the conception of the infinite (*das Unendliche*). Now, although the Hegelian conception of the infinite as absolute system is not the same as the traditional Christian conception of the Infinite Being, nevertheless Hegel does take account of the changed meaning introduced into the term by the Christian conception of God.

FROM FINITE TO INFINITE

For the Greeks, the infinite was the indeterminate, essentially a negative term. The Greek mind gave positive weight to formal *limit*, so that the limit was the innermost boundary that separated one thing or form from another, each constituting part of the whole economy of being and of thought. Limit butted upon limit, even the gods being "parts" of the cosmos. With the interposition of the concept of the high God, however, the term "infinitude" came to acquire a positive and determinate meaning. The biblical and especially the Christian mind placed the positive weight upon the infinite glory of the high God, so that what had been seen positively as limited now came to be seen negatively as finite. For in the wake of this conception, to call something that is limited "finite" is to name it from the vantage point of the unlimited divine fullness. The term "finite," then, properly signified the radical and unqualified dependency of the creature upon the Creator.

Nowadays, however, as seen in the previous reference to Sartre, the term "finite" has been claimed also with deliberate resolution in order to name the autonomy of the human sphere taken in itself and with exclusion of that theological vision; hence, "finite without limit." And so nowadays, to say "finite" is not thereby to imply "infinite" in any but a merely conceptual and verbal sense, leaving it open whether the latter is grounded in the former or vice versa. But equally, to say "the limited is finite and the finite is not infinite" does not rule out the possibility that the finite may be grounded in the infinite. There may yet be an infinite without which there would be no finite. That is the current nub of the proof. For proof always exists in context, and the challenge today is not, as it once was, to establish finitude against limit (though that too must be done); but also, even when what is limited is shown to be finite, it is still required to show that the finite is such that it must acknowledge the reality of the infinite precisely as the high God. The proof, then, is an inquiry into the finite—that there is the finite and what its character is—as much as, or even more than, it is a proof of the infinite. For whether the proof succeeds or not, it will tell us even more about ourselves than it will about God. And if it does succeed it will have shown that the *alpha* (qua limited starting point) must harbor within itself (qua finite) the *omega,* that is, the Infinite Being reached through the conclusion.

ST. ANSELM'S CLARIFICATION

It is just this putative pre-presence that makes the ontological proof so attractive—attractive yet problematic. It is a curious feature of the ontological proof that, since its first formulation, it cannot be quite banished from the human mind. It returns again and again in various forms: in St. Anselm, if not earlier in St. Augustine; in St. Bonaventure and Blessed John Duns Scotus; in Descartes, Spinoza, Leibniz, and Hegel; and in the recent lively philosophical discussion of the proof. The idea that motivates it is so powerful that it cannot quite be relinquished, yet so unique that it does not submit easily to demonstration.

The ontological proof is *sui generis,* both as an argument and in its conclusion.[9] First of all, as an argument: In his *Reply On Behalf of the Fool,* that is, the atheist, the monk Gaunilo of Marmoutiers objected to the proof in the form presented by Anselm of Bec in the *Proslogion.* Using the analogy of a perfect island, Gaunilo hoped thereby to refute Anselm's argument on the grounds that the mere possession of the idea of a perfect island in no way warrants the assertion that such an island actually exists. Anselm readily granted the point but replied that the idea he had in mind—of a Being than which none greater can be conceived—is not at all like the idea of a perfect island (which in truth is not a coherent idea at all); and that it is as unlike every other idea as the Being it presents is unlike every other being. The trouble with Anselm's reply, however, is that our language moves by analogies, by likenesses and their correlative unlikenesses. Indeed, Anselm himself appeals to the distinction between a painting in the mind and a painting in reality in order to set up the distinction between the unique idea existing in the mind and that same idea also existing in reality. He thereby recognizes that our terms are embedded in a web of other terms, so that one does not break out of them any more than one breaks out of the whole interconnectedness of language, except into silence. To say "light" is to suggest "dark," and to say "is" is to imply "is not."

It seems, then, that to the extent to which the argument is unique, it forsakes the common logic needed for the demonstration even while it draws the force of its conclusion from that same logic. It would be too much to charge Anselm with a straightforward inconsistency, and yet it is at least curious that he rejects the argument from analogy in the reply to Gaunilo, even while he relies upon a general analogy in order to determine the names of God in the remaining chapters of the *Proslogion.* And yet such a criticism somehow misses the force of the argument. In its own way the argument accommodates the correlative nature of linguistic terms by reducing thought to the contrast of absolute being and absolute nonbeing. The force of the argument is meant to carry thought through the irreducible linguistic correlation of *is* and *is not,* in which both have equal status as terms, to the absolute nonreciprocity in reality of *is* over *is not.*[10]

---

9. St. Anselm, *Proslogion* and *Reply to Gaunilo,* as well as Gaunilo, *On Behalf of the Fool.*

10. In the later chapters of the *Proslogion,* Anselm employs the principle: God is whatever it is (absolutely, i.e., in every respect) better to be than not to be.

This nonreciprocity is disclosed in the conclusion, too. As to what is concluded: if the Being than which none greater can be conceived is so unique that it stands in relation to none other, does not that status violate the very dynamism of proof that seeks to establish relationship? And yet, the power of the idea carries us beyond the idea itself, provided we can in some sense extend ourselves towards what is more intelligible than any possible conception. It is in this sense— which I do not claim was acknowledged by Anselm, except perhaps in the prayer with which he entered upon his proof—that Anselm's form of the ontological argument approaches the *via negativa,* carrying us beyond the web of language and thought. For both positions have in mind the same divine being. It is here, too, that—once again surprisingly—Anselm must meet Nicholas of Cusa. For Anselm's God, no more or less than Nicholas's, stands in no comparative relation with others, not even in a negative or differential relation with them.[11] *The* God is beyond otherness, beyond Plato's form of the Other, and beyond the Other articulated by recent students of religion. As has already been pointed out, the God indicated by Anselm's idea is no part of the totality of being. That does not mean that he is "outside" that totality, for that would simply constitute a new and greater totality of which he would be an integral part. He simply is not to be identified with either of such purported totalities or with any part of them. It is this denial that leads to the *via negativa.*

It is by a similar denial that Jacobi found "nihilism" to be truer than Fichte's transcendental system of philosophy.[12] It is this, too, that led John Scotus Eriugena[13] to the strange conclusion that, in the words of the master to his disciple, not only do we not know this high God, but God does not know himself. That is, God does not know *what* he is, not because he lacks knowledge, but because he is not a what, that is, because he transcends utterly all categories of being and knowledge. Such a conclusion is at once more negative and more positive than the pale Nothing (*Nichts*) waiting to be filled with the categories of Hegel's dialectic. It is sheer transcendence. And yet when we read St. Anselm we are reminded that this transcendence is, after all, Being. Now, the distinctiveness that Anselm finds in the Idea, St. Thomas finds in existential supereminence: Being at once most determinate yet utterly unlimited (*Esse infinitum primum et perfectum*). It is of this

11. See Anselm's *Monologion,* chaps. 15 and 16.

12. *Friedrich Heinrich Jacobis Werke* bd. 3, Leipzig: 1816: *Jacobi an Fichte* (1799). This "Open Letter" is available in English: *Fichte, Jacobi, Schelling: Philosophy of German Idealism,* ed. E. Behler (New York: Continuum, The German Library), 119–41.

13. *On the Division of Nature,* bk. II, chap. 28f.; cf. III, 19–23.

Being that we must say that creation does not add a whit more being than there is in God alone; indeed, an infinity less. And to this existence St. Thomas gives the name of Pure Act of being, *Ego sum qui sum.*

TRANSCENDENCE AND IMMANENCE ARE REALLY IDENTICAL

It is clear that such a God is no mere part of what is, nor even a whole within a larger whole. But when we speak of the transcendence of God today, the Enlightenment intervenes to cloud the issue. For it has translated the term "transcendence" into "that which is supposed to lie beyond this world"; so that "transcendence" is commonly understood as "other-worldly." In truth, however, nothing can falsify the conception of divine transcendence more than a separation between the terms "transcendence" and "immanence." If we take the etymological sense of the term "immanence" to mean "indwelling," "dwelling within oneself," we may, of course, extend it to mean "being contained within the universe, this-worldly." Now, the strategy of Enlightenment thinkers has been generally to narrow the horizon of interest by driving a wedge between "this world" and "the next," abandoning the term "transcendence" to the "other-world," which is in turn taken to be inaccessible, except perhaps to private belief. Considerations of transcendence can then be set aside in public discussion as mere personal opinion. And "transcendence" is then reduced in rational discourse to a non-serious term.

The reduction of the term "transcendence" to the periphery is further completed by the rejection of both terms; so that "this world" comes to mean not "that which stands in opposition to the next world" (the initial sense given to the terms by Enlightenment thinkers), but "the only world." And this sole world can be taken to be "the only world we can be sure of " (the sense given to the term by agnosticism), or "the only world we need consider" (the sense given by secular humanism), or "the only world open to rational discourse" (the sense given by positivism). Once this reduction of the term "transcendence" has been completed, it can once again be put to domestic use in what has been called "horizontal" transcendence (intentionality) in place of "vertical" transcendence (participation).

All of this stands in contrast to the meaning given these twin terms in the long Christian discourse that preceded the Enlightenment and that formulated the idea of the high God. Among the Schoolmen of the Middle Ages the term "*transcendens*" was used in a number of different contexts. Said of the relation of God to his creatures, how-

ever, it did not designate a different relation in reality from his intimacy with and immanent presence to his creatures. We may say, then,
that, when said of the divine, the two terms "transcendence" and "immanence" designate one and the same relation in reality. They do not
differ *in re*, but only *in mente*, only in definition. The distinction of
terms is a concession to the human mind as it deals with the real
relation of creature to Creator.

In the Schoolmen's tradition, the term "immanence" generally signifies the specific activity proper to organisms by which they can act
so as to transform themselves. Such activities as wanting, feeding, and
perceiving originate within the organism and have as their term a
change within that organism. Immanent activity of this sort is a primitive auto-determination. With human persons, immanent activity becomes the ability to communicate with another without loss of self, as
when I teach someone geometry without losing the knowledge of it
myself. With us too, however, there can be change, development, and
devolution, for I can gain new understanding through that teaching,
but I can also forget what I have once known. This "newness," however, is of quite another order than my new coat or my new suntan or
my new figure. To be sure, we undergo change and are only imper-
fectly immanent. Thus, the activity of perception is shot through with
physical interaction. Nevertheless, precisely *qua* perceiving (as distinct
from the transmission of light, the activation of nerve cells, etc.) it is
immanent in the sense that an agent initiates a process that alters itself.
And so a complex activity that is partly transitive and partly immanent
can be said to be "immanent" in that respect in which no diminution
of being results from it. In the jargon of the day, it is a "win-win"
situation. Thus, immanent activity means exchange without loss, as
when in friendship I may come to know myself better through knowing another well. "Indwelling" here means "dwelling with" and is the
basis of both friendship and citizenship. Indeed, the goods proper to
civilization, as distinct from its physical products, are built up through
the interplay of immanent and transitive activities, that is, of self-
determination and those other-determining activities that terminate
in products independent of their producers.

In the high God envisaged by St. Thomas's proof, however, immanence and transcendence do not merely interplay with one another,
they coincide. Complete beyond measure, his perfection does not
guard Him against change, but rather preempts the grounds for it.
In this fullness consists his transcendence. In such a divine abundance,
immanent activity is in the form of rich and intimate self-presence.
We must, however, obviate a possible misunderstanding. In his self-

presence, the Creator is acutely concerned with his creatures, for this is no longer the self-contemplating God imputed to Aristotle, indifferent to a universe he has not created. Such unawareness is clearly seen to be unworthy of the absolute perfection of the Creator God. St. Anselm tells us that this is the God of infinite compassion who entertains the highest interest in the good of his creatures. His presence to self is so fully and actually conscious that he is present to others by their being present to him within his own self-presence. The divine concern does not wait upon contact with his creatures, but arises rather in that creative self-presence in which creatures are present to the transcendent Source of their being. The real identity of divine transcendence and immanence calls us to recognize that the creature consists wholly and entirely in its relation to this transcendent-immanent "No-thing," as though to say, *"esse creaturae est adesse Deum,"* the being of creatures consists in presenting themselves to God.

Ordinarily, of course, relations presuppose terms. Thomas called such relations "categorial" or "predicamental." He also spoke of "transcendental" relations, such as those of the one, the true, and the good, relations that transcend all categorial relations and are confined to no type of being but are found throughout the whole range of being. But the relation of creation is unique. It is a nonreciprocal relation, a one-way dependence of the creature upon the Creator. For the creature participates in the creative gift of existence communicated by the Creator. The closest analogy is the relation of offspring to parent. But it is only an analogy, in which the difference outweighs the similarity. What is more, the believer attains religious maturity when he or she passes over from conceiving God in terms of parents to understanding parents in terms of God. Properly understood, the reversal discloses the unique character of the Creator God, on the one hand, and of the relation of creaturehood, on the other.

As to the relation, in it the creature has no existence independent of the relation, being constituted wholly and radically in, by, and through that relation. And yet, just because the unique relation of creation is the free and generous communication of *being*—that whereby each thing is and is everything it is—the creature receives its own integrity in and through that relation. The being of the creature, then, is that of a one-term, subsistent relation, or again, being in which the second term is the very relation itself.

The unique character of the relation called creation derives from the transcendent-immanent nature of the Creator. For God is not *a* being, like and unlike others. Nor is he the "highest being," the apex of the much discussed onto-theo-logical pyramid. God is, in the words of Nicholas of Cusa, so transcendent that he is not even "other" from his creation. He is not that Other so popular among recent philosophers and phenomenologists of religion. He is, says Nicholas, *non-aliud*; by which is meant, not that he is the same as us, but that he is so transcendent that he cannot be fitted into the correlation of same and other. God escapes the categories, even the fundamental ontological ones. For that very reason, however, God is closer to his creatures than they are to themselves. God, said St. Thomas, and St. Augustine before him, is most intimate to his creatures. Robert Sokolowski[14] says of the conception elaborated by St. Anselm—of a Being than which none greater can be conceived—that such a God is no part of the universe at all, takes up no room in it, displaces no creaturely being, and hence can be more intimately with and in his creatures than they can be with and in themselves. Creative presence is, to be sure, a unique order of presence.

To sum up, then, the unique character of this relation redounds upon the meaning of the terms "immanence" and "transcendence." Different in meaning, they are identical in reference and reality. The divine immanence is such that it transcends its creation utterly and absolutely, so that it is not even other to it. Here the spatial imagery at the root of the terms fails and the dissimilarity between God and creatures becomes explicit. By virtue of being no part of the universe, neither within it nor outside of it, by virtue of taking up no room or displacing any creature, such a perfectly determinate and actual Infinite Godhead can be said to be closer to each creature than it is to itself.

TWO PATHS WITHIN

In physical imagery, what is near is not far; closeness and distance oppose one another. Not so in human relationships. Physical proximity may go hand in hand with coolness and disdain, while physical separation need not diminish the intimacy of friends. Nor is the divine closeness spatial either. The search for such a God does not require a search beyond into some other world. It frequently takes religious form as a search within, but this religious interiority needs to be distinguished from a modern form of human interiority with which it is sometimes confused.

At the beginning of modern times the anthropological turn received decisive shape in the writings of Descartes, who undoubtedly gave

14. Robert Sokolowski, *The God of Faith and Reason* (Notre Dame, In.: University of Notre Dame Press, 1982), especially chaps. 1–5.

expression to a widespread shift of interest. If early modern astronomy displaced man from the physical center of the universe, even more, for reasons too complex to enter into here, the upshot of the uncompromising mechanism of early modern physics—only recently coming under criticism from a minority of physicists—exiled from the physical world all that had been associated with the specifically human, so that "nature" was no longer conceived as a familiar world of colors and sounds, of finality and form. The Cartesian retreat within to an individual human interiority ended in the indubitable certainty of the *ego cogito*. This mental fortress was to be given other names by later philosophers: "self," "association of impressions," "mind," "transcendental consciousness," "ego," and "will to power." Among its names is "subjectivity," a concept that seeks to preserve what is distinctively human by a retreat from an alien world given over to "objectivity." The modern sense of "intentionality" is a newer concept that seeks to move out once again into the world from which consciousness had fled, but it rests upon that earlier flight.

Religious interiority is also a movement within, but it differs radically from such modern inwardness, for it does not fall back upon itself in retreat from the external world. Rather, it takes the whole world, spiritual as well as physical, along with it back to its creative source. Instead of anchoring the retreat in some defensive form of the inner self, religious interiority brings one out onto the "broad field" that lies open before God. This breadth infinitely transcends the distinction of inner and outer, of physical and psychic, as the infinite Source transcends its finite consequents. The relation is non-reciprocal just because the finite stands in absolute dependence upon the infinite. Once again, we anticipate such a relationship in our experience of parentage. We often look back to the adults familiar to our childhood and wish that we might have been able to relate to them in more equal fashion, as we would now were they still alive. This is the sometimes bitter and always sad recognition of a certain nonreciprocity between human generations. But these sources of our own personal formation are only relative sources, and so the relation is not pure nonreciprocity. Or again, we also anticipate such nonreciprocity in the experience of receiving a gift. Reception is no simple physical transaction, for the only adequate "return" is that of gracious acceptance. But the "reciprocity" of reception is itself nonreciprocal, that is, it does not conform to the law of equal action and reaction. It is a free acknowledgment that adds nothing physical to the original communication.[15]

15. K. L. Schmitz, *The Gift: Creation* (Milwaukee: Marquette, Aquinas Lecture, 1982).

THE PRESENT CONTEXT OF THE PROOF

I have dwelt upon the issue of the relation of creation to the Creator God in order to point out that the proof cannot be effectively presented or understood or even refuted as though it is a straightforward argument from nature as currently understood. The argument implicates a whole context and subtext including the human dimension of reality as well. Thus, the first way (*prima via*) cannot proceed from motion and nature in the sense presently given to them. The "nature" of which St. Thomas speaks contains within itself efficient, formal, and final causalities, and its "motion" is to be understood within an ontological context that recognizes immanent activity as well as transitive activity and displacement. Moreover, the term *natura* is broader and richer than our present term *nature*. The former is used of human and divine as well as of physical being. It simply means "the various modes of being appropriate to things, humans, or God." And we still preserve that meaning in such sayings as "It is in the nature of things," though we have largely emptied the term of its metaphysical meaning. Nowadays, "nature" tends to refer to what is neither God nor man but is simply physical. Indeed, it is usual to think of nature as over against, or at least distinct from, the human, the social, the cultural, and the religious. A proof that would begin with a conception of nature devoid of causality and principles is unlikely to convince. Nor should it. The traditional proof, on the other hand, moves within a context of agency, and of agency that is not reduced to mere mechanical force.

And so those who have some misgiving about the effectiveness of the Five Ways today are not entirely without grounds. To the extent that the rich polyvalence of the term *natura* (said of physical things, human beings, and God) remains intact, so that the intelligible nexus and the real context within which the proof moves is taken to be polyvalent, to that extent the proof may reach its goal. However, once modern dichotomies—such as the Cartesian dualism between the affairs of the mind and those of the body, or the Kantian between understanding and will—were able to force a separation of distinct (though related) meanings formerly associated within the term nature, the proof needed restatement, in order to overcome the new situation. Instead, it has frequently received a reduced statement, as though one could rise to the high God from the new sense of "nature," that is, from "mere nature," from nature alone devoid of ontological constitution, from a nature from which the human has been methodically excised, from a mechanical nature separated from intelligible principles.

Once the distinctions inherent in the polyvalence of the term nature had been broken down into separations, dichotomies, and oppositions, there could be no resolution into the transcendent-immanent unity provided by the Source. Instead, the unity was sought for in other ways: through dialectical argument that broke down oppositions by synthesizing them into an architectonic unity (Kant), by sublating them into absolute system (Hegel), by returning them to their mythical ground (Schelling), or by suppressing the question (positivism). None of these reached towards the high God to whom St. Thomas's proof is directed.

The finite, whether taken as a hard shell exclusive of radical otherness or as system conceived as self-contained totality, remains impervious to such an argument. If rational argument is able to move only within such an enclosure (as many Enlightenment and post-Enlightenment thinkers insist), the rational recovery of God is unlikely. For then the issue of God must be handed over to a faith out of touch with the highest capacities of human thought. It is likely, then, that the question of God will be surrendered to feeling, perhaps to a "transcendental" feeling, such as that expounded by Schleiermacher or the earlier misreading of Rudolf Otto. Or perhaps it will be reduced to a merely private matter, of no great general import for human affairs. Or, again, reason may be robbed of its integrity, without an end of its own, and in the form of instrumental reason it may be pressed to serve interests ultimately inimical to it (ideology): the interests of power, arbitrary will, emotion, greed, preference, or one or another form of irrational faith. The challenge of the proof—namely, of the rational recovery of the high God or its failure—puts everything to the test. For it tests not only the concept of God, but reason itself and the scope of rationality. Indeed, in the end it confronts our very selves, since the nature, character, and destiny of our humanity is at stake in the outcome. The greatness of Nietzsche was to recognize this even as he sought to overcome it.

It may not be true that, as the Grand Inquisitor put it, if there is no God, everything is permitted. But it is true that if there is no God, very different things are permitted. To which the secular humanist replies, If there is a God, is anything permitted? Can anything at all be done by human agency? Here again we meet the question of human liberty and divine will, and the issue of human dignity. To which a human reason, unburdened by unfounded obstacles, has every right to ask, If the proof proves that there exists the high God as an unconditional necessity upon which the very existence of the finite depends, can there be indignity in acknowledging such an absolute Giver and such an absolute endowment? That is the issue upon which the proof ventures, and its outcome is nothing less than the answer to the question, Who are we anyhow?

Trinity College, University of Toronto, and the
Cambridge Center for the Study of Faith and Culture

2 Reason and Reliance: Adjusted Prospects for Natural Theology

JAMES ROSS

Prospects for natural theology have brightened since the mid-century. The climate in philosophy and the skills of the philosophical theologians have improved. Several subjects have significantly changed shape, and new options have opened.

Rational certainty about God is more plausible than was believed in the Fifties. The notions of rational certainty are better understood now, in particular, how vast a range of rational certainty in no way depends on proof of any sort, and how much of rational certainty, even in the most important matters, has a significantly "emotional" and "voluntary" base. For example, neither demonstration nor any proof at all is needed (or available) for rational certainty about the most general life-structuring convictions, whether it be that rational clarity of conviction enriches one's life, that respectful love of others is an intrinsic value, that scientific inquiry into nature is justified and successful, or that God exists and has the personal interest in us that believers expect. In some of those cases no one even pretends to offer demonstrations. In others, including God's case, "proofs" far less elaborate than demonstrations[1] are satisfactory for theoretical certainty, though even they are not necessary for rational practical conviction.

Furthermore, faith has been rehabilitated. Faith is willing reliance on others thought better placed to know, as well as willing reliance on the regularities we find in nature and people, to indicate what we should believe. Faith is undeniably a source of knowledge, often more efficient than finding out for oneself, as the telephone book makes

---

1. I don't mean inductive versus deductive proof, as illustrated in R. Swinburne's *The Coherence of Theism* and *The Existence of God,* or in the framework of John Mackie's *The Miracle of Theism* but, as I explain below, (i) proof beyond a reasonable doubt, but short of demonstration, (ii) proof by clear and convincing evidence, and (iii) proof by a preponderance of the evidence—notions adapted from law—are more effective for changing minds.

clear. And where faith falls short of knowledge, it often supplies rational certitude, even about the most expensive and conservatively entered human undertakings, especially in engineering (bridge and theater design), naval architecture (hull design), applied science (nuclear power plants), and sometimes even in our formal logical and mathematical disciplines.[2] Faith is a foundation for rational certainty, maybe not a rock-bottom one but an indispensable one. In fact, trust is the very fabric of social conviction and the golden thread of science.

There is no longer a responsible debate about whether there can be knowledge by faith,[3] that is, knowledge by way of our willing reliance

2. What most philosophers know about logic, and why it is so, is taken on faith from teachers and texts. Even our notions of validity and formal reliability are packages of faith. For example, most philosophers do not know that the notion of "logical consequence" is seriously and responsibly disputed, so much so that "relevance logics" and "deviant logics" are a growing industry; see John Passmore's *Recent Philosophy* (LaSalle, Ill.: Open Court Publishing, 1985), ann. bib. nn. 5–7, pp. 126–27. Logicians who insist that the principles of quantified modal logic (Systems S-4 and S-5) are true have the authority of white-coated actors in toothpaste ads.

See J. Ross, "The Crash of Modal Metaphysics," *Review of Metaphysics* (December, 1989), 251–79. See also Nathan Salmon, "The Logic of What Might Have Been," *Philosophical Review*, XCVIII, no. 1 (January 1989), 3–34, for arguments that the principles of modal logic are false. The interpreted modal logics simply provide ontologies for tinker toys. Worse, the Baysean calculation of the probabilities of good and evil used by Swinburne is philosophical costume jewelry. There is no world that is impossible for a good God to have created, just because of the evil in it.

3. I have argued several points about knowledge by faith that bear repetition: (a) that faith leads to knowledge follows even from austere notions of knowing like Chisholm's *Theory of Knowledge* (Prentice-Hall, 1969), see my "Testimonial Evidence," *Analysis and Metaphysics*, ed. Keith Lehrer (Dordrecht, The Netherlands: D. Reidel Pub. Co., 1975), 35–56; (b) that a correct interpretation of Aquinas requires that there be cognition (knowledge, short of scientific demonstration) by both natural and divine faith, see my "Aquinas on Belief and Knowledge," in *Essays Honoring Alan B. Wolter*, eds. William A. Frank and Gerard Etzkorn (St. Bonaventure, N.Y.: Fransciscan Institute Press, 1984), 243–69, and the discussion of cognitive voluntarism in my "Eschatological Pragmatism," in *Philosophy and the Christian Faith*, ed. Thomas Morris (Notre Dame, In.: University of Notre Dame Press, 1988), 279–300; (c) that the problem of "faith and reason" has to be analyzed with both faith and reason regarded as sources of knowledge without confusing cognition in general with "scientia," the output of Aristotelian demonstrative science, see my "Aquinas on Faith and Knowledge" cited above; and my earlier "Aquinas on Faith and Reason" in *The Challenge of Religion Today*, eds. J. Smith, F. Ferré, and Joseph Kockelmans (New York: Seabury Press, 1982), 83–103. See also chaps. 1 and 2 of Ross, *Introduction to the Philosophy of Religion* (New York: Macmillan, 1969); (d) that faith is a proper and indispensable basis for knowledge in the most important matters, especially when one is motivated by what is to be gained from the believing (say, immortal life; see Aquinas, *De Veritate* 14, 1), and that this is the view of both St. Augustine and St. Thomas, see my "Believing for Profit" in *The Ethics of Belief Debate*, ed. G. McCarthy, *AAR Studies in Religion*, 41 (Atlanta, Ga.: Scholars Press, 1986), 221–35; (e) that there really are things that we can never come to understand without first beginning by believing; see my "Unless You Believe You Will Not Understand" in *Experience, Reason and God*, ed. Eugene Long, The Catholic University of America Press: Washington, D.C., 1980), 113–28. In fact, believing first in order to understand later

on others and on some of the regularities we discern, but only about what sorts of things are best or better known that way.[4] To think we do not know that PCBs are dangerous in the water supply because *we* have not established it or even read the proof is just being foolish, not philosophical. There is a societal conviction that varies in quality, depending upon how much internal scrutiny it contains as a cognitive institution, on which we rely to find out, without strict reasoning and even without any conscious inquiry[5] at all, about fusion, fission, the benefits of fluoride, the dangers of chlordane, the age of galaxies, whether we need vaccinations or flu shots, and AIDS: *fides ex auditu,* said St. Paul.

Many people find out about God by taking the wise ones seriously: Gautama the Buddha, Abraham, Moses, Jesus, Socrates, and Plato, as well as their own parents, families, and communities. Such construals of life are typically reinforced by a culture that construes the world as the arena for a divine drama, in terms of which individuals conceive themselves (as workers, martyrs, leaders, ideologues, the faithful, the chosen people, etc.), having a place, a character or role in history, so that belief is strengthened into "gut instinct." Greek Orthodox spiritual teachers talk of one's belief, as conviction matures, "descending from the head to the heart," and before that, not being worth very much toward enlightenment.[6] The fact that hideous falsehoods can be believed that same way—just as errors are believed as a result of science—does not make the social institution that causes conviction less a source of rational belief. Similar convictions are generated the same way about how to understand one's own history (e.g., as of opportunity or repression). The animism of Native Americans did not amount to knowledge (if taken literally and not metaphorically), we

---

applies to every acquired human excellence, since without having the excellence one cannot see why it is satisfying to have, and why it is excellent, but at most that it is, and even that has to be taken on faith most of the time. By acquired excellence I mean Olympic-level skills at sports, at thought, at writing, and even at being morally right or mathematically disciplined; see my "Musical Standards as Function of Musical Accomplishment," forthcoming in *The Interpretation of Music: Philosophical Essays,* ed. Michael Krausz (Oxford: Oxford University Press, expected 1992).

4. For that is basically the difference between faith and reason as sources of cognition; the difference between relying on someone or something to tell us what is so and finding out for ourselves. The proper ambit of faith is not a patch of the cognitively deformed but a realm, not our unconditioned responsibility for finding out, for which faithful, reliable, perhaps knowledgeable spokespersons or signs can be found.

5. For example, a person can know that AIDS is a dangerous disease, even a virus, without ever having inquired into what a virus is or whether viruses are living things.

6. You can observe for yourself that beliefs have locations by noticing that certain beliefs have "head" associations and others are located in the chest and others in the stomach, detectably by the feelings associated.

think; the pantheism/animism of seventy percent of living humans is not, we think, literally correct. But that says nothing about the rationality of their convictions, or the rationality of the "sociology of knowledge" by which their convictions were generated. A social system that hands along truths about food and mixed truths and errors about health and how to live, and superstitions about God and "science," might do perfectly well to hand along an improved product. Because of the "garbage in, garbage out" principle, a social transmission system that has perfect integrity as a means of rational belief, when judged by its product, may be unjustly ridiculed. Besides, philosophers think the "reliability" of the system has something to do with the rationality of relying upon its outputs, proposing to measure reliability by the truth of the product. But for many products there are not alternative sources. As Augustine pointed out about the Christian faith, and we would have to point out to Hottentots resisting our teaching them science, "unless you believe, you will not understand." There is no way to get to see that this process works, without first becoming an initiate and making it work.

You cannot get into a position to evaluate until you become an insider. There is no access to the reliability of the "system" from the outside, any more than there is access to the standpoint of musical, philosophical, or aesthetic mastery of judgment, except by discipleship first. Augustine told a Manichee friend who wanted everything proved, "You are suffering from an illness only God can cure." (God's cure would be to move the friend to belief.) You simply cannot get into the position of competent cognitive appraisal of the most important channels of belief without talent matured as an apprentice, journeyman, and master (and thus a disciple) of the "way," whether it be how to play the piano, construct arguments, live justly and humanely, or live a fulfilled life.

So faith emerges as a means, a universal and effective means of knowledge. That is news, recent news in philosophical theology, and in epistemology in general. Of course, it is no news to Aquinas, Augustine, and Cicero that the fabric of human knowledge is the woof of trust and the warp of independent inquiry. But even they would have been reluctant to assign trust a major place in any science but divine science (theology). Moreover, there came a time, after Descartes had to clean out the hand-me-down prejudices that clogged the way of the new science, when an extreme of scientific caution required doing everything for oneself (or trying to), taking nothing on faith, relying on no one. That myth is still handed to high school students who are simultaneously "cooking" the results of their lab assignment so as to get the textbook's results and not to have to repeat it. Extreme self-reliance was just a wave in the sociology of science. Parallel processing is the wave of the future. Thus, the basic currents for human knowledge remain two: faith (reliance) and reason (finding out for oneself).[7]

There is an even more important advance going on now, the recognition that *feelings function cognitively to ground rational certainty.*[8] Feelings are knowledge-making. Yet feelings are not reasons, though their happening may be (a serious stomachache is reason to call a doctor). Against the background of our beliefs, feelings convert glimmerings into convictions and determine, supplement, and transfigure appearances.[9] Further, the satisfaction and stability of deep feeling hardens belief into rock-bottom commitment. That can, unfortunately, produce stubborn opposition to the truth just as easily as steadfast support for it. For only refined feeling correlates directly with quality of conviction. By stabilizing, configuring, and even supplementing the "presentation" of things, feeling does for cognition what glossy advertising does for desire.

Feeling functions cognitively both in our relying on others (faith: "I feel I can trust her"; "I feel secure relying on him"), and in our finding out for ourselves (reason: "Yes, that argument is elegant, satisfying"; or "No, that hypothesis is flimsy, tinselly"). Feelings, especially refined feelings (see III below), (1) *disclose* the quality of things and sometimes their real natures by transforming appearance into meaning, for instance, by making a mark on clay or a faint rustle cry "Danger! (Snake)"; and (2) they *configure* convictions, that is, make the content emerge by drawing the supporting pieces into a pattern, the way we detect a conspiracy. But they do even more than that, as I will explain below.

As a result, *cognitive voluntarism*[10] seems to be the most plausible

7. See also my "Unless You Believe You Will Not Understand," cited above.

8. There have been a number of books and articles on the cognitive function of feeling and emotion recently. Most mistakenly treat feelings as no more than detectors and trained feelings as refined detectors of the presence of features in things. Feelings certainly are detectors. But the profound function of refined feeling is as *cognitive transformers*, devices that configure the sensible and intelligible features of things into distinct intelligible patterns, for instance, to reveal who or what sort of person one is meeting, by whether one is "comfortable" or not. So most of the recent work on the functions of feeling falls short of what I have in mind here.

9. Recall Sartre's saying "an emotion is an affective transformation of reality," something made clear in the fable of the Fox and the grapes.

10. *Cognitive voluntarism* is explained in my "Believing for Profit," cited above, with further additions here. The heart of cognitive voluntarism is that belief is not the output of an evidence-weighing machine (that can be thrown out of kilter by prejudice, illness,

general account of experiential knowing, one that opposes "evidentialism," "representationalism," and "foundationalism," and holds, instead that, on the whole, we believe what we want and because we
want to (allowing both for compulsion by "evidence" and compulsion
by want), within a cognitive-voluntary system that has a targeted finality (the survival-then-fulfillment of the active person, in a basically
hospitable environment).[11] So "believing what you want to" is not the
pathology of religion and madness; it is the engine of adapted cognition. Instead, mad, irrational belief is willful and compulsive, out of
touch with the conditions of environment and the aims of our cognitive system.[12]

Believing, not at will but willingly, is both the form[13] of empirical
knowledge (and so, of induction, of all pattern discernment, as well
as of abstraction and genuine conception), and the form of reliance
on others, which involves the additional element of personal trust.
Thus religious faith, even strictly divine faith,[14] is not structurally deviant among cognitive states; it is typical of the cosmic extensions of
experience we have to make in a universe too large to explore by

etc.) but that, on the whole, we believe what we want (within limits) and, in large part,
believing what we want results in cognition (or at least warranted belief that may, of
course, not be true) because of the *targeted finality* of our cognitive faculties within a
reasonably hospitable environment.

Of course, just because the system is one of believing for profit, "wishful thinking"
can be a losing proposition for unrefined feeling and untrained understanding, or
ungoverned vice, or in a hostile environment. For instance, if almost everything (say,
in a jungle where we were suddenly transported from our urban life) were bad to eat,
our desire to "try it out," which increases, the hungrier we get, by suppressing the
behavioral control of our belief that "what is strange or ugly is probably bad to eat," so
as to induce us to eat worms, maggots, ants, and termites, would soon lead to our
demise. Even to know that rats are a better guide to what is edible than pigs would take
a lot of pain or a lot of insight [especially since rats now eat plastic and wire coverings
and insulation, but not frozen fish, see M. Smith, *Polar Star* (New York: Random House,
1989).

11. See my paper "Believing for Profit"; see also Aquinas, referred to therein.

12. Sanity requires a reasonable match between reality and desire, like a stone being
skipped on water; psychopathology has desire skipping on images (reflections), labeled
"the real" but actually on tangents.

13. By the "form" of reliance, here, I mean the "inner mechanism," the working
structure. Enjoyment, "liking it" (this can be low-level as well as intense) is what makes
us rely. As Aquinas said, "delectation is the form of faith." For Aquinas, "form" in this
context means "the first act," that is, the activity exercised. See my discussion in "Believing for Profit," mentioned above.

14. By "natural faith in God," I mean a general reliance on the whole cosmos to be
the work of God, a theistic conceptual (interpretive) set (see chap. 2 of my *Introduction
to Philosophy of Religion*) in contrast to divine faith, supernatural faith caused by sanc-
tifying grace, a "Jesus the Savior" conceptual set. Interpretive sets can be carried far
beyond their religious authorizations, e.g., by those who see God's intentions in everything they like, and divine punishment and displeasure in what they do not. Nevertheless, the very excess exhibits the existence of such conceptualization.

oneself: we make cosmic-construals to fit the targeted finality of our having knowing powers[15]; for example, our belief that scientific inquiry will disclose, or approximate, the meat and bones of the material world.

We have to have convictions that go beyond all the data and yet are not necessarily true in order to make sense of the data we have. For example, we have beliefs about the origin of the earth, about inertia, about relativity; that there were *homo sapiens* from 35,000 to, perhaps, 90,000 years ago (but much less than the quarter of a million or even two million years we had thought, mistaking *homo erectus* for our species), at most a millisecond in the "hour" of earth's life. We think the cosmos is about 17.5 billion light years in "diameter," with a single "evolution" of heavy elements from hydrogen in supernovas, and so forth (though some of us postulate dark galaxies that have accelerated past that fraction of the speed of light where their mass captures all their light, thus accounting for some of the "missing 90% of the matter" of the universe but requiring that the cosmos be much "older" than the slice visible from earth appears). Some even believe the "gaia" hypothesis, that the earth is a single living system where the lives of its living parts depend wholly on the health and life of the whole, just as cell life, normally, depends entirely on our whole bodily life and cannot long outlive it.[16] Others believe history is targeted on the return of Jesus, on a unification of consciousness (Teilhard de Chardin), and a post-historical community of saints.

For many, such convictions are paradigmatically rational. And that might well be true, depending on how conviction was reached and with what sort of trust.[17] We habitually and willingly believe that phys-

15. Cognitive voluntarism can be epitomized as: "humans believe what they want (with some wants compelled, of course) controlled by (within the general magnetic field of) the targeted finality of the human cognitive system (like magnetic north), which, unlike the animals' similar systems, is not directed to preservation of the species, but to fulfillment of the individual." The target, for Christians, is life with God. Yet in the description of "the targeted finality of our knowing powers," I do not need to sneak "God" or "life with God" in; for ordinary purposes (with the exception of things that depend on human completion and real freedom, see my "Mindful of Man," forthcoming) the cognitive powers can be treated as targeted on human flourishing, e.g., excellence in loving, learning, practical wisdom, etc.

16. The "gaia" hypothesis is a scientific analogue of Plato's "World Soul" and of the many primitive religious ideas of the "earth mother," and of "the living planet."

17. After all, millenialists and war-survivalists have similarly general beliefs (as do believers that apricot pits cure cancer) that most of us consider mad, and sad. Traditional "scientific" medicine often considers "wholistic" medicine mad, though there have been notable convergences, especially in sports medicine, allergy medicine, and psychiatric medicine; chiropractic, acupuncture, massage, and physiotherapy have been given place, as well as nutritional and exercise therapy for all sorts of disorders.

ical reality is mathematically intelligible and that the future will be like the past, though there is no reason in principle why that should be so, any more, say, than that thought-reality should be mathematically intelligible—which very few people at all believe or even care about.[18] How firmly we hold one or another of those usually implicit convictions depends on what explanatory power we accord it and how deeply we need it, what the "payoff" is. Such beliefs are not immune to refutation by experience, among the sensible anyway. Still, adherents will simply replace those disconfirmed with the nearest tenable facsimile—unless all trust has suddenly "gone down the drain," as when love is disillusioned—just the way we adjust metaphors to new technology.[19]

Advances in philosophical theology met setbacks too. The modal arguments for the existence of God that advanced like Chicago commodities through the late Seventies bottomed out in the Eighties, when a few people realized that the "possible worlds semantics" for Quantified Modal Logic,[20] used for the more highly touted versions, is a hideous platonistic fairytale[21] that conflicts with the divinity it is used to demonstrate. Nevertheless, the classical insights of Avicenna, Duns Scotus, and Leibniz underlying the modal arguments are innocent of the malignant ontologies and of the extensionalist basic logic, and will survive after extensionalist quantified modal logic has gone the way of the hula hoop.[22]

18. However, a study of Disney animators would reveal a mathematical intelligibility through and through, unless they all involve "NP-complete" outcomes.

19. When explanatory metaphors meet limits, we make new ones. That is what people did with mechanical models of the brain (animal spirits), then pneumatic (pressure, etc.), then chemical, then electrical models, then electrochemical ones, then computational ones. We remake metaphors to save and renovate our basic convictions. So, too, the cosmos is the carving, the claywork, the clockwork, the stage-design, the mis-en-scène, the story, the song of God.

20. J. Ross, "The Crash of Modal Metaphysics," cited above, and Ross, "God, Creator of Kinds and Possibilities," in Rationality, Religious Belief and Moral Commitment, ed. Robert Audi and William Wainwright (Ithaca, N.Y.: Cornell University Press, 1986), 315–34. I showed, I think, that the principle "no things, then no names" commits all ontologies for extensionalist quantified modal logic (QML) to a world of abstracta (whether or not they are divine ideas), or to Lewis's parallel plural worlds of individuated possibilia. Both options require that "being" be logically exhausted by limitation (by kinds and natures and individuals). But that principle is demonstrably false, indeed inconsistent, as was recognized from ancient times, e.g., by Parmenides, Plato, Aristotle, and every later classical metaphysician, including Spinoza and Leibniz. Nor can that result be avoided by regarding "being" as the logical product of individual possibilia. Furthermore, possibility cannot be prior to actual being; that would be an absurdity. The ontologies offered for the logic have no prospect whatever of being true.

21. Or an incoherent Neo-Augustinian Neo-Platonism.

22. The basic arguments are found in St. Anselm, Avicenna, Duns Scotus, Descartes,

There is, however, a dangerous threat to the hard-won clarity and care earned in philosophy over the decades that comes from a new salient: the abandonment of disciplined thought—in favor of rhetorical flourishes and slogans—because of the "futility of philosophy," as Richard Rorty[23] diagnosed it, and as a few others deconstruct the bipolar opposition of "true or false" to make a "postmodern" hermeneutics, in which science has no more access to truth than palm-reading or poetry.

Granted, the promises of analytic philosophy were mostly get-rich schemes with watered stock. Granted that diligent acolytes tried for decades to achieve the analyses, definitions, and reductions promised by the vague schemes of Russell, Carnap, Quine, Goodman, Putnam, Chomsky, Davidson, Sellars, and Chisholm, to name just a few of the thinkers of quality, ambition, and dedication. Granted, the scandalous failures to explain counterfactuals and to analyze "S knows that P," or anything else of significance, justify disenchantment. And even allowing that the new "puritans" of "epistemology naturalized" (Quine), of evidentialism, foundationalism, "explanatory coherence" in epistemology, and the "new methodists" of computationalism, functionalism, and connectivism in philosophy of mind (cognitive science), will also fail because of thin blood inherited from "logical fundamentalism"[24] and an archaic and anachronistic formulation of their problems. Still, that's no reason to give up clarity for clamor. It is better to make

and Leibniz, without those ontological commitments, of course, though there is some reason to think St. Anselm thought there were Platonic Forms, at least as divine ideas, which makes rather fine company for Plantinga, whom I criticize for that view. The earlier contemporary adaptations by N. Malcolm, "Anselm's Ontological Arguments," *Philosophical Review* 69 (1960), 41–62, Charles Hartshorne, *The Logic of Perfection* (La-Salle, Ill.: Open Court Publishing, 1962), and J. Ross, *Philosophical Theology* (Indianapolis, In.: Bobbs-Merrill, 1968) do not commit to an ontology for quantified modal logic, as does Plantinga's later version (*The Nature of Necessity*, Oxford: Clarendon Press, 1974), though the earlier versions also seem committed to the false claims that whatever is necessary is necessarily necessary and whatever is possible is necessarily possible. There is a way to formulate the reasoning without those commitments and even without a commitment to the false "whatever is possible is necessarily possible." I explain this in "The Passing of the Modal Proofs," in *Truth and Impossibility*, forthcoming.

23. *Philosophy and the Mirror of Nature* by Richard Rorty (Princeton, N.J.: Princeton University Press, 1979), and its sequels in papers and books.

24. Logical fundamentalism is an overextension of an impulse that comes from Russell, Frege, and Carnap and can be epitomized in the notion: "if it can be given a representation in first order quanitification, and not a simpler (say, propositional) one, then that is its "structure," no matter what *it* is." For instance, see Davidson on the logical form of English; cf. S. Kripke, *Wittgenstein on Rules and Private Language* (Oxford: Blackwell, 1982), p. 70, n. 60, for what I take to be disbelief at Davidson's idea. I explain "logical fundamentalism" in "The Crash," cited above, as the idea that first order quantification tracks the bones of reality, and that everything represented in the logic is to be given an element of the ontology.

radical realignments of analytic convictions than to join the "philosophy is dreck" evangelists, making intellectual significance into a contest of clamor, cliques, and political posturing.[25] That is near enough to happening in history, literary criticism and philosophy to deserve a warning.

I

Some obstacles to faith have gone away. Before saying more about proof, faith, and the cognitive function of feeling, I want to say something about the lost obstacles.

Some obstacles died out, the way verificationism did, after generating a vast theological literature.[26] Some obstacles became kinky, the way thoroughgoing religious skepticism did, displaying some disorder of the understanding (as I think Wittgenstein regarded any challenge, or response to one, for the justification of a cognitive practice as a whole, whether of knowing, science, religion, aesthetics, or mathematics). Skepticism and noncognitivism are not a going industry in philosophy at the moment, except for a recrudescence in "postmodern" deconstruction that I mentioned, which is much more targeted against claims for science than on religion.

Other obstacles were co-opted into advantages. The sleek scientific discourse of the logically literate, like David Lewis, was also cultivated by philosophical theologians like Alvin Plantinga in the upperclass accent of symbolic logic, in particular, in the moued tones of quantified modal logic, along with an ontology of abstracta to interpret the logic. God was given a scientized description as the being that exists in all possible worlds and is maximally great in every one.[27] Done well, the argumentation looks formidable. Philosophical theology made a comeback.[28] By using the scalpels of its disdainers, it achieved the glitter of neurosurgery and even made *Time* (April 7, 1980).

25. See Vincent Descombes, *Modern French Philosophy* (New York: Cambridge University Press, 1982) for an entertaining, illuminating, and richly quotational survey of the situation, which, if anything, is worse than I describe it. My impression is captured neatly by Jacques Bouveresse's (whimsical? vitriolic?) essay "Why I am so very Un-French," *Philosophy in France Today,* ed. Alan Montefiore (Cambridge: Cambridge University Press, 1983), 9–33.

26. I list many of those books and papers in the notes to chap. 7 of *Portraying Analogy* (Cambridge: Cambridge University Press, 1981), where I discuss the noncognitivity attack.

27. Alvin Plantinga, *The Nature of Necessity* (Oxford: Clarendon Press, 1974). Also see Michael Loux, ed., *The Possible and the Actual* (Ithaca, N.Y.: Cornell University Press, 1979), for a fine explanation of the relationship of ontologies to interpreting logic, an informative bibliography, and a representative set of essays by the persons involved in the subject. See also the more recent paper by Nathan Salmon cited above.

28. I speak of a comeback measured against the situation at the 1958 publication

Another obstacle became an advantage: the decline of evidentialism. Scientific knowledge had been considered superior to religious conviction just because belief was kept proportionate to the evidence.[29] This is "evidentialism" as Locke first stated it, a position that triggered a long "ethics of belief " debate[30] and laid down principles taken as "obvious" and "not worth arguing about," until they were pulverized in the course of unconnected road-building in philosophy of science.

The new story from Harvard about the underdetermination of hypotheses by data (Duhem–Quine), the inscrutability of reference (Quine, Putnam), that "entrenchment" of predicates is the basis of induction (Goodman's reworking of Hume's "custom"), and the "many versions, many worlds" of Goodman,[31] said unequivocally that scientific commitment goes beyond the evidence. (Of course, every ordinary true predication, e.g., "My sweater is torn," does, too, and in the same way, as Duns Scotus noticed around 1300.) In fact, Goodman's *Languages of Art* in 1968 made it basic that visual and all other sensory perception "goes beyond the data," as did Jerome Brunner in *Beyond the Data Given*; perception is constructive (supplementing, modifying,

---

of Flew and MacIntyre's *New Essays in Philosophical Theology* (New York: Macmillan). Religion was said to be meaningless for the most part and false in the remainder by most of the essayists. Yet about one third of all philosophers in the *Directory of American Philosophers* (early Seventies) listed themselves as interested in or specializing in philosophy of religion, even though most publication through the Sixties was critical, claiming religion is meaningless, nonsensical, noncognitive, false, contradictory, or "all of the above." Some well-written essays were very influential, like Mackie's and McCloskey's famous articles about the problem of evil in which Empedocles's and Lucretius's and Hume's charges were repeated.

Anthony Kenny's *The God of the Philosophers* in the Seventies (Oxford: Clarendon Press, 1979) and J. Mackie's *The Miracle of Theism* (New York: Clarendon Press, 1982) are examples of good analytic philosophy against which opposition skills were rapidly developing. There has been a marked shift. Being "pro-religion" is "in" among hundreds of philosophical theologians. Yet philosophical theology now falls outside the "establishment" in philosophy, as indicated by how few major analytic philosophy departments have specialists in philosophical theology (or philosophy of religion) and how unlikely they would be to look for one. Still, two generations of very talented people have renewed philosophical theology and keep it strong now, with fine journals and conference books as well as many new books on all areas, and a new thrust of philosophizing from the standpoint of religious faith, for which impetus Alvin Plantinga, William Alston, and Thomas Morris are especially to be praised. Moreover, among their notable accomplishments is the rehabilitation of thinkers banished by philosophy in general: St. Augustine, Aquinas, Scotus, Calvin, Bonaventure, and the Arabians, who are almost totally ignored otherwise in philosophy.

29. "The bulk and weight of the evidence" was "increased by heating it with love," to use a phrase of Sir James Fitzjames Stevens, *Liberty, Equality and Fraternity* (London, 1894), 344.

30. See McCarthy, *The Ethics of Belief Debate*, cited above.

31. This is not to be confused with D. Lewis's *On the Plurality of Worlds* (New York: Blackwell, 1986), a theory of parallel but physically inaccessible "large objects like this one." Goodman's irrealism is the view that there is no "this" world, except relative to a "true version" of it.

ignoring, and rearranging the sensory "data"), and both conception and judgment are constructive, too. Paul Kolers's experiments with reading (some published in *Scientific American*) display similar construction (a notion since appropriated by hermeneuticists). Those were the watchwords of Goodman's (and Gombrich's) new aesthetics, based on perceptual psychology. That led to a larger metaphysical doctrine: "the world is the product of art and discourse," that we *build* the experienced world.[32]

Still, as Putnam said, the success of science is not a miracle. There must be an explanation of it. How can we succeed by going beyond the data? There are two main options (combinable, too): (a) that science is a self-refining activity we take on *trust*, revising it by its outcomes (predictions, unifications, applications, etc.), the way we learn to steer a boat or play a violin, toward "satisfactory" understanding of wider and wider fields of phenomena. That position goes circular about the "data" for revising our science. Or (b) we *make it up*, making reality along with our versions of it, like stage designers perfecting their craft, where the object is believability, convincing substantiality.[33] That's the new pragmatism, trying to get such a tight fit between prediction and outcomes that there is no room for a relevant competitor to what *our* theory "refers" to (internal realism). Thus, we made "careers in plastics" (*The Graduate*) and "careers in microchips," and in arbitrage, not from "pregiven" reality, but by thought-architectonics in plastic reality. That is Goodman's "well-made worlds" in *Ways of Worldmaking*.

32. There is much to say in behalf of the constructive aspects of perception, and even of judgment; after all, nature does not come equipped with its own classifications, say into "thermoplastics" versus "ectoplastics." Even one's lap is a projected object, based in the reality of sitting as opposed to standing or lying down. So is one's figure (as object of admiration or vexation). Still, wholesale irrealism—"there are as many worlds as there are true world versions"—is neither compelled nor even invited by those considerations. Just the opposite, in fact: just as the perceptual illusions form a system that argues not against the veridicality of the senses but is both a condition for and a map of the veridicality of the senses, so our classifications are a (crude) map of the foundation in reality required for their success.

33. There is a lot to be said for both accounts, especially of perception and art, but not enough for either to carry the day beyond being a small paragraph toward explaining the success of science. Some deluded writers (Rorty in his three articles in *London Review of Books*, 1987) say American and Continental thought have finally converged, that "we make the world," and that we make the difference between "true" and "false"— a refined materialistic, conventionalized subjective idealism. On the contrary, the success of science is a stable comprehension of things (expressible in mathematized abstractions), with the object of comprehending all of nature, with "reductions" where appropriate. The object of science is to be "streetwise in the universe," to comprehend it. For that we need a story about understanding that has been unfashionable since it last appeared in Descartes's wax example (*Meditations, II*), Rene Descartes: *Meditations on First Philosophy* (New York: Cambridge University Press, 1986).

Regardless of the prospects for such accounts of the success of science, the new story from Harvard, as I said, dynamited the principles for "evidentialism" and for "foundationalism" to explain successful science. Philosophers, with no interest in religion, noticed that faith, trust, reliance on others better placed to know, is integral to science as a communication system, as well as a source of the premises in the discovery process itself.[34] For example, we rely upon the laws of nature to be the same everywhere, regardless of the position or motion of the observer, an article of Einsteinian faith whose confirmation depends on our accepting it first.[35] Moreover, we rely on processes of measurement and experiment that are the best at hand and are vindicated by their outcomes or replaced. So faith was rehabilitated, brought in from the cold and recognized to be a way of getting knowledge. The integrity of science demanded it. Science depends on faith, as the betrayals proved.

"Faith" is no longer the paradigm of "unjustified belief " or "belief that contravenes the evidence," or "belief held against the demands of reason," as Locke and Hume, and even C. J. Ducasse (*Nature, Mind and Death,* 1948) thought, but *rational* trust in those who *ought* to know and, equivocally but relatedly, reliance on the patterns in things. Even non-thinking animals display what Santayana called "animal faith," staking their lives hour by hour until they lose.

It does not matter that the new irrealism (Goodman) or Putnam's internal realism, or Quine's naturalized epistemology (with its subtended behaviorism) is itself hopeless. They dislodged the evidentialist's keystone. The arch of evidentialism collapsed, and with it, foundationalism and obstacles to rational faith as part of religious epistemology. Now we can incorporate the much older tradition that divine faith perfects natural faith.[36] And now we can critically reappraise the longer history of *cognitive voluntarism*, whose key elements were employed by Augustine and Aquinas[37] and remained in the bloodstream of philosophy at least as late as Descartes's account of error as due to the will, *Meditations,* and were reintroduced by William James (*The Will to Believe*) after having been unceremoniously ousted by British

34. See the heated assertions that lying, plagiarism, and faking results in science is a betrayal of the fabric of science. If old evidentialism were right, no one could justifiably rely upon anyone else, and so everyone could lie, because every scientist would have to do everything over. That illustrates how silly and unconnected to the actual practice of science philosophical accounts of rationality can become.

35. See remarks to similar effect in John Passmore's *Recent Philosophy,* cited above, pp. 111–14.

36. That grace perfects nature.

37. See "Believing for Profit," cited above.

empiricism (Locke, though even Locke had to regard conviction as falling under the power of the will in order to castigate credulity and unsupported belief so severely).

We trust because we want something.[38] Reliance is, itself, a mode of satisfaction. That's the basic psychological mechanism for "taking someone's word for it" as well as for "relying on what things do." A hunter relies on the flight patterns of turkeys because he wants to eat some. We trust even an unprepossessing stranger for directions, going long distances on slight word if there is no one else to ask. Need overrides caution. We distrust strange meat, strange shapes, and strange tastes. But hunger can countermand disgust, making us eat the native's unidentifiable food and even eat the all too clearly identifiable snake, lizard, ant, maggot, or eye. We can, even against resistance, trust people we don't like when we want something badly: medical care, banking, home repairs; sometimes, amazingly, to get love and intimacy. We can even trust people we do not trust, in desperation or passion.

Augustine says, *"nemo credit nisi volens"* ("no one believes unless he wants to"); not that you can believe at will or even disbelieve at will, though the power of the unconscious is awesome at rejection, and impressive at accommodation, regardless of the evidence. Nevertheless, the will is the engine of believing, not the understanding, except in the few cases of the "manifest vision of truth," of compelling obviousness, as Aquinas explained it. And even the compelling obviousness of one's mortal wounds can be willed away, say, as a medic urges one to live, sometimes with success. The rest of the time, when evidence does not compel belief, the will supplies the commitment.

Aquinas says it is reasonable to believe someone for the good to be gained from doing so, that is, to believe for profit. That was Augustine's view in his *On the Profit of Believing (De Utilitate Credendi)*. In fact Augustine says the unbeliever is *in extremis,* suffering from a sickness only God can cure, exactly in the position of the patient who must trust the doctor or die. (How else could such savage medicine have been practiced on England's Charles II in 1685? See *Great Medical Disasters,* Richard Gordon, Dorset, 1976.) In particular, Aquinas says it is reasonable to believe Jesus for the sake of attaining eternal life: "[T]hus we are moved to believe what God says because we are promised eternal life as a reward if we believe. And this reward moves the will to *assent* to what is said, although the intellect is not moved by anything which it understands" (*De Veritate,* 14.1). Aquinas clearly

38. See papers on Aquinas cited above.

thinks "believing for profit" is a natural paradigm on which grace builds.[39]

Seventeenth-century science idealized finding out for oneself, Descartes's antidote for groundless and false received opinion. The success of science wore out the ideal by making parallel processing part of the very energy of discovery and proof (see James Watson, *The Double Helix*). We now know you cannot do science by yourself or by watching everything everyone does. You cannot even guarantee the size of the spoons you buy, much less calibrate the beakers, read the x-rays, or measure the accuracy of electronic measurers, or replicate every important experiment you depend upon. Science is a web of dependence and trust. That's why we regard faked results with such horror.[40] As Aquinas reported Cicero, the reason every lie is against reason is that it tears the fabric of community. A fortiori for lies in science. In science, public rational certainty is only incidentally a function of the evidence *you* have for it, and much more a matter of the process by which you derived it and how it fits into what "everyone" is confident to say.

So evidentialism died, and foundationalism along with it—though plenty of philosophers still promenade those corpses in the wheelchairs of argument. And faith, rehabilitated as a means of knowledge, coordinate with one's own inquiry, now stands as a source, not only of rational certainty, but even of scientific knowledge. That's how most of us get most of our scientific knowledge. The knowledge of God is gradually moving into configuration with our knowledge of universal inertia and of the gravitational effects of dark matter.

Another obstacle died out, after causing a vast literature, because the game was not worth the candle, as I said,[41] namely, the irritating, ignorant wrangle over whether religious discourse is somehow meaning-impaired. To those who reflect on how information is conveyed in natural language, it is certain that mainstream religious discourse meets stringent conditions for cognitivity, though much of the discourse is craftbound. Religious discourse shares meaning-differentiation features, like analogy, metaphor, and denomination, that are universal in both unbound and craftbound discourse. We can even explain how nonsense is generated from sense,[42] accounting for a vast subtext of

39. See the references in the articles cited above.

40. Robertson Davies, in *The Lyre of Orpheus* (New York: Viking, 1989), says "Faking is the syphilis of art," p. 465.

41. See notes to Chapter 7 in J. Ross, *Portraying Analogy* (Cambridge: Cambridge University Press, 1981), for books and papers representing the hundreds of efforts to accommodate that dead doctrine.

42. See Ross, *Portraying Analogy,* chap. 7, cited above. Particularly note the account

religious talk (as also occurs in stock-market appraisals, "psychobabble," science, philosophy, art, music, and everywhere else), that is as loony and without content as you could ever imagine. So much, then, for the longstanding noncognitivist annoyance.[43] But enough on the resurrection of faith for now.

II

Demonstration and other kinds of proof need to be reconsidered. Demonstration is a very restricted kind of proof because it has to eliminate all counter-possibilities. I mean not only that the conclusion has to follow validly: "not *possibly* . . . [the premises], and *not* . . . [the conclusion]." The reasoning has to exhaust the field of relevant possibility (usually by allowing a contradiction to be deduced from the negation of the conclusion) or by providing for a *construction* of the conclusion from the premises entirely by permutations permitted in the logic. Thus, a demonstration has to eliminate every relevant, "Suppose, instead . . . ." Demonstration is like cabinet-making; it requires a lot of tools, very skilled craftsmanship, and a devoted and cultivated clientele, and it can't be used in iron bridge-building.

Being demonstrated is a special status for something certain, a kind of public and impersonal certification. Exactly what that certification amounts to, what it adds to personal and collective sureness, was never crystal clear, even in days when philosophy had Euclidean science as a model. What it would amount to now is even more puzzling, when we know that being demonstrated (e.g., a Euclidean theorem or a theorem of Newtonian mechanics) does not amount to being unqualifiedly true and assures no particular grip on the real world.

One thing has been obvious all along (though it is overlooked often enough): "being demonstrated" is not a necessary condition for "being

of how nonsense is generated as "fallout" of the meaning-adaptation of words. Apparently anybody can do what madmen, preachers, poets (doctors, lawyers?), and phenomenologists do routinely.

43. There was a political factor, too, in the drying up of the cognitivity debate. It died out in ethics, aesthetics, and especially metaphysics around the time other postwar figures like Quine, Sellars, Davidson, Goodman, etc., firmly shifted interest to logic, philosophy of science, and "naturalized epistemology" (the explanation of knowledge by entirely physical processes). A. J. Ayer's favorite thesis, that metaphysics, ethics, and religion are meaningless, was simply abandoned. The establishment got tired of it. Interest turned in the Sixties and Seventies to theories of meaning for whole languages (Davidson and Dummett, Grice), and to epistemology naturalized (Quine) as functionalism (Putnam), to accounts of personal identity (Bernard Williams and D. Parfitt), and to Rawls's *Theory of Justice* (Cambridge, Mass.: Belknap Press of Harvard University Press, 1971) and allied subjects. "Establishment" philosophers lost interest in the discussion of religion almost entirely.

known" or for "being the object of rational certainty," not even in mathematics, much less in religion or science. In fact, "being demonstrated" is not a well-traveled path into scientific status. There is not one (non-formal, non-trivial[44]) point in the whole of philosophy that is regarded by philosophers generally as having been demonstrated. That, after two and a half millennia! So demonstration can't be what we are after generally; why, then, in the case of God?

Why does anyone insist that the existence of God be demonstrated, especially people who never try to demonstrate anything? It seems to be the fault of believers (including Plato's and Aristotle's broad *Theos*) who offered to provide the assurances. Among Christians, Augustine offers an argument in Book II of *De Libero Arbitrio,* and Anselm surprises practically everyone with the force and clarity of his reasoning in *Proslogion.* Aquinas, Scotus, Ockham, Descartes, Leibniz, Spinoza, and even Locke contrived to offer what were supposed to be conclusive arguments.

Still, why should anyone, nowadays, who grants that nothing of importance can be demonstrated in philosophy or seldom attempts such a feat, ask that the existence of God be demonstrated as a condition for believing it?[45] There seems to be a confusion over what it is reasonable to believe, even to be strongly convinced of in structuring one's life, and what is a proper part of our world-science.

When Plato, Aristotle, Plotinus, Augustine, Anselm, Avicenna, Averroes, Maimonides, Aquinas, Scotus, Ockham, Descartes, Leibniz, Locke, Spinoza, Berkeley, Newton, Kant, and Peirce[46] constructed their formidable reasonings, their objective was not religious but scientific, to make a coherent world-picture based on rigorously thought-out principles. (Notice, where the question of God's existence has been answered negatively, even taking Empedocles, Lucretius, Hume, Nietzsche, and Sartre into account, nothing remotely approaching the rigor and discipline of a demonstration is offered. Why?)

---

44. The only formal results I know of that appear to have any philosophical significance are (i) that numerical infinities, infinite sets, classes, etc., have a subset in one-to-one correspondence with the whole; (ii) that there are truths of arithmetic (and of every system rich enough to be a model of arithmetic) that cannot be deduced from any axiomatization that does not include the truth in question; and (iii) some trivial notions about validity, the difference among material, formal and strict implication, the consistency of systems, and the like. In other words, nothing of substantive philosophical importance is demonstrable at all, and all demonstrations by philosophers (as when I say "it's demonstrable that your view is inconsistent") are framed in a narrow context of common assumptions, for the time not disputed. That's what I mean by saying "demonstration is tightly context-bound."

45. Could it be because you might risk (or fear to) so much by disbelieving it that we need a justification for unbelief (see Pascal)?

46. There are a few dozen "demonstrators" still living, like Charles Hartshorne.

The inquiry among the main philosophers was not over what to believe about the being of God, but over what reasoning to accept as decisive on the issue. They mostly seemed to think decisive reasons on the issue were available, despite their vast range of other differences, not decisive as to what to believe—for most thought they already knew that—but decisive as to carrying the "scientific" burden of proof, decisive in settling the matter without leaving any uncovered counterpossibilities.

Many of the philosophers' ontologies required the being of God (e.g., Plato, Aristotle, Plotinus, Aquinas, etc.), and some philosophers based their whole theories of knowledge on the veracity or illumination of God, as did Augustine (*De Libero Arbitrio*) and Descartes ((*Meditationes*, III and VI), and so needed demonstrative certainty about God. Others base their whole physical science on the divine order of nature resulting from divine wisdom, as did Leibniz and Newton. Others think "God is a Geometer," as Keppler did, to account for why the simplest and most orderly of scientific hypotheses are to be expected to be true. Some think God is a rational spirit "who does not play dice with the world," as did Einstein, explaining why "messy" hypotheses, like the Heisenberg indeterminacy principle, are not the basic truth. Even if, unlike those thinkers, you do not intellectually employ belief in God as a foundation for scientific knowledge, or otherwise live in theistic conviction, you might still appreciate (more notionally and less existentially than they, no doubt) why the great thinkers seek rationales to decide the issue by exhausting the possibilities.

Besides, the case that there is not rational certainty, objective and well-founded, about the being of God is virtually a "non-starter."[47] For mistaken arguments, carefully constructed, do ground rational conviction; they can even have true conclusions. What if they fail to eliminate all the counterpossibilities? Rational certainty does not require this, any more than a justification for a perceptual claim has to eliminate all counterpossibilities. The whole issue of whether believers in God have rational certainty of the sort held by those, say, who believe that AIDS is a fatal disease, is a recent invention, framed in evidentialist assumptions and assigning the classical "demonstrations" a role both less than and irrelevant to the one they served. The issue still

47. A line of reasoning that succeeds at demonstration will, of course, ground rational certainty, if it is appreciated. But it may ground it just as well without success at demonstration. It may even ground rational certainty when it is mistaken. For instance, I do not think Descartes's certainty that humans are a unity of distinct substances was irrational or in some way reprehensible; he was merely mistaken.

remains for philosophers to find rationales for or against the existence of God that actually exhaust the options and do so decisively.

There is nothing knowable by a demonstration that cannot be known with certainty without one, and that includes mathematical and logical theorems. So demonstrability is not a gateway condition of knowability for anything. Therefore, showing that a purported demonstration fails (or that all of them do) does not discredit the claim to natural knowledge of the existence of God.[48]

Moreover, many people think God's existence is recognized and encountered, that it is known by a kind of awareness, whether or not it is demonstrable. In fact, recognition of God's reality is a matter of educated construal, something like the insight by which we recognize that the cosmos is mathematically intelligible. That kind of cognition is more a matter of training and refinement than a particular group of considerations; it is more like learning how to understand the music of J. S. Bach or acquiring historical understanding.[49] So "demonstration" is not even appropriate for vindicating the knowledge claims typical of certain believers in God.[50]

Arguments that meet my conditions for demonstration[51] [namely, (1) validity (2) and true premises (3) that are publicly accessible (4) without epistemic circularity and (5) reliably and methodically decidable, and (6) that also exhaust all counterpossibility for the conclusion], if there are any for the existence of God, may have nothing whatever to do with changing minds. In fact, that is to be expected. Something else is needed.

Demonstrations need a lot of level ground among the parties. That's why they are not good persuasive devices from "insiders" to "outsiders." Demonstrations require too much in the way of shared knowledge to serve parties who have opposed commitments about a very important conclusion. They serve even less well when parties opposed over the conclusion are also opposed over the underlying considerations, for

48. Some people misunderstood the First Vatican Council to have affirmed that our actively being able to demonstrate the existence of God is a condition for our having natural knowability of God; e.g., I think Garrigou-LaGrange thought so; see my *Philosophical Theology* (Indianapolis, In.: Bobbs-Merrill, 1969).

49. For instance, a chromatic scale played in fourths.

50. The ice has been broken on whether unbelief is a reprehensible condition ethically, see Mark Talbot's "Is It Natural to Believe in God?" *Faith and Philosophy* 6, no. 2 (April 1989), 155–72, with its thought-provoking quotations from Calvin.

51. I wrote about the conditions for demonstrations in *Philosophical Theology*, chap. 1; *Introduction to Philosophy of Religion*, chap. 1; and "On Proofs for the Existence of God," *The Monist* (Aquinas Centennial Issue 1974). I think by adding the requirement that "counterpossibilities have to be exhausted or blocked," the older rigid notion is clearer.

instance, over whether an infinite regress of inclusive causes is impossible or whether the movement of material things has to begin with a first movement (like winding a clock).

A genuine demonstration rules out all counterpossibilities. Thus, a heavy investment of feeling in an anti-theistic outcome will raise a "counterpossibility," no matter what consideration is offered.[52] There is always something a dedicated nonbeliever would deny rather than accept the conclusion. For instance, a teacher of mine said that if I could derive the existence of God from the principle of noncontradiction, that would amount to a reason for him to doubt that principle. Such regression of doubts from conclusion to premises is not unreasonable; it is a device for inquiry. Thus, the better the argument you offer, the more the ignorant you may make your opponent.[53]

We cannot find a large enough field of common assumptions to exclude such a trade-off of doubts, not even for the sincerely inquiring and somewhat inclined unbeliever, especially if he or she is "smart" but not an expert. So we have to talk about what causes conviction.

An argument is convincing about a hard point only when it goes right up to the edge at which you are not willing to doubt, and leans on that edge to leverage your belief. You can't do that with arguments about important things that make the whole meaning of your life. That is not a defect in the religious situation.[54] We simply do not rest such important matters on the thin reed of argument. The same holds in mathematics for those with a dedicated, lived-in conception of the subject.[55]

There can be no demonstration of the existence of transfinite numbers for a mathematical intuitionist because the form of thinking that yields the conclusions, "indirect proof,"[56] comes into doubt just because it yields such conclusions. The intuitionist "needs" no such numbers. ("God made the natural numbers, man made the rest.") So one side uses indirect proof to establish the existence of transfinite num-

52. The antecedent probability of a semantically consistent hypothesis, for a particular person, depends partly on how badly he wants it to be true; otherwise doubt may be just transferred from the conclusion to whatever consideration is advanced for it.

53. The explanation of that point is to be found in both George Mavrodes's *Belief in God* (New York: Random House, 1970) and my *Philosophical Theology*.

54. Or in the moral situation; or in our knowledge of the objectives or the foundations of perception, or of mathematics; or in our certainty about the external world.

55. There does seem to be some irresolvable dispute between intuitionists and others that cannot be settled by any argument as to whether the principles of excluded middle and bifurcation of predicates are universal truths rather than local devices.

56. Indirect proof is deduction of the existence of something, say, a prime larger than one million, by deduction of a contradiction from the denial that there is such a number.

bers by deducing a contradiction from the assumption that there are no such numbers, just the way I would prove that there is a prime that is the immediate successor of ten and argue, in the same form, for the existence of God. The other side says the argument is invalid because "indirect proof " is invalid to prove existence; only construction amounts to existence.[57]

Demonstrations are commendations in a "scholarly" world. They are orderly arrangements of considerations so as to command the conclusion, from those sharing enough to be disposed to be commanded. So, purported demonstrations of what one does not believe, based on diversely interpreted considerations[58] one already knows about, are simply annoying. They dress up in formal robes just what we object to.

For instance, in the discussion of the reality of "the external world," no "demonstration" will settle a real dispute. Both sides know all the considerations and all their patterns. Neither side can make a new *ad hominem* circumstantial argument whose price is some principle the opponent cares about and assigns the same weight as does the other. So some other sort of proof may be far better for changing minds.

There are also other kinds of proof: (i) what puts the matter beyond a reasonable doubt; (ii) what makes the matter clear and convincing; (iii) what tips the scale of belief. From law for example, we can find non-demonstrative "proofs" that are high in persuasive power as well as reliability. In fact, that is the basis for their comparative ranking into "proof beyond a reasonable doubt," "proof by clear and convincing evidence," and "proof by the preponderance of the evidence." Even the latter, as the victories of tobacco companies have made clear, can require an enormous body of scientific evidence and expertise and can be weakened or discounted by all sorts of challenges.

Nevertheless, sometimes wholly circumstantial evidence can amount

57. Quantified reasoning with empty names, like "unicorn," that deduces, e.g., the existence of unicorns from the contradiction that would result from admitting that "all unicorns have only one horn" and asserting "there are no unicorns" is obviously mistaken. This is analogous to the intuitionist's objection to the indirect proof: expressions are taken to be designative and put into phrases where a contradiction is made from a denial of the existence, say, of a real number larger than N (the number of the natural numbers). There can be no rapprochement between the parties, not by any demonstration, anyway.

58. See the discussion of "considerations" in Ross, "On Proofs for the Existence of God," cited above. Examples of considerations: "being cannot be accounted for by causation because causation supposes being"; "whatever is moved is moved by another"; "whatever begins to be is caused to be"; "whatever possibly exists, exists necessarily or contingently." Notice, when you write the key consideration briefly, you can see that demonstrative form is simply an iron bridge to the conclusion. The real question always is "Will I accept such a consideration as decisive, if the bridge can be made?"

to a proof "beyond a reasonable doubt," even of a capital crime. I mean that without a "smoking gun," and without eyewitnesses or even a corpse, enough evidence of means, motive, and opportunity, and the absence of any other reasonable hypothesis, can cause conviction beyond a reasonable doubt. Circumstantial evidence can accumulate against our background knowledge to "proof beyond a reasonable doubt," like snow blowing against a fence till we can walk over on it.

First, a proof beyond a reasonable doubt is not shaken by one's showing there is a semantically consistent counterpossibility. For one thing, semantic consistency is not sufficient for real possibility.[59] For another, bare possibilities don't engage doubt,[60] nor do remote ones. Relevant possibilities have to compete for likelihood with the judgment under inquiry in order to raise doubts. You might have been vaporized by the time the light leaving your face was processed by my brain, and so no longer exist when I "see" you; this is a bare possibility, but it does not lead to reasonable doubt.

Second, a proof by clear and convincing evidence generates conviction (and often certainty when the elements are true) even when one may admit there are other relevant, and not wholly unlikely, possibilities. One might wonder about other possibilities, not entirely unlikely, whose likelihood is worth taking into account. So maybe the colors of things are not in the things, as some scientists say. Yet, I think the case is clear and convincing that they are (despite significant counterarguments), just as that the air around a dead animal smells. That the case is clear and convincing means I am sure the conclusion is true; not that the sureness guarantees truth. Moreover, that the case is clear and convincing means I am objectively justified in my certainty (but not that my opponents will agree on that or on the grounds that I accept).

59. I have given the reasons in *Truth and Impossibility* and "Aquinas's Exemplarism, Aquinas's Voluntarism," *Catholic Philosophical Quarterly*, LXIV, no. 2 (Spring 1990). Consider: "he talks faster than light." Consistent, yes; possible, no. The basic consideration is that verbal possibilities (semantic consistencies) involve "overflow" conditions, conditions that go beyond the meanings of the words and are "incorporated" by their designative roles. So verbally, "thinking birds" are possible; but whether such are really possible depends on whether the "overflow" conditions required in nature for thinking things conflict with those for being a bird. Not sure? How about "thinking electrons"? If you are in doubt, you grant my point. Thomas Reid made an argument for the same point based on the idea that there may be necessities in nature that we do not know about. I thank Josefine Nauckhoff for pointing out Michael Hooker's paper on Reid to me.

60. If "ifs" and "ands" were pots and pans, there'd be no need of tinkers. It is a common mistake in philosophy to say a person will doubt what he sees or says (or ought to), if we show him he might have been mistaken, and under these very conditions. Rather, he should say, "So what? I wasn't." (I might have been killed, too; but I wasn't.)

The order of the universe, the unsettling idea that ours is the only intelligence, even the only life,[61] in the universe, that our understanding is not the product of any other intelligence but only transient and without final meaning, all may converge to create a clear and convincing case that reality has to have one cosmos-explaining, intelligent being. For a philosopher to say that this cannot amount to a case of clear and convincing evidence (even though it is not beyond reasonable doubt) is simply to legislate in the face of the facts.

You may have a clear and convincing case for something without having independent clear and convincing evidence for the nonoccurrence of each defeating condition.[62] Philosophers often mix those things up. Thus you may allow that the mysteriousness of evil, the unrelieved oppression of the innocent, and the apparent triumph of the unjust are reasons for doubting what you are certain of without sharing those doubts yourself but only wondering about how it all "goes together."

Third, considerations can configure into conviction even though they do not put the conclusion beyond reasonable doubt or make a clear and convincing case but simply tip the scale so that the balance of belief shifts to affirmation, though with some fear of error. Many who do not think there is a clear and convincing case for genuine human responsibility, not defeated by psychophysical determinism, may still find the preponderance of evidence from personal experience sufficient to cause affirmation. That is called proof by the "preponderance of the evidence." Preponderant evidence is not just "more," it *tips* the scale so that it *settles* to affirmation, to belief. This is a success situation.[63]

61. Arthur Clarke is said to have remarked that the most momentous scientific question is whether we are the only intelligent beings in the universe, equally momentous either way, a kind of apex of human existence when we first come on the answer.

62. You may know a minor took your car for a joy-ride because a neighbor says he saw him get into it. Of course, the FBI might have commandeered it; gangsters might have used it to kidnap the minor; a "private eye" might have borrowed it; your wife might have persuaded the neighbor to lie because she ran out of gas; and so on, forever.

63. For these purposes, I am assuming there really is a contest of considerations supported by admissible evidence on both sides. In that situation, the failure of the plaintiff to persuade tips the scale against him and for the defendant. In short, in civil cases, the plaintiff has the responsibility to load the scale with enough admissible data to tip it in his favor; otherwise, it falls by operation of law in favor of the defendant, a more constricted system than we have in practical life.

In the theological case, considerations can tip the scale to rational conviction, short of clear and convincing evidence, but still not require an exercise of faith in the conclusion, rather, a genuine cognitive construal of one's own, even if the result is only true belief (or rationally justified belief, leaving truth aside). I think the being of God is a suitable object for belief by a preponderance of the evidence (as weighed and sorted

This discussion of proof beyond reasonable doubt, by clear and convincing evidence, and by tipping the scale of belief displays how there can be fully rational conviction, even knowing, that is less than scientific demonstration.

Ordinary conviction, taken as a whole, is a tissue with threads of solid knowing (with many different bases, of the sorts I have mentioned and others to come) and some small webs of our having found things out for ourselves. But it is generally held together with various kinds of faith—reliance on others or on social processes for faithful reports of actual findings out. Our responsible believing is not, for the most part, knowing, though a far larger portion of it is knowing than philosophical accounts usually allow. For they confound the standards of objective science with the conditions for individual cognition.

Within such a general approach, rational conviction about the existence of God can come from convergent wondering about the mystery of the being of the cosmos, about the fact that in the trillions of galaxies there is only evil here on our planet (as far as we can tell), about the mysterious exhilarating obviousness of intelligent life and love visible on the bloody face of a newborn human, and about whether something as marvelous as human love and understanding could come about without intention and be extinguished, person by person, and finally and forever with the death of the species. Convergent *disbelief* in the thought-out alternatives, based upon their violation of a "good scientific story" requiring simplicity and beauty and economy, is a pretty fair basis for rational conviction, perhaps amounting to knowledge, but in any case, to a justified conviction about God, just as such reasoning can be such a basis in art, science, music, and even investments.

These are considerations that *transfigure*[64] our world and can configure the galaxies into manifesting God, just as knowing how to read can turn mere marks into "Do not infest your mind with beating on the strangeness of this business" (*The Tempest,* V.1), or the right understanding can detect the *Dies Irae* in a wedding march or find the faces

---

individually). It can come out both ways for different thoughtful persons. That's why, whatever the defects of unbelief, it is a rational certainty for some people. Talbot's paper (cited above) and the tendency of "reformed" epistemology and the long "ethics of belief " debate (see the McCarthy book cited above) will now invite a backlash, because believing beyond the evidence, against God's existence, will be said to involve not so much a failure of evidence for God as a moral failure to develop the cognitive functions of feeling to discern and configure it, and will invite the charge that we have dulled our sensitivity with trash, like a soap opera addict who regards all serious stories as tedious and bad.

64. See chap. 2 of *Introduction to Philosophy of Religion,* cited above.

of the Presidents in a scattering of dots. It is not argument that carries the day, but discernment that satisfies the rational appetite.

More important than anything I have said yet is that feelings function cognitively at all levels to disclose considerations, to connect the elements of proof short of demonstration, and even to reveal the logical connections to us and what *are* the relevant factors. Above all, feelings configure experience into conviction.

III

Feelings function cognitively in the basis for certainty. Most people don't ever ask why we have to train feeling as well as understanding. Why sensitize young people's responses by exposure to pets, poets, painting, architecture, theater, novels, decoration, decorum, dance, argumentation, law, and even wilderness and zoos? And why teach them the critical appraisal of some or all? Many suppose it is for the young to "appreciate" and perhaps "enjoy," get pleasure from such things, and in a few cases be able to tell good from bad. That's the "Romper Room" version of refinement.

A "person of refinement," even as that notion was understood in the eighteenth century and surely in much of the nineteenth, is a "person of taste," a person who habitually tells the good from the bad, the excellent from the rest, and finds enjoyment in the best. A person of refinement enjoys the excellent by second nature, but is able to transfer such judgment to all human activities. Refinement is the ability to detect quality virtually anywhere, whether or not one is able to produce it, explain it, or teach it.[65]

Training makes for refinement, whether in thought (philosophy, mathematics, history, physics, sociology, law), expression (writing, dance, painting, drawing, sculpture), action (statesmanship, politics, business), or any other mode of excellence. Some refinement of understanding (literature, languages, philosophy) and of feeling (art, history, music) is more general and more easily transferred than others (formal logic, accounting, engineering). But the object of all is the same: the integration of feeling and understanding into effortless excellence of judgment, performance, expression, and enjoyment. This holds

65. The notion of "refinement" had popular corruptions, of course, in prissy, conformist, mannered dandies and worldlings, in foppish dilettantes, learned triflers, nincompoops, and sage rubes. Breeding in horses, dogs, and roses can be overdone, as well as "cultivation" of people, not just to being silly or outright mad, but to being perverse and evil. So we can "refine" feeling to cultivate the thrill of evil, self-regarding willfulness, a craze of cruelty, the exaltation of fury, and the cold self-containment of disdain, contempt, and contumely. But that takes nothing away from the real thing.

whether we are talking of an olympic diver who does not need to "word out" his actions, but plans them by imaginary prevision with feeling, and so only has to notice the feeling to achieve the previsioned actions, or of the writer who has to smash words around in bunches to make edges that will express his thoughts. The philosopher is worse off, working harder, because he or she has to battle with the words like a writer but elude their beguilement,[66] their tendency to appear to do the work once they fit together, instead of revealing how little work has been done, and how arthritically.

The cognitive refinement of feeling can only be learned by apprenticeship because it requires mimesis. It requires the fully invested "doing the same" with which an infant son walks like his father (from first walking to last) and with which all children learn their parents' language(s). Mimesis is the only path to refinement of cognitive feeling.

Beyond detection of features of things, and being an elaborate analogue computer (the way a diver's feeling monitors and modifies a performance too elaborate and too rapid to think about), feelings configure disclosures ("I could *see* he was lying"; "He infuriated me; I suddenly *saw* he did not care at all."). Beyond that, feelings transfigure events, creating meaning, making as great a change as meaning does from mere marks to "If the eye were an animal, sight would be its soul." Making that sort of meaning *is* conviction, operative conviction.

Feelings configure considerations into convictions. That's how we arrive at the most important and the most general, basic, and stable convictions by which we live and die.

Do you think you could ever solve the basic disputes about the foundations of morality; the role of heterosexual love; the place of family, of children, of religion, of loyalty and love in one's life; of the extent of individual liberty, respect for law, deliberate opposition to the law, and rebellion against love; the place of personal power and physical force, of desire and lust, cruelty, pride, punishment, revenge, forgiveness, neighborliness, speculation science and wonder, poetry and health, inquiry, work and play, making and using, and enjoying, and the time to be allocated to each, fast enough and well enough to live rationally as long as you have? And yet every one of those commitments, once habitual, is final, irrevocable, life-determining, and more important than your money.

66. See Aristotle's remarks in *The Topics*, Wittgenstein's comments about the fly in the fly bottle and the like, and Aquinas's remarks about imagination. See also my "Mindful of Man" section, "The Imagination Is the Master of Falsity," forthcoming.

They are just a few things we live and die by. Do you think you could ever figure out enough about all those and more to make your conclusions the framework of your (only) life? You have to live by reliance, not what you figured out, just to make scope enough for reason to be of any use to you, to do anything significant for you. You have to live basically by refined feeling, by the product of mimesis. No wonder there is no real luck for the ill-reared.[67]

Practical wisdom, knowing how to live well and what for and having the means and resolution to do it (Augustine), is the product of refined feeling functioning cognitively, not of speculative reason (for which feeling functions, too), even at its best entangled in a web of disputes.

Now, to explain the epistemological importance of all this, I have to remark that rationalist conceptions of knowing have finally been rejected. The conception, found in Plato, Augustine, and Descartes (and one that sneaks back into every discussion about skepticism) is this: "S knows that P if and only if P is true, and *it is not possible* that S believe P on the grounds or in the conditions in which S does, when P is false." As long as that notion dominated, there was not much point in talking about the cognitive functions of feeling.

Now we know that most ordinary knowledge is of a kind where, though we might in indistinguishable circumstances have believed the same thing when it was false, because our believing is reasonably grounded (evidentially or by reliance) and is true, it is knowing (absent defeating conditions). I cannot forbear pointing out that if that is what ordinary empirical knowing is, then the only thing that could prevent ordinary religious believers from actually knowing that God exists, after giving it the sort of thought I mentioned above and becoming convinced, is that the belief is false. In a word, they know God exists if God does exist. And that meets the most stringent test their opponents consistently impose.

We acknowledge an indefinite list of "defeating" conditions, conditions whose presence or absence will defeat what is otherwise sufficient for knowing. So if it turns out I was tricked into belief, even when it would otherwise be all right, or that there was an accidental correlation of truth and my believing without orderly causation, or there was a betrayal by a trustworthy person or a loss of fidelity in a transmitter, then what would otherwise have been knowledge is defeated, even if the belief is true. Adequately based true belief, without defeating conditions, is ordinary cognition.

Undefeated justified true belief is ordinary empirical knowledge,

67. Apart from the intervention of grace.

but not all of it. Ordinary cognition is the knowledge by which we live and die. It is the kind of knowledge we use to decide the matters of greatest import, requiring the care of a noticing person disposing of his most important interests; the knowledge that the stove did not relight after we shut it off, that a building is reasonably safe, that a dog is not going to chew the electric wires, that poisons are not present in food or air, that a baby is positioned to breathe freely.

The prudent person settling his most important business with a high degree of risk aversion and a loathing of uncertainty, except over small things, wants little of articulated argument and more of satisfaction with his expectations. He is a cognitive voluntarist, ripe for both grace and temptation. That's how salespersons prey on the greedy, through the very cognitive devices, wishful thinking, that customers use to find a bargain. The difference between the dupe and the smart shopper is in how much desire distorts reality.

When the outcome of our consideration is supposed to be stable and coherent as a basis for our life, we rest far more on feeling than on argument of any kind. It is amazing how many things we "bet our life" on, with only habitual reliance and no other thought. Yet how much hesitation a small change of conduct designed to gain eternal life calls up in those who have not divine faith.

Practical wisdom, the ability to live wisely and well, is the product of good training and example, internalized by your *mimesis* of refined understanding, feeling, and even passion. Yes, passion. A life without passion is feeble and furtive. Passion has to be made part of refinement, then, made to reveal and to found conviction, and not just sexual passion, but envy, anger, fear, hope, eagerness, energy, excitement, exaltation, joy, sadness, sorrow, and despair. The violent feelings have to find place in refined cognition.[68] So, too, philosophy without feeling is philosophy without springs. It's like bicycling with training wheels. Words milled in fury that sputter a little convey comprehension better than mincing passionless professional patter.

Practical wisdom is more reliable and more appropriate than science for making a life. Even in philosophy, wisdom counts above cleverness and mere intelligence. So when David Lewis tells us there *are* all the ways things might have been, and all the things, too, ranged in other worlds unreachable physically from ours, but otherwise like ours and just as real as ours, the elegance of his argument, the adroit way he avoids traps others are gored in, avail nothing to persuade us. The

68. See Flannery O'Connor's "The Violent Bear It Away," Flannery O'Connor, *Collected Works* (New York: Viking Press, 1988), and the poetry of Brother Antoninus in David Kherdian, *Six Poets of the San Francisco Renaissance, Portraits and Checklists* (Fresno, Cal.: Giligin Press, 1967).

idea is a non-starter. It offends wisdom; it does not have the "feel" of quality. The same is true of Platonists about mathematical objects who are physicalists otherwise; theirs is polyester ontology. So in the end, even in intellectual matters, there is a dispositive appraisal (at least for a time) in which our training and acquired refinement count far more than any argument. We arrive at conviction: Lewis's plurality of worlds is, at bottom, science fiction, not philosophical science.

Many intelligent people rest their theistic convictions on divine faith (on the confident expectation that the promises of Jesus will be fulfilled). They look at theistic argument less for conviction than for a scientific schematism for things, the way they would read an explanation of electrical generators, already sure the electric company produces electricity but wanting to know in a schematic way *how*. Since they believe the cause of religious conviction is divine grace, they need no argument to reinforce its rationality. But they do get satisfaction from having an explanation, something that is undeniable to anyone "who understands electricity" in contrast to one who does not. So argument and explanation don't increase certitude or substitute for revelation; they supply another kind of satisfaction: the understanding that is one of the rewards of believing for those who seek to understand what they have first believed (Augustine).

Finally, when practical wisdom evaluates the considerations about God, some believers find the force of the case against God, based on evil, to be reversed. They notice that: (a) There is no religiously neutral description of what is problematic about evil. (b) It cannot be evil for a good God to make death, pain, the mindless destruction and cruelty of the animal world, or wrong to make animal consciousness with its dominating rages, terrors, and rapaciousness; otherwise the case is closed from the statement of the problem: res ipsa loquitur. Besides, God's relationship to creaturely pain cannot be a determined exercise of omnipotence to get rid of it, as the life of Jesus makes clear. He healed only a token among sufferers and raised few dead. (c) It cannot be evil for God to make free creatures who do monstrous evil, otherwise the case would be closed. (d) There can be no genuine *problem* of evil if God does not exist; for then what is there to complain about and to whom? So the conviction of believers and nonbelievers alike about the mystery of evil and the "broken" condition of mankind who "contrive evil from their infancy" (*Genesis*) testifies to the being of God and to the divine mystery and transcendence. The problem of evil is not a problem for God; it is our problem with understanding God. If there were no God, there would be no problem of evil. But there is; so?

The same can be said of the "silence" of God at Golgotha, on the beaches of Japan in the sixteenth century, and at the Holocaust in the twentieth. If there is no God, there is nothing missing; there is nothing to wonder about, nor anything else to expect, except worse, later. And if God exists, God must share and transform evil so that the good are truly not harmed, and the evil are damaged in ways only divine love can repair. (See similar remarks by both Marilyn Adams and Eleanore Stump.) So the problem is that we cannot see how that is to be done; the problem is ours.

Is there any world so replete with evil that a good God could not create it? Is there any world made impossible by the evil in it? Which one? Why? If none, then how could the nonbeing of God be entailed or even made probable by the evil on earth?

The general subject of *configurations into conviction* is not part of post-seventeenth-century epistemology. Yet, we need to go beyond talk about faith, central though it is in the life of the mind and life in general, to consider how feeling functions in conviction.

Feeling creates conviction by combining satisfaction (fulfillment in some respect) with reliance (which is itself a kind of satisfaction in dependence, like lovers holding hands) into an outcome that is our conviction. Two kinds of satisfaction suffuse something we assent to. That's how we, those who did not discover anything or even repeat the inquiries, know that there are micro-particles, electrons, molecules, atoms. We rely on the community that says it did find out, and we get satisfaction and rewards by doing so. Thus we are convinced.

That is faith that amounts to knowledge, when the social institution is integral. So also is your conviction that the heart pumps blood, that oxygen is brought to the brain by the blood, that cells somehow communicate to one another directions to differentiate into diverse organs so that liver cells don't produce kidney cells. Such convictions come from natural faith, assisted by (but not transformed by) feeling, configuring the assertions of others into conviction.

But you have other devices far more powerful, vast inputs of feeling that atomize and rearrange the pieces of "data" for belief. Call them *conviction capacitors, convictors.* We have "operative beliefs" that convert data ("evidence" is too restrictive a word because feelings count too) into conviction (both as to content and as to assent).

The capacitors are operative beliefs that are not objects of belief but accumulate data and feeling until a cognitive threshold is reached and a conviction is discharged, arranging belief into a new pattern (say, accepting the view that there is a personal redeemer, or forming a deep distrust of bearded men), often almost undislodgeable thereafter. Frequently these convictions are impervious to all evidence, changeable only by a bleeding away of feelings, of the satisfactions gained from the viewpoint; for example, "that I care about him/her" or "success is increasing my wealth and power"; convictions like that can hemorrhage; for example, when one becomes crippled, unjustly imprisoned, or the victim of malice.

Convictors (such operative networks of energy and structure) work like neuroses. Neuroses are actually only cognitively deviant convictors; they generate physical movement, desires, feelings, and belief, but in a framework where feeling is not a well-founded test of truth. You can identify neuroses from the pattern and compulsion toward disorderly outputs like compulsive handwashing, pointless sobbing, false laughter, pointless lying. You can acquire powerful intellectual software (even convictors that may not be consistent with one another) in favorable circumstances, just as you can acquire neuroses in unfavorable ones. Similarly, there are disorders of the understanding, intellectual convictors, that function in philosophy and science the way neuroses do in personal interactions.

Consider some ordinary examples. A certain amount of repetition and peer pressure may convince you the "Porsche NNN" is the car to own, the best, most prestigious, and so on, while someone else is wholly unaffected. A whispered hint from the social doyen may convince you that Beacon Hill is the only place to live. Someone else is repulsed by such conspicuous materialism. A sarcastic high-school teacher embroiders on the Inquisition, giving a wrong story about the Church's repressing science, and "organized religion is bad" becomes a lifelong certainty impervious to argument.

The kinds of convictors are as varied as people and their experiences. They are modulated by attitudes toward risk, avoidance of cognitive dissonance, love of symmetry, fear of punishment, desire to be right, love of saying "I told you so," love of being praised, desire to be cuddly, satisfaction in repelling strangers. The modulating attitudes have as many "values," comparatively, as there can be diatonic melodies. In fact, there are so many convictors and so many threshold states and modifications that I wonder how we could ever get true beliefs about anything important (unless we were designed to).

IV

In a word, cognition is more a corporate, collective state than we might have thought. We can read off collective behavior (say, the widespread certainty that blue jeans—or whatever the fashion is—are what one wears) the presence of awarenesses and desires that are generational, national, and even cultural, the result of the collective conscious and the collective unconscious. Convictors affect moral virtue, intellectual virtue, and even mental health. For instance, things that are considered individual failings (for example, littering or cigarette smoking) may be caused—and improved—by manipulating the collective consciousness, as shown by the success of anti-smoking displays and the recent social turn against public inebriation. Similarly, there is a return to the idea that we should cultivate public examples of virtue and emphasize certain praiseworthy traits (like environmental care).

The idea that our cognitive powers are targeted, aimed at our own flourishing, and, by grace, targeted beyond at life with God, is part of what I call "cognitive voluntarism," a wholly distinct explanation of knowledge by experience (in contrast to the representationalist/evidentialist/foundationalist cluster of ideas for the last three centuries). Cognitive voluntarism is the view that humans, for the most part, believe not because they are compelled by the evidence but because they *want* to (sometimes even being compelled by wants operating as "convictors"[69]) because assenting appears to advance their "apprehended good." Both Augustine and Aquinas (with differences) think our cognitive powers have basic drives (of which the rational appetite, the will, is the chief drive), and thus have a targeted finality that is no natural end, but rather, life with God.[70] Cognitive voluntarism may offer a better explanation of the rationality of religious belief and of the success of science than does any competing view. But that is promissory, requiring a separate essay about the objectives and successes of science and what it is like to be "streetwise in the universe."

University of Pennsylvania

69. As Aquinas explained the non-meritorious faith of the bad angels.
70. See my "Mindful of Man," forthcoming.

3   On the Very Strongest Arguments
GEORGE I. MAVRODES

I think that there have been, and still are, philosophers who have thought that natural theology can satisfy the very highest standards of philosophical rigor. Perhaps Thomas Aquinas is the best-known historical example.[1] Some of the more prominent recent essays into natural theology, however, appear to be somewhat more modest in their claims. Alvin Plantinga, for example, has formulated and defended an interesting version of the ontological argument. After an extensive discussion, he expresses his own judgment of the argument by saying, "I think this version of the Ontological Argument is sound."[2] He goes on to say, however, that "it must be conceded, however, that [this] argument is not a successful piece of natural theology." And he soon adds that arguments of this sort "cannot, perhaps, be said to *prove* or *establish* their conclusion."[3]

Another recent attempt at theistic argumentation is that of Richard Swinburne. He defines a concept for which he uses the phrase "good deductive argument," and then announces that "I shall argue that (neither separately nor in conjunction) are any of the arguments which I consider for or against the existence of God good deductive arguments."[4] And this despite the fact that he recognizes that there are deductive theistic arguments that are valid and whose premises may well be true. His own positive attempt at theistic argumentation is an extended and cumulative inductive argument whose conclusion is that

1. I am supposing that, in applying the term "demonstration" to arguments *quia* (from effects) as well as to arguments *propter quid* (from essences), Thomas means to imply that the former are just as good as the latter. If this reading of Thomas's views is not correct, then perhaps Thomas is not an example of the sort of philosopher I have in mind here.

2. Alvin Plantinga, *The Nature of Necessity* (London: Oxford University Press, 1974), 217. By "sound" Plantinga evidently means that the argument is deductively valid and that its premises are true.

3. Ibid., 219, 221.

4. Richard Swinburne, *The Existence of God* (New York: Oxford University Press, 1979), 13, 14.

"on our total evidence theism is more probable than not."[5] The language of that conclusion certainly seems to be more modest than that of, say, Thomas.

In this paper I want to explore this modesty somewhat more fully. I am inclined to think, indeed, that it would be better for natural theologians to return (at least sometimes) to the more robust language of Thomas, and to claim (for better or worse) that they are proving and demonstrating the existence of God by means of good deductive arguments. But the main substance of the paper is the exploration of the factors that might go into making the *strength* or *goodness* of a deductive argument.

It seems fairly natural to suppose that some arguments are indeed better than others, stronger in some important way. Maybe we even have an idea of an argument that is as strong as an argument can possibly be—perhaps that is what is sometimes called a "knock-down drag-out argument." And if we could turn out a theistic argument that was that strong, then we could legitimately claim to have proved the existence of God. What would such an argument have to have?

We can get a start on that question by asking what it is that people like Plantinga and Swinburne think is lacking in those arguments they think are not successful pieces of natural theology, not good deductive arguments. In the interesting cases, what these arguments are said to lack does not seem to be a virtue of truth or logic. Plantinga flatly claims those virtues for his ontological argument. Rather, he says that his argument is not a success in natural theology because that discipline "typically draws its premises from the stock of propositions accepted by nearly every sane man, or perhaps nearly every rational man." And he adds that "the central premiss of [this] argument is not of this sort."[6]

In a similar way, Swinburne defines a *good* deductive argument as one whose premises are "known to be true by those who dispute about the conclusion, [and] which are valid." And he observes that there are, of course, valid theistic arguments whose premises may be true but are nevertheless disputed by atheists, and so on.[7]

Given these stipulations, I would be pretty much at a loss to suggest a theistic argument that would count as a good one, a success in natural theology. It looks like a rather unpromising project. But how shall

5. Ibid., 291.

6. Plantinga, ibid., 219, 220.

7. Swinburne, ibid., 7. Though Swinburne is not entirely clear on this point, I interpret him here to require that the premises be known by everyone who debates about religion.

we understand the stipulations themselves? We can take them, if we wish, to be nothing more than arbitrary pieces of terminology—stipulations of a sense for the expression "natural theology," and of a (rather technical) sense of "good."

If we were to do that, however, we would probably be missing something important in the claims of these philosophers. It seems to me, at any rate, that people like Plantinga and Swinburne intend to suggest that arguments that have these features are (or would be, if there were such arguments) better, preferable, stronger, more reliable, more valuable, and so forth, than arguments that lack them. Consequently, to say of a theistic argument that it is not a success in natural theology, that it does not prove its conclusion (Plantinga), or that it is not a good deductive argument (Swinburne), is at least to say that it falls short of some genuine ideal. And maybe it also says that the argument in question is weaker than some other actual argument. It is that claim that I want to explore here.

Both Plantinga and Swinburne try to specify the ideal in terms of universality. The successful piece of natural theology would have premises, according to Plantinga, that are accepted by nearly every sane man or nearly every rational man. Swinburne's good deductive argument would have premises known to be true by the people who argue about religion. But why should we suppose that this sort of universality would be a "good-making" characteristic of an argument?

Probably the answer that comes most readily to mind is something like this: an argument that had this property would do something good—an epistemic good—for a whole lot of people, maybe for everybody or almost everybody. It would provide them with a way of knowing something that they did not know before (or, at least, that they might not have known before).[8] And no argument that was not universal in this way could do this good thing as widely. Hence, this universality represents a genuine ideal for an argument.

This idea invites some further precision and clarification, but it will be useful to have some short way of referring to the idea we are trying to clarify. I will say, therefore, that an argument that has this property we are trying to identify more clearly is a *compelling* argument.

We can make a first stab at defining such a type of argument (in the spirit of Plantinga and Swinburne) as

(C1) An argument is compelling if and only if it is sound and everyone accepts it.

8. Cf. Swinburne: "The point of arguments is to get people, in so far as they are rational, to accept conclusions." Ibid., 7.

This is a fairly simple and straightforward definition, and it has about it the flavor of universality that we can detect in the Plantinga and Swinburne ideals for natural theology. But perhaps it goes too far. That is, many of us will suspect that there are no such arguments as this at all, or at any rate none of much interest or importance. There seem to be so many ways in which a person might fail to accept an argument—by failing to understand it, for example, or by never having heard of it or thought of it—that probably no argument actually satisfies the condition in (C1).

A substantially weaker condition yields

(C2) An argument is compelling if and only if it is sound and everyone who understands it accepts it.

This invites two further clarifications.

1. For the purposes of this paper I will say that a person accepts an argument if and only if he believes the conclusion of the argument and he believes that the argument is sound.

2. I propose to understand the universal generalization in (C2) and its successors and alternatives as "law-like" rather than "accidental." That is, I will assume that a claim such as "Gödel's argument for the incompleteness of arithmetic is compelling" supports (entails?) an indefinite range of counterfactuals, such as "if Margaret Thatcher were to understand Gödel's argument then she would accept it," and so on.[9]

Now, it seems fairly clear that there are sound arguments that do not satisfy the condition in (C2). In the ordinary sense of "understand," at least, it seems quite possible that someone should understand "Adolf Hitler died of a heart attack" without knowing whether it is true, and without having any belief about its truth. But, presumably, either that proposition is true or else its denial is true. We can think, then, of an argument that contains the true member of that pair as a premise, and whose other premises (if any) are true, and whose logic is valid. It would seem that there could be a person who understood that argument, but who did not accept it because he did not know the truth about Hitler's death.

It is also possible that there are arguments that would satisfy the condition in (C2) if it were interpreted as an accidental universal, but that do not satisfy it when it is interpreted, as I propose to do, as a

9. In a recent discussion of this topic, I heard it suggested that Gödel's argument for the incompleteness of arithmetic was an example of the strongest possible sort of argument, and that it had the sort of universality we are exploring. I am going to use Gödel's argument as a convenient stalking-horse (or whipping-boy).

law-like universal. It is not hard to think of examples. (C2) thus seems to specify an interesting property for arguments, a property that not nearly every argument has, even if it has the virtues of truth and validity. But that does not guarantee that (C2) captures the somewhat vague notions of strength and goodness with which we began.

As for strength, we might begin by noting that some arguments are harder to understand than others. Gödel's argument, for example, seems to be a good bit harder than many of the arguments in Euclid's geometry. And Thomas's arguments for the existence of God are probably not the easiest arguments a student will come across in the history of philosophy. That suggests the following exercise in comparison. Suppose for the moment that Gödel's argument is compelling in the sense of (C2). That entails that everyone who understands it accepts it, and if anyone else were to understand it then he or she would also accept it. But suppose also that there are only, say, a thousand people who do understand the argument, and another 10,000 or so who would understand it if they were to study it. It is just too difficult, we may suppose, for the rest of us. Those suppositions are compatible with the claim that Gödel's argument is compelling in the sense of (C2). And now think of another argument (perhaps, say, for the existence of God) that is sound[10] but not compelling. We may suppose that this argument is understood by about a million people, of whom about half accept it, and there are another 20 or 30 million who could understand it if they studied it, again with an acceptance rate of about half. Which of these is the stronger (or better) argument for its conclusion?

In thinking about this question we must remember that, by supposition, both of these arguments are fully valid. And both of them have true premises and true conclusions. They do not differ in those respects. But they do differ in at least two interesting, and perhaps important, ways. First, one of them satisfies the condition in (C2) and the other does not. Second, the numbers of people who in fact do, or can, accept them differ greatly. But in this example these differences pull in opposite directions.

The property identified in (C2) seems to me, as I said earlier, to be an interesting property. Perhaps it is also a "strength-making" property in an argument, though that doesn't seem at all clear to me. At the very least, it seems a lot clearer that something like "accessibility"

10. If it is false that God exists, then there is, of course, no sound argument for his existence. But if it is true that God exists, then the task of constructing a sound argument for his existence is trivial. For a further discussion of this point, see George I. Mavrodes, *Belief in God* (New York: Random House, 1970), 22–28.

or "ease of understanding" is a strength-making property when combined with soundness. And that is because accessibility is an important factor in the utility of an argument for important epistemic purposes—extending one's knowledge, extending the range of one's true beliefs, providing reasons for one's beliefs, and so forth. But in our example, the argument for God's existence wins hands down along that dimension. Gödel's argument contributes to the epistemic well-being, as we might say, of a thousand people, and has the potential of doing the same for another 10,000. But the theistic argument contributes to the epistemic well-being of half a million, and its potential is in the tens of millions.

Of course, there is another dimension along which Gödel's argument wins. It has the interesting property of being compelling, while the theistic argument does not. But why should that be thought to be a strength-making property of an argument? Why take it to be a virtue in an argument, rather than just an interesting property? In what way is an argument better if it satisfies the condition in (C2)?

In thinking about this question it is important not to confuse (C2) with (C1). An argument that was compelling in the sense of (C1) would be universally accessible (in fact, it would actually be understood and accepted by everyone), and would seem to make a very wide contribution to epistemic projects, much wider than my hypothetical theistic argument. But compellingness in the sense of (C2) is compatible with extremely limited accessibility. It is quite possible that there are arguments that are far from compelling in the sense of (C2), but that are far closer to the universality of (C1) than any argument that does satisfy the condition in (C2).

Perhaps we could say, rather cautiously, that compellingness in the sense of (C2) *may* be a strength-making property in an argument. But if so, then it may be overridden by other properties, in the sense that some arguments that lack compellingness may be stronger than some that have it. Compellingness, then, would not be sufficient to identify or characterize the strongest arguments.

That suggests that we might improve on (C2) by including a requirement of accessibility in the *definiens*. How could we do that? If, for example, we were simply to include the clause "and everybody understands it," then we would get something that is equivalent to (C1). But that seems unsatisfactory. The following, however, might be more promising:

(C3) An argument is compelling if and only if it is sound and everyone who understands it accepts it and everyone who studies it understands it.

And I propose to construe the last clause, just as the second, in terms of a law-like generalization.

The condition in (C3) is, of course, at least as restrictive as that of (C2) and it seems to be more restrictive. It requires that a compelling argument be such that everyone who studies it understands it. "Studies" is, of course, a somewhat vague term. If we take it in its ordinary sense, however, and assume that only some finite and "reasonable" effort is envisaged, then there certainly seem to be arguments that do not satisfy this condition.

If there is some argument that satisfies the condition in (C3)—I think that there is no plausibility at all in supposing that Gödel's argument does that, but let us imagine that the "classic" argument that there is no largest prime number does—then we could try to assess its strength in comparison with those we have been considering. It is consistent with (C3) that the argument in question should be one that is in fact understood by only a few people, say a thousand. In that respect the classic argument would match my earlier characterization of Gödel's argument. But there would be some plausibility in saying that its potential was much greater, greater in fact than that of my hypothetical theistic argument. For the last clause seems to guarantee that, in some important sense, an argument that satisfies the condition in (C3) is accessible to absolutely everyone. All it requires is some study, study such as anyone can give it.[11]

It seems plausible to think that the potential of an argument, in the sense we have just been using, is a strength-making property. At least it seems that an argument with great potential is, so far as that goes, a better argument than one with less potential. For it seems that the former at least could have a greater epistemic impact than the latter. An argument that was compelling in the sense of (C3), in fact, could have a universal epistemic effect.

"Could have," however, is not the same as "does have" or "will have." It is quite possible that some argument that is not compelling in the sense of (C3) has a much greater epistemic significance than any argument which is compelling in that sense.[12] For there could be an argument that satisfied the condition in (C3) but that was nevertheless "unattractive," in the sense that it did not attract many people to study

11. Anyone? Even small children, or people who are mentally defective, or those suffering from severe psychoses, and so on? For the time being I will ignore these problems.

12. I suppose that if there are, in fact, any arguments that satisfy the condition in (C3), then their epistemic impact is far less than that of many other arguments that clearly do not satisfy it.

it, to spend time and energy on it, and so on. And there might be another that really excited a lot of people, though not all of those who studied it were able thereby to understand it. And the latter argument might contribute to the epistemic well-being of many more people than the former.

Now, attractiveness also seems to be a strength-making property of an argument. If I could reformulate a theistic argument in some way that would induce twice as many people to think about it carefully, and if I could do that without losing any of the other virtues that argument might have, then I would think I had improved it significantly. If that is so, then it would seem that there could be an argument that was not compelling in the sense of (C3) (and so had less potential than one that was compelling in this sense), but that on account of its greater attractiveness, contributed to the epistemic well-being of many more people than did some compelling argument. And so even if compellingness in the sense of (C3) is a strength-making property, it seems to be neither necessary nor sufficient for identifying the very strongest sort of argument.

So far we have been trying to make precise and explicit the idea of an argument that has a sort of universal "punch." (C1) does express that idea in a fairly straightforward way—it is just the idea of an argument that is universally accepted—but it seems likely that nothing satisfies the condition in (C1). (C2) restricts and weakens the condition significantly, but preserves a sort of universalistic "flavor" by making the qualification a universal generalization. But now it seems plausible that some arguments that do not satisfy the condition in (C2) may well have more epistemic punch, may in fact be closer to the ideal of universality, than many arguments that do satisfy that condition. Attempting to close that gap we formulated (C3), adding another restriction to the condition, again a universal generalization. But it seems to suffer the same fate as (C2).

We could continue along this general line, hoping that eventually we could come up with a formulation that would capture the greatest epistemic punch an argument could have. But maybe every such attempt is doomed to fall prey to the sort of counter-example strategy that has already been employed here.

At any rate, there are no doubt some who will say that the whole positive strategy so far has been misdirected. I have been construing the strength of an argument as being a sort of function of the number of people to whose epistemic well-being that argument does (or could) contribute. But it may be suggested that the real—or at any rate, the philosophically significant—strength of an argument is more a matter of quality than of quantity. Perhaps Gödel's argument is accessible to no more than a few people. But it may do something better than many a more accessible argument, better than many a more attractive argument, and so on. In fact (so it may be said), Gödel's argument may be highly inaccessible and unattractive and yet it may do the very best thing that an argument can do. If so, it is absolutely top-drawer, a real knock-down drag-out argument. And so perhaps it sets a standard at which theistic arguments can aim, but that they cannot achieve.

What might that good thing be, the thing that Gödel's argument does and that perhaps no theistic argument is able to do? In a vague sort of way, it might be suggested that the sort of argument for which we are groping is one that confers upon its conclusion a maximal epistemic solidity. I think that words such as *establish, demonstrate,* and *prove* are sometimes used with an overtone of this sort. What is established or demonstrated is somehow epistemically secure, as secure in the realm of knowledge as anything can be.[13] And this, it might be said, is what compelling arguments do. They make their conclusions secure. And that is an achievement of high value.

Now, we might or might not be satisfied with the clarity of this explanation—that is, with the clarity of the idea of epistemic solidity, security, and so on. I think that I do have some grip on that idea, and so I cannot complain that the sort of explanation just sketched leaves me entirely cold. On the other hand, to the extent that I do understand the idea, I would not suppose that maximal epistemic security belongs uniquely, or in any special way, to compelling arguments.

Let us imagine that there is some argument—call it A_1—that satisfies (C_1).[14] It has premises, P and Q, and a conclusion, R. Since (C_1) requires that A_1 be sound, R will be a truth, and in A_1 R will be validly derived from truths. But those facts cannot be special or unique to A_1, or to arguments that satisfy (C_1). For there are plenty of sound arguments that do not satisfy (C_1), and in all of them true conclusions are validly derived from true premises. In fact, R itself must be the conclusion of many sound arguments other than A_1, arguments that do not satisfy (C_1).

Here, no doubt, it will be suggested that we have gotten sidetracked. The special quality of compelling arguments cannot be explained purely in terms of truth and logic, it will be said. No, we must somehow bring in something like reliability, or maybe the idea of an especially

---

13. Cf. Plantinga: "The policy of accepting only the incontestable promises security but little else." Ibid., 221.

14. Any argument that satisfies (C_1) also satisfies (C_2) and (C_3).

strong epistemic "grip" on a truth. Perhaps, indeed, the various conditions formulated so far were not entirely satisfactory in this respect. We should not have satisfied ourselves with the notion of "accepting" an argument, or believing it, but should rather have insisted on knowledge.

Well, let's try knowledge. We can construct a sort of analogue of (C1), generated by replacing "accepts" by "knows."

(C4) An argument is compelling if and only if everyone knows it to be sound.

In what way would an argument that satisfied this condition be more reliable than one that did not? Or in what way would it give us a stronger grip upon its conclusion?

It is true that (C4) determines a set of arguments that (at least if it is not the null set) consists entirely of sound arguments, all of them having whatever virtues all sound arguments have. But that is not a unique feature of (C4). There are many different ways of determining many different sets, all of which consist entirely of sound arguments. For example, the condition, "the arguments that Mikhail Gorbachev knows to be sound," determines just such a set. Very probably it determines a larger and more interesting set than does (C4), because it is likely that Mr. Gorbachev knows a lot of things that not everyone knows. And all of the arguments in this set have all of the virtues that all sound arguments have.

What if someone says that we don't have a fully reliable way of discovering what arguments belong in the Gorbachev set, since we don't have a fully reliable way of telling what it is that Gorbachev really knows, as distinguished from what he merely (and perhaps mistakenly) believes? This seems to me to be true. But is the situation any different with respect to (C4)?

If there is an argument that satisfies (C4), then of course I will know that argument to be sound (since presumably I fall within the scope of the universal quantifier). It doesn't at all follow that I would thereby know that this argument satisfied (C4). There are, after all, a lot of things I know that not everyone knows—almost everything I know falls into that category. Whatever may be the case with the Gorbachev set, it doesn't seem that my reliability in picking out "the arguments that I know to be sound" is lower than my reliability in picking out the arguments that satisfy (C4). I would suppose, indeed, that it is many times higher.

There might be someone, I suppose, who holds that the only things anyone knows are the things everyone knows. This seems to be so implausible a suggestion that I have a hard time getting up any steam over it. But we might at least notice that, on this view, the existence of God will not be any worse off than Gödel's theorem. Since not everybody knows either of them, nobody knows either of them.

But maybe someone holds a somewhat more plausible version of this principle. She holds, that is, that the only things anyone knows are things everyone would know if they understood them, or studied them, and so on. This would invite us to formulate the following condition:

(C5) An argument is compelling if and only if anyone who understood it (or studied it, etc.) would know it to be sound.

Given the knowledge thesis just cited, an argument that satisfied (C5) would seem to have at least a chance of deriving a conclusion from a piece of knowledge, and thus of generating a piece of knowledge. But an argument that did not satisfy (C5) would have no such chance. Thus it might be plausible to hold that (C5) does, after all, identify a set of arguments that have a unique strength.

It might, of course, turn out that (C5) identifies the null set—that is, that there are no arguments at all that satisfy it. That will be the case if there are no propositions that are such that anyone who understood them would know them to be true. I myself do not know whether there are any such propositions, and I have no idea of how one is supposed to discover whether there are any.

Even if there are, however, there seems to me to be a further difficulty. Why should we suppose that propositions of this sort are any better, either as knowledge or as the sources of knowledge, than any other truths? There are lots of things that it seems to me that I know, and that I have no inclination at all to think would be recognized as truths by everyone who understood them, and that seem to me to be just as firmly parts of my knowledge as anything else that I know. Of course, I might be mistaken in that. Is there some reason to think that I am in fact mistaken in that?

If I am not mistaken there, then (C5) does not seem to fare any better than the other conditions we have tried. Possibly there are some other conjectures that I have not thought of, and that are more promising. So far, however, I am inclined to think that the ideal of universal compellingness that seems to lie behind criteria such as those of Plantinga and Swinburne does not identify a genuine virtue of argumentation. If it is a fact that theistic arguments compare unfavorably in strength with arguments of some other sort, then we don't yet seem to have a clear idea of why that is.

The University of Michigan

4 Hermeneutic Philosophy and Natural Theology

JOSEPH J. KOCKELMANS

I. INTRODUCTION

In this essay I would like to reflect on the status of natural theology today from the perspective of hermeneutic philosophy. By hermeneutic philosophy I understand the kind of philosophy developed and promoted by Heidegger, Gadamer, and to some degree also Ricoeur. Yet in this essay I shall also describe briefly how I understand my own position within the hermeneutic movement.

In the first section of this essay, I retrace briefly the genesis and development of natural theology; in this section I dwell on the metaphysical views of Aristotle, the Stoa, St. Augustine, Anselm, Bonaventure, and Scotus on the one hand, and on the Aristotelian tradition of Albert and Aquinas on the other. I make a special effort here to explain natural theology's concern with proofs for the existence of God in connection with the development of large metaphysical systems developed in modern rationalism. I also speak briefly about the empiricist concern with natural theology. Finally, I focus briefly on the views on natural theology of Kant and German Idealism.

In the second section, I describe what I understand by hermeneutic philosophy and indicate its typical limits. In the third section I turn to the modern scene. Here I focus on contemporary criticism of metaphysics, in general, and of natural theology as a form of *metaphysica specialis,* in particular. Then I try to explain the view of hermeneutic philosophy in regard to the question of why today arguments for the existence of God, even if logically valid, are of no importance philosophically or practically. I also indicate in what sense proofs for the existence of God remain meaningful for those who already believe in God. Finally, I conclude these reflections with some brief observations on negative theology, and the use of analogical and symbolic language in both natural and sacred theology.

Before concluding these brief introductory reflections I would like to say a few words about the expression *natural theology* and the different meanings the term has been given over the centuries.

The word *theology* itself is very old. Its original meaning must have come very close to what we now call mythology.[1] For the word *theologos* was used first for the poets and writers who wrote about the nature and the origin of the gods. Although Aristotle still used the word *theologos* to refer to poets and authors who speak about the gods,[2] he also introduced the term *theologia* as a technical term to refer to that part of first philosophy that, taken to be distinct from "ontology," is concerned with the separate and immobile being, namely God.[3] The term "natural theology" was introduced in the Middle Ages to distinguish philosophical reflections on the existence and essence of God from sacred theology, which takes its point of departure from the Scriptures as well as from tradition. In the tradition of Wolff, natural theology becomes a form of special metaphysics; in that tradition one customarily makes a distinction between *metaphysica generalis* and *metaphysica specialis*; as for the latter, one distinguishes cosmology and psychology from natural theology. It is perhaps of some importance for the understanding of natural theology's concern with proofs for the existence of God to note that in the sixteenth century the notion of natural religion was developed, which eventually would prepare the way for the typical kind of deism that became prominent during the period of the Enlightenment, and which eventually would reduce Christianity to a religion in which the good moral life is practically the only thing that still counts.[4] It is understandable that in such a context the arguments for the existence of God have a meaning quite different from the one they once had in a predominantly Christian context. I shall return to this point later.

II. HISTORICO-CRITICAL SURVEY OF ARGUMENTS GIVEN FOR THE EXISTENCE OF GOD[5]

It is well known that arguments for the existence of God were already developed in classical antiquity. Jaeger has shown[6] that such

1. Cf. Plato, *Republic*, II, 379A.
2. Aristotle, *Metaphysics*, I, 983b28f.; III, 1000a10.
3. Ibid., XI, 1064a29–1064b5.
4. Cf. my essay, "Reflections on the Interaction Between Science and Religion," in *The Challenge of Religion: Contemporary Readings in Philosophy of Religion*, ed. Frederick Ferré, Joseph J. Kockelmans, and John E. Smith (New York: Seabury Press, 1982), 296–316.
5. For what follows, see D. Schluter, "Gottesbeweis," in *Historisches Wörterbuch der Philosophie*, ed. H. Ritter (Stuttgart: Schwabe, 1975), vol. 3, cols. 818–30.
6. W. Jaeger, *The Theology of the Early Greek Philosophers*, trans. Edward S. Robinson (Oxford: Clarendon Press, 1947).

arguments were proposed when philosophers began to realize that it is not possible to answer the question concerning the mode of Being of God. According to Xenophon,[7] Socrates once observed that we do know the great works that God brings about but he himself remains invisible; he remains hidden behind the things he has created. This means that God cannot be grasped immediately; our insight into his being and his mode of Being is something we had to learn to conclude from things we do know immediately. In the language of Scholastic philosophy, one could say: the statement "God exists" is not a *propositio nota per se quoad nos*;[8] it is a statement that needs proof and argument. Yet from the context within which the arguments were developed, it is clear that the primary intention of such arguments was not to lead a human being from something known to something completely unknown, nor from being an unbeliever to the insight that God indeed does exist; the basic intention, rather, was to give "explicit expression for thought to the elevation of the mind toward God."[9] In other words, the arguments were meant to unfold methodically, systematically, and logically the conclusion that is contained in all spontaneous, unreflected knowledge of God.

The arguments for the existence of God that were given in the Christian world must be understood from the same basic concern. In other words, these arguments, too, were meant to show that the God about whom our revelation speaks and whom we do not see, but in whom we firmly believe, indeed actually can and must exist. The arguments thus try to show that, in comparison with the numberless finite things that are given to us in direct experience, there nonetheless also must be one being that is one and infinite; it is an absolute being that is in and of itself, and that can be grasped as an understanding and willing being. Different authors interpret this common insight in different ways. Later such arguments for the existence of God were developed mainly in metaphysics, taken as natural theology.

In the course of time, many arguments for the existence of God have been proposed. Some of them have been proposed in treatises of a non-metaphysical, but rather scientific, nature. According to metaphysics, these arguments are the result of an impermissible transgression of territorial boundaries. There are other arguments that take their starting point in man's self-awareness, such as the eu-

---

7. Xenophon, *Memorabilia*, IV, 3, 13.
8. Thomas Aquinas, *Summa Theologiae*, I, q.21, a.1.
9. G. F. W. Hegel, *Vorlesungen über die Beweise vom Dasein Gottes*, ed. G. Lasson (Hamburg: Meiner, 1966).

daemonologic or deontological arguments for the existence of God. For metaphysics, such arguments cannot lead to anything except some probable statements, as long as they cannot be brought back to strictly metaphysical reflections. The argument that rests on the realization that the acceptance of the existence of a divine being is virtually universally human does not live up to the criteria metaphysics has formulated for such arguments.

The arguments that are taken to be important from a metaphysical point of view are the following: the cosmological, ontological, and teleological arguments, and the arguments that rest on the "*gradus entis.*" These arguments assume quite different forms in the works of different authors. This explains why such arguments have a close affinity with the kind of metaphysics in which they were developed.

The oldest argument for the existence of God is the teleological argument that concludes the existence of God from the governance of the world (Aquinas's fifth way). "We see that things that lack intelligence . . . act for an end . . . Hence it is clear that not fortuitously, but designedly, do they achieve their end. Now whatever lacks intelligence cannot move towards an end, unless it be directed by some being endowed with knowledge and intelligence. . . . Therefore some intelligent being exists by whom all natural things are directed to their end; and this being we call God."[10] The argument was given first by Socrates[11] and then taken over by Plato[12] and Aristotle.[13] In the Stoic philosophy it was considered the most important argument for the existence of God. In the early Middle Ages the argument is quoted by William of Conches and Petrus of Poitiers, among others. It received its sharpest formulation in the *Summa Contra Gentiles* of Aquinas, who attributed this formulation of the argument to Damascene. The argument runs as follows: "Contrary and discordant things cannot, always or for the most part, be parts of one order except under someone's governance, which enables all and each to tend to a definite end. But in the world we find that things of diverse natures come together under one order, and this not rarely or by chance, but always or for the most part. There must therefore be some being by whose providence the world is governed. This being we call God."[14]

With the exception of Ockham, who does not mention the argument, this proof for the existence of God is found in the works of all

10. Thomas Aquinas, *Summa Theologiae*, I, 2, 3, c.
11. Xenophon, *Memorabilia*, I, 4; IV, 3.
12. Plato, *Philebus*, 28D.
13. Aristotle, *Fragments*, 13, 1476a11–32.
14. Thomas Aquinas, *Summa contra Gentiles*, I, 13, no. 35.

leading philosophers of the Middle Ages and the Renaissance. In Leibniz, we find an argument from the preestablished harmony that is quite similar to the teleological argument. Yet the physico-theological argument introduced by William Derham and discussed by Kant is really a different kind of argument. It presupposes that the world is somehow similar to an enormous clockwork; such a clockwork presupposes a World-Builder.[15]

Although one cannot say that Plato developed arguments for the existence of God in his works, nonetheless a number of ideas there were used later in arguments for the existence of God; this is true not only for Aristotle's argument that starts from movement, but also for the argument *de gradibus entis*.[16] Yet Aristotle was the first author to create a formal argument for the existence of God.[17] His best-known argument starts from the motion found in the universe, where motion is understood in terms of his potency-act doctrine. The argument was taken over by many scholastic philosophers, notably by Aquinas, who calls it the first and more manifest way.[18] Much of contemporary criticism of this argument, which criticism presupposes conceptions of modern physics not found in Aristotle and rejects his potency-act scheme, is, from the perspective of metaphysics, really beside the point. It is of the greatest importance to observe here that Aristotle introduced a formal argument for the existence of God after he had rejected Plato's doctrine of the forms and after he had gone through some period of "nihilism," wondering, and doubt. Aristotle's uncertainty concerning a possible move from Plato's Ideas to the notion of one God (*ho Theos*) can be followed in his *Eudemian* as well as his *Nicomachean Ethics*.[19] Thus it is important to note that Aristotle does not raise the issue of proofs for the existence of God within a religious context, but rather in a strictly philosophical, metaphysical, and ethical one.

During the time of the Patristic and early Christian era, Greek Church Fathers began to incorporate arguments for the existence of God into their sacred-theological investigations. In other words, they created a sacred theology in which they took their point of departure from the Scriptures, but in which they also incorporated ideas from

15. Immanuel Kant, *Critique of Pure Reason*, B, 648ff.
16. Plato, *Laws*, X, 6–9; *Timaeus*, 28C–29D; *Symposium*, 210E–211C; *Republic*, VI, 16–19; *Phaedrus*, 245C–E.
17. Aristotle, *Physics*, VIII; *Metaphysics*, XII.
18. Thomas Aquinas, *Summa Theologiae*, I, 2, 3, c.
19. R. A. Gauthier and J. Y. Jolif, *L'Éthique à Nicomaque*, 2 vols. (Louvain: Publications Universitaires, 1970), vol. I, pt. 1, pp. 10–61 passim; vol. II, pp. 561–63, 814–15, 853–60, 896–97.

Greek philosophy (Plato, Aristotle, and the Stoa). The proofs for the existence of God were meant to build a bridge between what can be known about God on the basis of reason alone and what God has revealed about himself in the Scriptures. The arguments were meant to show not so much that God actually exists (because that was known through the Scriptures and accepted in faith), but rather that the Christian's belief in God is not irrational. These Church Fathers, however, did not develop any new arguments for the existence of God. This we find for the first time in the works of St. Augustine. Augustine obviously does mention other arguments as well, such as the teleological argument, the argument that starts from the changeability of all natural things,[20] the argument *de gradibus entis*. Yet, among the arguments he developed himself, the argument that concludes from the existence of unchangeable truths the existence of God as the Truth is best known.[21] This argument has some similarity with the argument "*ex possibilibus*" of Leibniz. It is interesting to note that Leibniz himself explicitly refers to Augustine's argument.[22] For our present purposes it is important to note that Augustine developed these arguments in order to bring the skeptic and agnostic to the realization that God indeed exists; furthermore, the arguments were meant to convince the believer of the rational credibility of what he had already accepted in faith.

The arguments for the existence of God play an important role in scholastic theology. One was led to develop such arguments in view of the fact that the Scriptures suggest that such arguments are possible and important.[23] Furthermore, the arguments were developed in order to build a bridge between what can be known by reason alone and what has been revealed by the Scriptures. Thus it is essential to stress the point that in Medieval and Renaissance Scholasticism the arguments for the existence of God have no meaning and function independent of sacred theology; proofs for the existence of God belong in "fundamental" theology, where the rational credibility of the articles of faith is discussed. They do not have there the apologetic function they will receive in the seventeenth and eighteenth centuries.

The arguments for the existence of God developed in the period of Scholasticism usually rest on arguments that already were hinted at by Greek and Patristic authors. Yet Anselm's ontological argument is

20. St. Augustine, *Confessions*, X, 6.
21. St. Augustine, *On Free Will*, II, *iii*,7–*xv*,39.
22. G. W. Leibniz, *New Essays Concerning Human Understanding*, trans. A. G. Langley (Lasalle, Ill.: Open Court, 1949), 503–04.
23. Cf. *Wisd. of Sol.*, 13:1–5; *Rom.* 1:19–20.

an exception. In his *Monologion*,[24] Anselm had already developed the argument that proceeds from the degrees of perfection we find in the universe. This Platonic argument was discussed by several authors before him, notably Augustine and several leading Augustinian theologians. In his *Proslogion*,[25] Anselm introduced a new type of argument that later would become known as the ontological argument.[26] The argument begins with the major premise that we all believe God is that being than which nothing greater can be thought. Such a being cannot exist in someone's mind alone. Therefore there is absolutely no doubt that something than which nothing greater can be thought exists both in the mind and in reality.[27]

Although some authors in the Middle Ages and the Renaissance have accepted this argument as valid, most leading theologians have rejected it. The argument was later reformulated by both Descartes and Leibniz,[28] and in that form it was held by many to be valid until Kant refuted it in 1781.[29] Hegel has tried to prove the validity of the argument,[30] but many contemporary authors feel, following Frege,[31] that the argument is not valid.

Aquinas developed five arguments for the existence of God; these arguments were all known in the Scholastic tradition. He calls them Ways to indicate that they are to lead the mind to the insight that it is not unreasonable to believe in God. In addition, Aquinas also wanted to lay the foundation for what he was going to say as a theologian about God's essence and his attributes.

In the modern era, since the time of Descartes, arguments for the existence of God were not developed in order to justify "the preambles to the articles of faith,"[32] but rather to provide certain metaphysical systems with a *fundamentum inconcussum*.[33] In addition to this, God's existence was to be "justified" in light of the evil present in our world.[34]

24. St. Anselm, *Monologion,* chaps. 1 and 2.
25. St. Anselm, *Proslogion,* chaps. 2 and 3.
26. Immanuel Kant, *Critique of Pure Reason,* B, 620ff.
27. St. Anselm, Proslogion, chap. 2.
28. Descartes, *Meditations on First Philosophy,* Meditation 5; Leibniz, *Philosophische Schriften,* ed. C. J. Gerhardt (Hildesheim: Olms, 1960), VII, 261.
29. Immanuel Kant, cited above.
30. Cf. Dieter Henrich, *Der ontologische Gottesbeweis* (Tübingen: Mohr, 1960), 189–219.
31. Gottlob Frege, "Über Begriff und Gegenstand," *Vierteljahrschrift für wissenschaftliche Philosophie,* 16 (1892), 192–205, 200ff.
32. Aquinas, *Summa Theologiae,* I, 2, 2, ad 1.
33. Martin Heidegger, *What is a Thing?* trans. W. B. Barton, Jr. and Vera Deutsch (Chicago: Regnery, 1967), 98–106.
34. G. W. Leibniz, *Theodicy: Essays on the Goodness of God, the Freedom of Man, and the Origin of Evil,* trans. E. M. Huggard (Edinburgh: Clark, 1952).

This made it necessary to distinguish first between a general metaphysics that would have the form of an ontology (a study of being as being) and one or more forms of special metaphysics, particularly natural theology. Finally, arguments for the existence of God were then often also used apologetically in an effort to defend the attitude of the believer against the attacks of the views of nonbelievers.[35]

After this brief summary of the most important arguments for the existence of God and the contexts in which they originated, I turn to a brief reflection on the question of how I understand my own position within the hermeneutic philosophical movement. I shall make a special effort to stress the limits intrinsic to philosophical reflection.

III. ON HERMENEUTIC PHILOSOPHY AND THE LIMITS OF PHILOSOPHICAL REFLECTION[36]

Like many other contemporary philosophers, hermeneutic philosophers, following Heidegger, have gradually come to believe that it is necessary to adopt a critical attitude in regard to all classical conceptions of philosophy. But in criticizing the classical, metaphysical views, our interest is positive in that we firmly believe that in these classical conceptions an ideal shows itself that until now has never completely materialized. Instead of denying philosophy's history, we want to make this history into an explicit subject matter of philosophical reflection, in order to bring to light and unfold the genuine meaning of this ideal, seen for the first time in Greece by Parmenides and Heraclitus. In this process of retrieve, we try to maintain what has been genuinely great in the philosophies of the past.

We agree with the Greek philosophers that the subject matter of philosophy is to be found in Being. But instead of focusing our main interest on the beings, the *onta,* we turn our attention to the finite totality of meaning or the Whole, in and through which, as far as their meaning is concerned, the beings can manifest themselves as the beings they are. With Descartes and Kant, however, we are convinced that in reflecting upon the Whole, man should take his point of departure in human subjectivity. But in opposition to modern philosophy, we do not conceive of this subjectivity in terms of a thinking substance, a closed monad, a passively registering knowing device that develops impressions into ideas with the help of certain laws of asso-

35. Cf. A. Cottier, *Der Gottesbeweis in der Geschichte der modernen Aufklärungsphilosophie. Descartes-Spinoza-Leibniz-Wolff-Kant* (Bern: Luthy, 1943).

36. For what follows, cf. the first chapter of my book, *The World in Science and Philosophy* (Milwaukee: Bruce Publishing Co., 1969), 3–54.

ciation, a pure consciousness, or even the place where the Absolute materializes his self-awareness in absolute knowledge. Man experiences himself immediately as a being who finds himself in a world and who, in whatever he does, thinks, feels, or desires, knows that he has a not-yet-articulated knowledge of that world. It is from this pre-ontological understanding of the world that philosophy must take its starting point in its attempt to answer the question concerning the meaning of the Whole.

The interpretive analysis of the mode of Being characteristic of man shows that the human subjectivity is essentially intentional; man *ek-sists*, stands out toward the world, necessarily transcends himself and things in the direction of the world. Thus man is not an ego wrapped up in itself, nor is he a complicated mechanism causally interwoven with his environment. From the very beginning, and in the deepest core of his being, man manifests himself as a being that is in and toward its world. It is in and through his dialogue with the intramundane things and his fellows that man, from the perspective of the Whole, lets the beings and the world be what they are, uncovers them, articulates their meaning and, thus, brings this meaning to light.

The moment one realizes that man is nothing but a project of the world, and that his existential orientation toward the world can accept various, concrete forms, the question immediately becomes: Which one of these relations with the world is the most primordial one? Whereas Descartes and Kant felt that our relation with the world is originally and primordially a cognitive relation that is constituted and preserved in *theoretical* knowledge, we claim that theoretical knowledge and science are only special, and even derivative modes of man's fundamental orientation toward the world. Man's orientation toward the world originally takes the form of a concernful preoccupation with intramundane things and his fellows. Man does not rise to theoretical speculation or attain science except by taking his point of departure in his concernful preoccupation.

From these brief reflections, very important consequences necessarily follow. First, it is clear why we believe that traditional philosophy since the time of Plato and Aristotle, in questioning itself about the problem of the Whole (i.e., the problem of Being), has directed its attention too one-sidedly to intramundane things. It is also clear that in modern philosophy the things themselves have been considered too one-sidedly as objects of theoretical knowledge and, specifically, as objects such as they appear in empirical science. In this way beings were replaced by objects, things by objectified entities.

Another important consequence of the preceding reflections is that hermeneutic philosophy has to adopt a radically critical attitude in regard to classical *metaphysics*. First of all, metaphysics, instead of focusing on the totality of all possible meaning, centered its entire attention upon beings in an effort to locate a "being of all beings" as ultimate efficient and final cause of the totality of all things. Furthermore, every form of *metaphysica specialis* maintained this ontic attitude and, in addition, turned to entities that manifestly lie far beyond the realm of experience a human being can actually reflect on. In this attitude, hermeneutic philosophy is certainly deeply influenced by Kant's first *Critique*; yet its own position is notably different from that defended by Kant, who still left ample room for two or even three forms of *metaphysica specialis*.

We must now turn to a few other important elements of our conception of philosophy, namely its essential historicity and the idea that philosophy consists of critical reflection upon man's experience.

With Hegel we claim that man is essentially temporal and historical and that, if man himself is essentially historical, every human manifestation participates in this historicity as well. This means, among many other things, that man's philosophy is essentially historical, too. In trying to find their own way within the realm opened up by Hegel's view on the historicity of philosophy, many contemporary philosophers argue that this historicity is ultimately rooted, on the one hand, in the essentially historical character of the Whole itself, that is, the totality of all meaning, which shows and hides itself in various epochs of man's history in various ways, and, on the other hand, in man's own historicity.

From this it follows at once that there never can be a perfect philosophical synthesis. Each philosophy tries to understand the world on which it reflects. Since this particular world is not identical to *the* world, and *the* world is not identical to the Whole, but merely consists of the peculiar way in which the totality of all possible meaning shows and hides itself at a particular moment of man's history through a limited number of partly articulated "worlds," and each philosophy itself is essentially co-constituted by that world, it is obvious that philosophy never can escape the limitations of its own historical condition. In other words, we agree with Hegel that the differences in philosophical perspectives should be comprehended in terms of the continuing development of the truth taken as the process of gradual unveilment and concealment. The only point in which we cannot follow Hegel in this respect consists in the fact that Hegel sees the various philosophical perspectives as elements of an organic unity or system, in which the one element is as necessary as the other, and posits that necessity is constitutive of the life of the Whole. We, on the other hand, try to understand later philosophical syntheses as free consequences of earlier forms of thought and, therefore, definitely deny that individual philosophies and epochs of philosophy's history have emerged from one another according to laws based on the necessity of a dialectical process.

This brings us to another element in Hegel's conception of philosophy that is of great importance to us here, the idea that philosophy must be considered as a critical reflection of man's experience upon itself. In the *Phenomenology of Spirit,* Hegel posits that philosophy is the "science" of the experiences made by consciousness. In the book's introduction, the author states that the philosopher should not put himself in the place of the various human experiences; his task is merely to decipher them as history makes them available to him. In revealing the imminent logic of man's experience in all of its sectors, the question is no longer limited, as was the case in Kant's *Critique of Pure Reason,* to discovering what conditions make our scientific experiences possible. Hegel's problem is one of knowing how social, moral, aesthetic, and religious experiences are possible and, therefore, one of deciphering man's fundamental situation in the face of the world and of other men. What Hegel really wanted to do was to understand the social order, economic and legal systems, works of art, science, technology, ethics, and religion as so many ways for man to confront the limitations of his own condition. From this point of view, it is understandable that Hegel defines "experience" as the dialectical process that consciousness executes upon itself. Experience here no longer simply means our merely theoretical and reflexive contact with the sensible world, as it did in Kant; the word here reassumes the "tragic" resonance it has in common language, as for example when a man speaks about what he has lived through.

Hegel interpreted this idea in an idealistic way and explicitly defended the view that, through thought, the philosopher, and the philosopher alone, can get at the truth about all experiences, integrate them, go beyond them, and, from the depth of his wisdom, obtain the revelation of the real meaning of world history, to which other men simply submit by faith. We reject this idealistic interpretation and claim that to be a philosopher is to actualize an essentially human possibility and that it thus is nonsense to flatter oneself with the idea that one can exhaust man's religious, moral, political, judicial, social, and aesthetic life and all other modes of man's ek-sistence within the purely philosophical ek-sistence.

Philosophy is the explication of our pre-philosophical life in and with the world. It reveals to us something of the truth that is still concealed in it in an implicit way. It brings our original understanding of the world and of ourselves, basically mediated to us through the tradition to which we belong, over into an authentic understanding. Philosophy is not, however, only a determinate elaboration of our everyday knowledge concerning the world and our being in it; first and foremost it is a destruction of that knowledge. For when we start to think as philosophers and to pose philosophical questions to ourselves, we already have our opinions, conceptions, ideas, and insights, whatever their root and origin may be. As everyone knows from his own life, it is very difficult to escape from the power of the "self-evidence" of these preconceptions, because these preconceptions govern our thought without our knowledge. "Reduction" and criticism are necessary processes here, and, as Hegel has already shown, such processes manifest themselves first and foremost as a destruction of our natural and naive certainties.

The problem, however, is much more complicated than it seems to be at first sight. For in the domain of our pre-philosophical life, characteristic of our natural attitude, our life, which is rooted in the most original experience of our own being-in-the-world itself, is already "organized" in many ways. In the primordial experience, which is our being-in-the-world itself, all kinds of very fundamental but limited experiences announce themselves. The most important of these articulated and elaborated experiences are known as myth, religion, theology, art, politics, social theory, ethics, science, technology, and all other dimensions of our "culture." It is precisely this complex of articulated experiences, which are already elaborated in a nonphilosophical way, that philosophy time and again must try to understand in light of the truth of Being.

Thus, in addition to the dialectical relation between our philosophical reflection and the different philosophical currents that preceded it in our tradition, there is another set of relations (at least as essential as the one just mentioned) between our philosophical conception and one or more forms of nonphilosophical experience that, generally speaking, belong to the same cultural-historical period to which we ourselves belong.

In a certain sense, therefore, one could say that the history of philosophy is nothing more than a "dialectical" movement in which the philosophical dimension in man has tried continuously to comprehend all kinds of experiences that were evoked in part precisely by its own development. The philosophical dimension is inseparable from everything in a person's life that is not philosophy. That is why the philo-

sophical dimension must give to the different forms of nonphilosophical experience the possibility of developing independently, and even
of explicitly and repeatedly resisting and opposing the philosophical
reflection. On the other hand, however, we must realize that the different forms of nonphilosophical experience will never be able to take
over the task of the philosophical reflection itself, which at root is the
concern for the Whole.

In other words, philosophy itself does not have a title to constitute
meaning. For this is precisely the task of the different forms of man's
experience. Being nonphilosophical, however, these experiences are
not able to constitute meaning in a comprehensive manner. Experience wants to be reason but in each concrete case it materializes this
aim at first only inadequately. Furthermore, every experience presupposes a horizon of meaning that it cannot thematize itself. The perception of intramundane things, scientific research, the reflection of
man about his own destiny, the comport of society, the creation of
art—all of this is not yet philosophy, although all are obviously the
work of reason. Philosophy, which is essentially oriented toward these
different forms of experience and attempts to bring to light their
proper meaning within the Whole of meaning through critical reflection, knows that neither at the very beginning nor at the end will it
ever have at its disposal all the means with which it can once and for
all normatively prescribe what the function of each articulated form
of experience within the totality of meaning should be. The only thing
philosophy knows is that the constitution of meaning always has already begun, and that, although it has never completely succeeded, it
has never completely failed either. Philosophy's task is merely to unveil
what this process precisely consists of, within the perspective of the
totality of meaning, and how, in and through it, the Whole manifests
and hides itself at the same time.

IV. SOME REFLECTIONS ON NATURAL THEOLOGY[37]

In the preceding section I have defined philosophy as the critical
reflection on experiences that have already taken place. The meaning
of this reflection is to bring to light the "genuine" meaning of these

---

37. For what follows, cf. Thomas De Vio, Cardinal Cajetan, *The Analogy of Names
and the Concept of Being*, trans. E. A. Bushinski and H. J. Koren (Pittsburgh: Duquesne
University Press, 1953); Vladimir Lossky, *Théologie négative et connaissance de Dieu chez
Maître Eckhart* (Paris: Vrin, 1960); B. Montagnes, *La doctrine de l'analogie de l'être d'après
saint Thomas d'Aquin* (Louvain: Nauwelaerts, 1963); Battista Mondin, *St. Thomas Aquinas'
Philosophy in the Commentary of the Sentences* (The Hague: Nijhoff, 1975); R. M. Mac-

experiences by subjecting the immediately given to a process of critical mediation in such a manner that the critical reflection will not be permitted to become a substitute for the original experience. In view of the fact that, in any process of mediation, a framework of meaning is pre-understood that, as an a priori synthesis, is antecedent to the experiences to be reflected upon, all critical reflection has the form of an interpretation.

It will be clear at once that if philosophy is conceived of in this manner, those who engage in philosophical reflection have excluded the possibility of employing deductive argumentations. Taken in the sense indicated, philosophy does not prove anything (if the term "to prove" is taken in its literal logical sense), but merely examines and clarifies presuppositions and assumptions in a methodical manner. From this perspective, the entire application of logical procedures in the common sense of the term is left to the domain and competence of the sciences.

From this it follows at once that all forms of *metaphysica specialis,* in the sense of the tradition since the time of Wolff, including natural theology, are to be abandoned. For we find ourselves in the position of having to admit that, as philosophers, we cannot prove the existence of God and, furthermore, are unable to say anything about God's mode of being.

It is often said that this kind of philosophy, which defines man as Being-in-the-world, makes man exclusively into a this-worldly being in a theological sense. It is often said also that this kind of philosophy is inherently atheistic and that it gives to man the place that formerly in philosophy was held by God. Others have claimed that hermeneutic philosophy is caught up in sheer indifference to the question of God's existence. The position of hermeneutic philosophy is, rather, that a philosophy that thinks from the perspective of the happening of the truth of Being is simply unable to address today, in a meaningful manner, the question of the existence of God. For to speak about God's existence and his essence in a meaningful manner one must be able to say what the word "God" is to signify. But this presupposes

Inerny, *The Logic of Analogy* (The Hague: Nijhoff, 1961); Paul Ricoeur, *De l'interprétation. Essay sur Freud* (Paris: Vrin, 1965); "Le symbole donne à penser," in *Esprit,* 27 (1959), 60–76; *The Conflict of Interpretations: Essays in Hermeneutics* (Evanston, Ill.: Northwestern University Press, 1974); Martin Heidegger, *Phänomenologie und Theologie* (Frankfurt: Klostermann, 1970); Joseph J. Kockelmans, "Signs and Symbols," in *Essays in Metaphysics,* ed. Carl Vaught (University Park, Pa.: The Pennsylvania State University Press, 1970), 181–212; "On Myth and Its Relationship to Hermeneutics," in *Cultural Hermeneutics,* 1 (1973), 47–86; "Heidegger on Theology," in *The Southwestern Journal of Philosophy,* 4 (1973), 85–108.

that one knows the essence of divinity, and that in turn presupposes that one understands the essence of the holy. But in the world in which we live, a world that is preoccupied with technology and science, with domination and control, the notion of the holy has lost its meaning. In the final analysis, this kind of philosophy refrains from speaking about God out of respect for the boundaries that have been set for thinking by the truth of Being itself.[38]

Yet we obviously do not deny the possibility of a regional ontology of religious phenomena. But one should realize that regional ontologies are not philosophical disciplines in the strict sense. Rather, they limit themselves to a descriptive and interpretive analysis of the basic structure of those entities and the relations that exist among them, which, taken together, constitute a clearly defined but limited realm of meaning. Thus in the conception of philosophy developed here, there is the possibility and necessity of developing regional ontologies of "nature," of man, of social phenomena, of aesthetic phenomena, of religious phenomena, and so forth. Once the regional ontology of religious phenomena, commonly known as phenomenology of religion, has been sufficiently developed, we, as philosophers, can then critically reflect on our religious experiences as well as on the formal structures brought to light by phenomenology of religion. However, since, as philosophers, we cannot reflect on any experiences except those that we ourselves have had and that have given us something worthy to think about, and in view of the fact that our own religious experiences originated from the religious tradition in which we grew up, our critical reflections on our religious experiences will have to be concerned with our experiences of the Christianness of Christianity, for instance. But of that we have knowledge only through God's revelation, known to us through the Scriptures and the Christian tradition, as mediated to us by both kerygma and sacred theology. And in such a perspective there does not seem to be any need for a natural theology. Since we believe in God, there does not seem to be any need for a proof of his existence; and since God has spoken to us through the Scriptures and the Christian tradition, there does not seem to be any need for a speculation of God's essence and attributes.

Yet all of this obviously does not mean that it would not be good for a believer to convince himself that it is not at all unreasonable to believe in God. The classical *quinque viae* all draw attention to specific sets of facts in which the religious mind confronts the Transcendent.

---

38. Martin Heidegger, "Letter on Humanism," in *Basic Writings*, ed. David Farrell Krell (New York: Harper and Row, 1977), 193–242, 216–30.

To a religious person, the discovery of harmony and order in the universe, for example, can become an occasion of faith, just as the inability to explain disorder may induce religious doubt. Both the believer and the nonbeliever are puzzled by order and disorder. If one were to attempt to "deduce" the notion of a Supreme Being from the idea of order, one merely would commit a logical error.[39]

Furthermore, one should realize also that the entire universe is more understandable in its various aspects under the assumption that God exists than it would be if everything had to be explained by mere chance.[40] One even wonders whether or not, in such a position, chance would not become what all other people have called God. Finally, one should not forget that, in the modern world, new versions of old arguments have been proposed, such as Paley's teleological argument, and that, in addition, completely new arguments have been developed, such as the axiological proof, which tries to establish the existence of a highest Value, or the eudaemonic argument, which aims to prove that man's striving for happiness presupposes the existence of a highest Good, or even one of the moral proofs for the existence of God that try to show that God exists either by starting from the existence of an objective moral order or from the concrete experiences of conscience that all human beings appear to share. There are obviously other arguments, such as that which rests on the notion of entropy, or the various arguments proposed in contemporary cosmology; yet these arguments, too, are "valid" only for a person who already believes in the existence of God and now convinces himself that his belief and faith in God are not irrational or even unreasonable. It should be noted that some of these arguments simply have no power of proof, whereas others will be meaningful only to those who have the appropriate knowledge of the relevant science.

But let us return to the main issue: natural theology. Even if one were to take the conception of philosophy proposed here in its minimal form, then there still would be some important issues that would make any involvement in natural theology questionable to us. All natural theology implies at least two basic assumptions: (1) Man is capable of proving the existence of God, and (2) man is able to know the essence of God (at least to some degree) by means of analogy. As for the first assumption, it seems to me that Kant's critical philosophy and the entire literature it evoked have shown convincingly that it is im-

39. Cf. Louis Dupré, "The Teleological Argument," in *The Challenge of Religion*, 128–38, Conclusion, 135–36.
40. Cf. Peter Bertocci, "The Wider Teleological Argument for a Personal God," in *The Challenge of Religion*, 139–59 passim.

possible for man to prove the existence of God, although it is virtually impossible to account for all aspects of the human reality if one were to exclude the possibility of God's existence. This is true particularly for the moral domain.

As for the second issue, all those who have defended the possibility of a positive, natural theology assumed that the concepts and words used to articulate them, which man developed in a long historical process in his concern with things, his fellows, and events, can be employed also in our thinking and speaking about God. They were of the opinion that at least some concepts and words can be applied to God, because these concepts and words can be employed analogically. They all agreed that man cannot find concepts and names that would be adequate to properly designate God. In this sense, almost all philosophers of the past, in some form or other, have subscribed to a kind of apophasy and, thus, to a negative theology. Yet the idea that God is ineffable has practically always been combined with some form of positive theology: Although, strictly speaking, God is ineffable, we nonetheless can have some knowledge of him. For God created all things; thus, the names we use to refer to the things he created may be applied to God within certain limits stipulated by two conditions: (1) The names are to be used analogously, and (2) they are to be applied to God *modo supereminentiori*. The main reason why most authors have tried to add some form of positive theology to a strictly negative one is to be found in the fact that if they were not to do so, they would exclude the possibility of God's revealing himself to man.

The conditions stipulated for man's speaking about God are interpreted by the various authors in different manners. The tension between the two conditions has given rise to different interpretations. Those who strongly stress the modo supereminentiori aspect will have to set very severe limits to a possible application of analogous concepts and words to God; on the other hand, those who focus mainly on the analogous character of the concepts and words we apply to God will have to minimize the meaning of the expression supereminentiori.

Most modern authors who have written on analogy take their point of departure in Cajetan's *The Analogy of Names*.[41] It should be noted that Cajetan, while claiming to be merely systematizing and developing the views formulated by Aristotle, Averroes, and Aquinas, nonetheless at the same time admits that the doctrine formulated in his treatise is not found in the same manner in the works of the three main sources quoted. The terminology suggested by Cajetan is not found in his

41. Cf. n. 37 above.

primary sources, and the distinctions proposed by him do not cover the much more refined distinctions of the leading medieval authors.

For our present purposes, the most important point to focus on is the fact that, for Cajetan, the analogy of attribution is to be limited to the analogy according to extrinsic denomination, "so that the primary analogate realizes the perfection formally, whereas the others have it only by extrinsic denomination."[42] From this it follows that, for speaking about God, this type of analogy is not important. Cajetan is fully aware of this and for that reason argues that in natural theology, as well as in sacred theology, all concepts and words properly applied to God are to be taken in the analogy of strict proportionality.[43]

Careful study of the documents of medieval philosophers, however, has shown first that according to the leading authors in natural theology the analogy of strict proportionality cannot be employed, because the infinite distance between God and created things excludes this type of analogy. It is obviously not correct to state: "God:his Being = created thing:its finite being." These authors, therefore, introduced in the analogy of attribution an analogy according to intrinsic denomination, in addition to the analogy according to extrinsic denomination as suggested by Cajetan. In the analogy according to intrinsic denomination, one must furthermore make a distinction between the analogy of many in regard to one ("being" in regard to accident and substance) and the analogy by participation and by essence ("being" in regard to God and created things). Note that in the latter case an infinite distance is again implied.

The main reason I believe that analogous concepts and words cannot be applied to God directly, but have a meaningful function only within the context of a symbolic speaking about God, are the following. First, the infinite distance implied in the analogy of attribution according to intrinsic denomination makes it impossible for us to have a positive idea as to what a given concept or name might mean when applied to God. This type of analogy implies that words applied to God have the same meaning as they have when they are applied to finite things, although what is so meant is infinitely different. One might argue that what these words mean in both cases is not infinitely different but merely the same taken in an infinitely different degree. Yet even in this interpretation, what one really claims is that the words have a meaning totally beyond our finite comprehension. In the statement, "God is good," the term "good" has an indefinite meaning. The

42. Cajetan, *The Analogy of Names*, p. 16.
43. Ibid., 28–29, 57.

statement expresses that God most certainly is not non-good. Yet what the predicate "good" might mean in a positive sense remains fully hidden to me.

More importantly, one should realize also that our concepts and words are meaningful only with respect to a given a priori framework of meaning. The term *a priori* here means nothing but the fact that the framework of meaning is a priori in regard to the application of the concepts and words in question, and by no means implies the doctrine of innate ideas or Kant's conception of the categories. Now it is the fact that all of our concepts and words function meaningfully only within frameworks of meaning, which makes any positive application of these concepts and words to God impossible. One might say that, when applied to God, the word "good" expresses that God is good regardless of the perspective one is willing to adopt. Yet, in that supposition, all words applied to God will necessarily have the same meaning. Anyone who thinks it meaningful to say that God is good most certainly did not mean to imply that one might as well say that God is just, omnipotent, or wise. We cannot avoid using our concepts and words, even when we speak about God, from the perspective of a certain a priori synthesis, although we know that having to employ these syntheses is precisely the reason our concepts and words cannot be applied positively to a Being who is beyond all perspectives.

These and other difficulties are the reason many modern authors believe that in our speaking about God, symbolism plays the leading role.[44] It is true that the application of symbolism necessarily implies the use of analogy, but in this context the problems raised in regard to the merely semantic interpretation of analogy no longer hold. To explain this briefly, the following remarks may suffice.

In each sign we make a distinction between the signifying and the signified (structure) and between the so-constituted sign and the thing designated (intention). Symbols are to be characterized by the fact that, in addition to these structural and intentional dualities, a third duality is to be admitted, namely one of meaning in regard to meaning.

44. Cf. E. Castelli, *L'Analyse du langage théologique* (Paris: Aubier, 1969); Paul Ricoeur, *The Conflict of Interpretations,* pt. V, ed. Don Ihde (Evanston, Ill.: Northwestern University Press, 1974); *The Symbolism of Evil,* trans. E. Buchanan (New York: Harper and Row, 1967); "The Language of Faith," *Union Seminary Quarterly Review,* 28 (1973), 213–24; "Philosophy and Religious Language," *The Journal of Religion,* 54 (1974), 71–85; "Le symbole donne à penser," in *Esprit,* 27 (1959), 60–76; Kenneth L. Schmitz, "Restitution of Meaning in Religious Speech," in *The Challenge of Religion* (New York: Seabury Press, 1982), 234–46; James Ross, "Ways of Religious Knowing," in *The Challenge of Religion,* 83–103.

The symbol implies the presence of a perceptible figure that refers to a "world" that itself is not perceptible. Symbols are employed particularly when we wish to point to a world of meaning to which man has no direct access through perception or through the sciences that presuppose perception. Symbols are, in principle, capable of achieving this task in that they imply a hermeneutic dimension in addition to the semantic dimension found in all signs. It is the presence of this hermeneutical dimension in symbols that explains that it takes a special science to elucidate symbols, a science of interpretation that is not interested primarily in the relation between the signifying sign and the signified entity (semantics), but in the relation between the literal meaning and the "hidden" meaning, which the first only "symbolizes." The literal meaning in an analogous way intends a second meaning that is given in no other way and, in some cases, cannot be given in another way. Thus analogy does not function here on the semantic level (as in all classical theories), but on the level of the relation between the immediately signified and the secondly signified. Analysis of the analogy that joins the literal meaning to the symbolic meaning is made difficult by the fact that the symbolic meaning is given only by means of an element in the immediately signified and nowhere else. The analogy in this case is like an intention contained in what is immediately signified by the literal meaning of the cultural or ritual words. This intention cannot be objectified in principle and, thus, it is impossible to translate it by other expressions. Living in the literal meaning, one is drawn by it beyond itself to a second meaning; thus it is the literal meaning that brings the analogy about by giving us the primary analogate within a determinate context. By the symbol one is drawn toward a "hidden" world, but the symbol itself does not (and in most cases cannot) articulate that world.

Although these reflections do not form a substitute for the classical, natural theology (taken as *metaphysica specialis*), one could perhaps say, nevertheless, that they express the basic concern of all forms of negative theology.

V. CONCLUSION

In the preceding reflections, I have rejected the possibility of a natural theology in the sense of Wolff, Baumgarten, and other rationalist authors of the precritical tradition. My reason for this position is that no philosophical justification can be given for this type of special metaphysics. Both Kant and Heidegger have, each in his own way, given convincing arguments for this view.

On the other hand, I have maintained the possibility of a regional ontology of religious phenomena. Yet I foresee serious difficulties with the circumscription of the range of the phenomena with which this discipline is to concern itself. These difficulties are connected with the fact that the people who belong to a religion that presupposes revelation (Judaism, Christianity) will defend the view that their religion is the only true religion. This seems to lead to the view that if Christianity, for instance, is to be taken as a religion, then it is also the one and only religion; on the other hand, if there are many religions, then Christianity cannot be one of them. I have not dealt with this implication because of lack of space. Yet, in my view, the issue deserves careful attention.

I have maintained the legitimacy of "arguments" for the existence of God in order to guarantee the credibility of religious faith. Yet I see no need for a philosopher's God, who is to guarantee the absoluteness of a metaphysical synthesis. Nor do I see any need for a justification of God's existence in light of the evil that surrounds us.

The Pennsylvania State University

5 Natural Theology and Positive Predication: Might Maimonides Be a Guide?

FREDERICK FERRÉ

One of the persistent sources of doubt about the value or possibility of natural theology is concern about the logic of theological language. Can human speech refer to the divine in any reliable way, or must our language, when used about God, be so heavily swathed in indirection, equivocation, and obscuration that the whole enterprise of natural theology must collapse?

I plan in this chapter to defend the logical possibility of a meaningful and important natural theology, though a natural theology freshly—and properly—chastened by recognition of the logical limits of human speech and argument. I shall not attempt to "do" substantive natural theology here, but instead to discuss the prior question of what the powers and limits of language allow for the natural theologian when argument commences. Above all, I want to dispute the idea that natural theology must somehow be abandoned simply because words used about God must have entirely different meanings from their normal ones. First, I do not believe that this logical situation is always the case; and, second, even if it should be true that our predication of positive properties to God must in a sense be ineradicably equivocal, this would not significantly undermine the properly understood enterprise of natural theologizing.

It becomes at once important to define this enterprise in the normative sense that I plan to defend. Natural theology, as I support it, is the theoretical effort of religious persons to consider the universal bearing of the God they worship on the world at large. This is a broader understanding than one that centers around "proofs" alone, since great ideas may be illuminating even though not proven. It is also a characterization that does not confine natural theology to its apologetic aspect. Natural theology is properly done by thinking beings who need to make connections in thought between the focus of their most intense values and their most comprehensive modes of experience.[1] Such thinking beings seek out these connections in the first place for themselves, in search of wholeness. Only secondarily is the convincing of other people, especially those outside the particular religious community of shared values, symbols, and stories, a compelling goal.

In my understanding of normative natural theology, then, religion and religious community are prior to and contributory to reflection and generalization. In the context of religious convictions, however, the same intellectual motives to think large thoughts coherently—to think connectedly as far as possible—motives that are behind the urge toward a unified science (or, at a more preliminary level, the urge to wider and wider extensions and applications of particular theories) function within religious communities and healthily motivate at least some religious persons. The path up to metaphysics, to theories of unlimited comprehensiveness, leads (as in Aristotle's case) through "the physics," when no special religious conceptions are at stake; the path up to natural theology, which in many ways overlaps in function and subject matter with secular metaphysics, leads through particular communities of value-saturated belief and practice.

Bowman L. Clarke makes a similar point by contrasting "revealed" with natural theology:

If revelation . . . deals with particular relations or manifestations of God disclosed in the uniqueness of certain revelatory events, involving both a particular reception and a particular communal context, there will be that aspect which can be said to deal with God as related to, or manifested in, any and every event without reference to any particular individual or community. This is the area of natural theology.[2]

Clarke continues by contrasting the purposes of "revealed" theology with those of natural theology:

Whereas the purpose of revelation is to make God efficacious within the lives of particular men and particular communities, the purpose of natural theology is to connect religion through its general ideas to philosophy, particularly to that area of philosophy which deals with the most general categories of existence—metaphysics.[3]

Tying natural theology so intimately to philosophy, however, and to

1. See my *Basic Modern Philosophy of Religion* (New York: Charles Scribner's Sons, 1967), chap. 3, for extensive development of the idea of religion as our most intense and comprehensive way of valuing.

2. Bowman L. Clarke, *Language and Natural Theology* (The Hague: Mouton, 1966), 80.

3. Ibid., 80–81.

metaphysics in particular, has its risks. If metaphysics is a leaking ship, then natural theology sinks, too.

It is, I hope, unnecessary in this essay to rehearse the recent controversial history of metaphysics and metaphysical language. Many today remain entirely unpersuaded that Clarke's "most general categories of existence" can meaningfully be employed in connection with a referent as all-encompassing as metaphysical comprehensiveness requires. Even those who, like myself, cautiously encourage venturing up to these unlimited levels of theoretical connection[4] must recognize that something peculiar happens to language when assertions are attempted about what, as Clarke put it, is "related to, or manifested in, any and every event." The normal "method of difference," in Whitehead's phrase,[5] is lacking when in the nature of the case no experience could fail to manifest these categories and no experiment could falsify claims made in their terms. Does language like this—so universal that it is incompatible with no possible experience—continue to communicate to minds whose thought and speech is normally forged in connection with boundaries, edges, and hot/cold or on/off binary choices?

On the other hand, if we are considering natural theology, not just secular metaphysics, how can God, the object of religious awe, be discussed in the same language that refers no less to garbage, toenail clippings, and dirty dishes than to the Maker of Heaven and Earth? God, for the religious community, is the most high as well as the most real. Among religious believers there is an understandable revulsion from desecrating the Holy One by speaking and thinking about Him in the shopworn categories applicable to our profane world. Can terms that serve to relate to every event also serve to refer to the One for whom all perfection is reserved?

Natural theology seems trapped between the philosophical drive to relate everything to everything else—in which case only language expressing similarities and connections will suffice—and the religious drive to distinguish God from everything else—in which case only language expressing God's otherness can be allowed. Either tendency, taken too far, could prove fatal to the enterprise. Metaphysical lan-

---

4. See *Basic Modern Philosophy of Religion,* cited above, chap. 13, "The Cognitive Possibilities of Religious Language," especially sec. II, "The Modes of Understanding," 388–396. Also see, in my *Philosophy of Technology* (Englewood Cliffs, N.J.: Prentice-Hall, 1988), chap. 8, "Technology and Metaphysics," especially sec. 8.2, "Metaphysical Thinking," 120–26.

5. "We habitually observe by the method of difference. Sometimes we see an elephant, and sometimes we do not. The result is that an elephant, when present, is noticed." Alfred North Whitehead, *Process and Reality: An Essay in Cosmology* (New York: Macmillan, 1929), 6.

guage denied the "method of difference" may find it impossible to define a clear referent other than some obscure, elusive Absolute; but language expressing nothing but differences between God and the rest of the world may end by allowing neither referent for thought about God nor anything to say about Him at all.

In this dilemma it may be instructive to turn to the thought of one who is remembered for grasping the latter horn—negative theology— and making it the sole touchstone of religious wisdom. I refer to Moses Maimonides (1135–1204), the great medieval Jewish thinker who may have more to teach us than is usually recognized. Maimonides is normally identified as the most extreme exponent of negative theology in the Judeo-Christian tradition. Thomas Aquinas (1224–74) respectfully wrestled with Maimonides in this guise and—though Thomas acknowledged the immense obstacles to merely univocal predication of positive attributes to God—he rejected his predecessor's seemingly unalloyed negative theology in favor of his own preferred "middle way" of analogy. Virtually all philosophical argument about Maimonides, pro or con, has followed Thomas's lead in interpreting the message of *The Guide of the Perplexed* as a relatively one-dimensional protest against any affirmative theology.

There is no doubt that Maimonides is one of the great scourges of heedless affirmations about God. Affirmations of positive predicates have the logical consequence, as noted above, of associating whatever is being described with other (inevitably "lower") things which are also suited, in their ways, to carrying the same all-purpose predicate. Against such "associations" Maimonides makes his strong objection.

Know that the description of God, may He be cherished and exalted, by means of negations is the correct description—a description that is not affected by an indulgence in facile language and does not imply any deficiency with respect to God in general or in any particular mode. On the other hand, if one describes Him by means of affirmations, one implies, as we have made clear, that He is associated with that which is not He and implies a deficiency in Him.[6]

The logical foundation of this protest is, as Maimonides puts it, "that an attribute does not particularize any object of which it is predicated in such a way that it is not associated by virtue of that particular attribute with other things."[7] But the religious motivation to avoid any such demeaning "associations" is above all compelling for Maimonides. His writing, even at points of maximum technical complexity, is constantly interrupted with his ejaculations of praise and honor for the

6. Moses Maimonides, *The Guide of the Perplexed,* trans. Shlomo Pines (Chicago: The University of Chicago Press, 1963), pt. I, chap. 58. Henceforth *Guide.*
7. Ibid.

One about Whom his arguments revolve. On every page, in virtually every paragraph, wherever God is mentioned, a phrase like "may He be exalted," or "may He be magnified and glorified," leaps out of the prose. Reading *The Guide of the Perplexed,* one is never allowed to forget that the main thing is piety. Arguments are in the service of adoration.

Refraining from affirmative predication, then, is recommended as a way of avoiding giving offense to God. Maimonides cites a parable of Rabbi Haninah: "It is as if a mortal king who had millions of gold pieces were praised for possessing silver. Would this not be an offense to him?" And later he interprets it:

He does not say, for example: What does this resemble? It is as if a mortal king who had millions of gold pieces were praised for possessing one hundred pieces. For this example would have indicated that the perfections of Him, may He be exalted, while more perfect than the perfections that are ascribed to Him, still belong to the same species as the latter. ... But the wisdom manifest in this parable lies in his saying: *gold pieces and were praised for possessing silver.* He says this in order to indicate that in God, may He be exalted, there is nothing belonging to the same species as the attributes that are regarded by us as perfections, but that all these attributes are deficiencies with regard to God, just as he made clear in this parable when he said: *Would this not be an offense to him?*[8]

Then Maimonides drives home his central point: "I have then already made it known to you that everything in these attributes that you regard as a perfection is a deficiency with regard to Him, may He be exalted, as it belongs to a species to which the things that are with us belong."[9]

Making affirmations of this sort, then, is rejected as impious, even though it may be impiety grounded in ignorance. Maimonides classifies it as "*unintended obloquy and vituperation.*"[10] Those who understand will go to great lengths to avoid such obloquy, since, "in view of the fact that *speaking ill* and *defamation* are acts of great disobedience, how much all the more so is the loosening of the tongue with regard to God, may He be exalted, and the predicating of Him qualificative attributions above which He is exalted."[11] The masses may well not be able to understand this logically subtle form of impiety for what it is; indeed, Maimonides advises against trying to inform them. "This notion ... should not be divulged to the vulgar. For this kind of speculation is more suitable for the elite who consider that the magnification of God does not consist in their saying improper things but in their understanding properly."[12]

---

8. *Guide,* pt. I, chap. 59.
10. Ibid.
12. Ibid.

9. Ibid.
11. Ibid.

What, then, is the proper way of understanding and magnifying God, and can there truly be another way than by affirmative predication? Maimonides insists, as we have seen, that negation, for those prepared enough to handle it intellectually, is the correct way. Its great virtue is, of course, that negation does not offend by implying inappropriate associations. But can the negative way actually give understanding and allow proper magnification? Maimonides recognizes the problem. If it is wrong to ascribe affirmative attributes to God, then "in what respect can there be superiority or inferiority between those who apprehend Him? If, however, there is none, *Moses our Master* and *Solomon* did not apprehend anything different from what a single individual among the pupils apprehends, and there can be no increase in this knowledge."[13] This unacceptable consequence would follow, however, only if "knowing more" (Moses more than the lowly pupil, or a learned adult more than the child that he or she was) must be defined as the possession of an ever larger collection of positive predicates. This is a false conception of knowledge. True, with respect to the things of which attributes are appropriately predicated, "he who predicates these attributes accordingly comes nearer to the apprehension of the true reality of the thing in question."[14] But with respect to God, for whom ignorant positive attributions are offensive, "you come nearer to the apprehension of Him, may He be exalted, with every increase in the negations regarding Him."[15]

Such growth in apprehension is illustrated by Maimonides as a kind of narrowing down from vague, global ignorance to greater and greater grasp of what is left from repeated negation. He gives the following example of how "particularization" can be achieved through negation:

[I]f there were a man in this house and you know that some body is in it without knowing what it is and would ask, saying: What is in this house? and the one who answered you would say: There is no mineral in it and no body of a plant—a certain particularization would be achieved and you would know that a living being is in the house though you would not know which animal. Thus the attributes of negation have in this respect something in common with the attributes of affirmation, for the former undoubtedly bring about some particularization even if the particularization due to them only exists in the exclusion of what has been negated from the sum total of things that we had thought of as not being negated.[16]

Thus negative theology is not to be confused with nescience or ag-

13. Ibid.   14. Ibid.
15. Ibid.   16. *Guide*, pt. I, chap. 58.

nosticism. Such unrelieved negative positions would, indeed, end in relativism and in an empty silence about God. But for Maimonides,

in every case in which the demonstration that a certain thing should be negated with reference to Him becomes clear to you, you become more perfect, and . . . in every case in which you affirm of Him an additional thing, you become one who likens Him to other things and you get further away from the knowledge of His true reality. It is from this point of view that one ought to come nearer to an apprehension of Him by means of investigation and research: namely, in order that one should know the impossibility of everything that is impossible with reference to Him. . . .[17]

The silence of Maimonides' negative theology, unlike the silence of nescience, is not empty but rich. As he writes: "The most apt phrase concerning this subject is the dictum occurring in the *Psalms* (65:2), *Silence is praise to Thee,* which interpreted signifies: silence with regard to You is praise."[18]

There is a problem here, however. For silence to be meaningful praise, it must have a specific referent to which it points. How is this established if only negation is allowable? Likewise, for the "particularization" of a situation to be achieved through repeated negations (as in a game of Twenty Questions), there must be a prior context of positive knowledge, a "sum total of things that we had thought of as not being negated." In Maimonides' example it was postulated that "you knew that some body" was in the house, and it was taken for known, as well, that all bodies must be either mineral or vegetable or animal. The negative way, if it is to remain a way of apprehension and magnification of God, seems dependent on a prior positive way of some such sort. Is Maimonides prepared to admit such a context?

His traditional image among philosophers of religion notwithstanding, the answer from Maimonides is emphatically, Yes. His motives for rejecting the careless use of positive predicates for God are not simply those of piety. There are epistemological and metaphysical reasons as well. Maimonides writes: "we are only able to apprehend the fact that He is and cannot apprehend His quiddity. It is consequently impossible that He should have affirmative attributes. For he has no 'That' outside of His 'What,' and hence an attribute cannot be indicative of one of the two. . . ."[19] Here, Maimonides the natural theologian, as we shall shortly see, comes to the support of Maimonides the negative theologian.

But Maimonides the "revealed" theologian stands prior to both his

17. *Guide,* pt. I, chap. 59.   18. Ibid.
19. *Guide,* pt. I, chap. 58.

other roles. Even he, despite his many warnings against "unintended obloquy," recognizes the "necessity" of providing a certain limited set of authorized positive predicates by which to designate and describe the Perfect One about Whom natural theology conducts its more abstract reflections.

[I]f we were left only to our intellects we should never have mentioned [affirmative] attributes or stated a thing appertaining to them. Yet the necessity to address men in such terms as would make them achieve some representation—in accordance with the dictum of the Sages: *The Torah speaks the language of the sons of man*—obliged resort to predicating of God their own perfections when speaking to them. It must then be our purpose to draw a line at using these expressions and not to apply them to Him except only in reading the *Torah*. However, as the *men of the Great Synagogue,* who were prophets, appeared in their turn and inserted the mention of these attributes in the prayer, it is our purpose to pronounce only these attributes when saying our prayers.[20]

Although extremely cautious about their use (he warns that "we are not permitted [even] in our prayers to use and to cite all the attributes ascribed to God in the books of the prophets"[21]), Maimonides wisely allows a way to satisfy the religious need for some authorized representations of God, so long as these are not licentiously wrenched from their context of worship.

Natural theology, in contrast, approaches God from the opposite side, not from the experience of particular communities or the language of specific stories, but from the universal or pervasive properties of things. To these matters, Maimonides turned without hesitation. The three principal metaphysical truths about God to be demonstrated are (1) that God exists, (2) that God is not a body nor a force in a body, and (3) that He is one, entirely simple, being. Maimonides was convinced that adequate demonstrations had long existed for all these points. In his view, Aristotle could hardly be improved on when it came to such demonstrations. The proofs are familiar ones to those who know Aristotle (or St. Thomas) and need not be more than mentioned here.

Maimonides' primary demonstration for God's existence is the argument from motion—that all movers cannot infinitely have been moved by something other than themselves, and that therefore there must necessarily be a mover responsible for all motion but moved by no other. "Now this is the deity, may His name be sublime; I am referring to the first cause moving the sphere."[22] Maimonides also uses the argument from generation and corruption—to the effect that if

20. *Guide,* pt. I, chap. 59.   21. Ibid.
22. *Guide,* pt. II, chap. 1.

everything were contingent, then there would be nothing in existence today, since "what is possible to a species must necessarily come about."[23]

Hence it follows necessarily, according to this speculation that if there are, as we perceive, existents subject to generation and corruption, there must be a certain existent that is not subject to generation and corruption. Now in this existent that is not subject to generation and corruption, there is no possibility of corruption at all; rather, its existence is necessary, not possible.[24]

This demonstration "is a demonstration concerning which there can be no doubt, no refutation, and no dispute, except on the part of one who is ignorant of the method of demonstration."[25] This was the first point to be demonstrated.

That point carries with it the corollary that, as a necessary existent, this first mover can have no·cause; and if it is necessary in its own essence, it can have no composition since its existence must not be distinct from its essence. If uncaused and uncomposite, then it cannot be a body or a force in a body, all of which are caused and composite, at the very least in the distinction between form and matter. This was the second point to be demonstrated.

Finally, a being whose essence is existence must be One and absolutely simple. "Accordingly, nothing at all can be associated with the necessary of existence."[26] This was the third point for demonstration. God's radical oneness—the doctrine that God has no "That" outside of his "What"—was the key point theoretically (if not religiously), as we recall, for rejecting attributions of common positive predicates to God.

These arguments are familiar and less impressive to most of us today than they were to Maimonides. But that is not the most interesting point. What is especially worth notice is that negative theology was not left hanging as mere negation; it was placed within a context both of authorized positive religious predicates and also of metaphysical argumentation. Maimonides had no qualms about using theoretical reason. "For the intellect that God made overflow unto man and that is the latter's ultimate perfection, was that which *Adam* had been provided with before he disobeyed. It was because of this that it was said of him that he was created *in the image of God and in His likeness.*"[27] Thinking metaphysically, Maimonides does not even feel required to draw back from the affirmation of real "likeness" between

23. Ibid.   24. Ibid.
25. Ibid.   26. Ibid.
27. *Guide,* pt. I, chap. 2.

man and God. He treats such a likeness as more than simply following out the consequences of the image metaphor. God is rightly held to be "the intellect as well as the intellectually cognizing subject and the intellectually cognized object, and that those three notions form in Him, may He be exalted, one single notion in which there is no multiplicity."[28] But this is not paradoxical or strange, since the same is true of human intellections as well. "For in the case of every intellect, its act is identical in essence; for intellect in actu is not one thing and its act another thing; for the true reality and the quiddity of the intellect is apprehension."[29] Thus, "the numerical unity of the intellect, the intellectually cognizing subject, and the intellectually cognized object, does not hold good with reference to the Creator only, but also with references to every intellect."[30] The difference between us and God is that we are only sometimes an intellect in actu and frequently are impeded in our intellections, while God is "constantly an intellect in actu and . . . there is no impediment either proceeding from His essence or from another that might hinder His apprehending."[31] Far from denying important continuities between man and God, Maimonides here affirms an extremely intimate point of relationship in kind. It may be noted that it is only within the context of technical, theoretical discourse that this is allowed; but if it were not for some such permission in these contexts, there would be nothing worth thinking about, and negative theology would be nothing more than nescience. Finally, Maimonides shows that the influence of natural and revealed theology does not flow only in one direction. If natural theology is essential to anchor a non-agnostic piety of restrained tongues on the one hand, so, on the other hand, can revealed religion confront and correct metaphysical speculations. Maimonides spends much effort discussing the doctrine that the world is eternal and necessary. At one point he assumes it as a premise[32] to be added to the other twenty-five premises he needs for his metaphysical demonstrations about God's existence, non-materiality, and simplicity—but he adds it only to show that whether it is assumed or not, the demonstrations themselves remain unaffected. Thus Aristotle's position affirming the eternity of the world is granted only as a hypothesis, not as something demonstrated or certain. Maimonides recognizes that Aristotle held it to be the most fitting view, but, on the other hand, that it runs counter to the biblical vision of God as creator. His own position is that "the premise in question is possible—that is, neither necessary, as is af-

28. *Guide,* pt. I, chap. 68.   29. Ibid.
30. Ibid.   31. Ibid.
32. *Guide,* pt. II, Introduction.

firmed by the commentators of the writings of Aristotle, nor impossible, as is claimed by the Mutakallimūn."[33] In that open situation, considerations other than theoretical ones alone may become decisive, Maimonides shows, some chapters later. Necessity and eternity, granted to the world, would seem to rule out purpose and creation for the deity. The two conflict. "For to me a combination between existing in virtue of necessity," Maimonides writes, "and being produced in time in virtue of a purpose and a will—a combination uniting these two—comes near to a combination of two contraries."[34] It all depends, he acknowledges, on how key terms are used.

[T]he assertion, as maintained by Aristotle, [is] that this being [the world] proceeds necessarily from its cause and is perpetual in virtue of the latter's perpetuity . . . but that it has always been and will always be as it is—just as the sunrise is indubitably the agent of the day, though neither of them precedes the other in point of time. But this is not the meaning of purpose, as we propose to conceive it. For we wish to signify by the term that it—I mean the world—does not necessarily proceed from Him, may He be exalted, as an effect necessarily proceeds from its cause without being able to be separated from it or to change unless its cause or one of its modes also changes.[35]

In this situation, the community of belief has a stake in the answer. Is the world a product of necessity, or is its cause "the agent that has brought about this diversity and has particularized it in the way in which we, the followers of *Moses our Master,* believe"?[36] Maimonides' answer shows that in at least some circumstances, like this, anthropomorphic concepts like purpose and freedom, drawn from the authorized imagery of a religious community, can come to the aid of theory when theory alone cannot decide the issue. Many unfortunate consequences afflict the necessitarian, Maimonides shows, which are escaped "if, however, we believe that all this has been produced through the purpose of one who purposed, made, and particularized it [the world]—as His wisdom, which cannot be grasped, required. . . ."[37] Most strikingly, the necessitarian view suffers by offending God's perfection:

Withal very disgraceful conclusions would follow upon it. Namely, it would follow that the deity, whom everyone who is intelligent recognizes to be perfect in every kind of perfection, could, as far as all the beings are concerned, produce nothing new in any of them; if He wished to lengthen a fly's wing or to shorten a worm's foot, He would not be able to do it.[38]

---

33. Ibid.
35. *Guide,* pt. II, chap. 21.
37. *Guide,* pt. II, chap. 22.

34. *Guide,* pt. II, chap. 20.
36. Ibid.
38. Ibid.

God "purposing," God "wishing," God "willing," God "making," God "producing"? Can this be Maimonides? Indeed, the leading historical advocate of negative theology not only permits himself to argue in these and similar affirmative ways, he also allows the vivid positive imagery of faith to have decisive impact on unsettled theoretical problems, just as he allows positive general conceptions of metaphysics to provide needed definite descriptions for the deity about whom, he argues in other contexts, it is wiser intellectually and deeper spiritually to withhold positive predicates rather than to affirm them.

Is Maimonides merely inconsistent? Some would say so, and even Maimonides warns against seeking an easy reading of his difficult and esoteric work. But if this is simple inconsistency on his part, it shows how difficult—perhaps impossible—it is to remain purely negative and still to engage in the theological task. I believe, however, that more can be said for his complex and multilayered position than that. I shall argue, in fact, that theologians today can find considerable guidance through contemporary logical perplexities from the thought of Maimonides, freely translated into our own idiom.

Today, natural theologians would be wise to recognize that the right way to argue for theism is not to take literally, and thus feel obliged to defend, the many detailed claims that are always woven together into the rich fabric of a religious world outlook, but to take the outlook as a whole, analogous to the many-stranded fabric of what Quine called a "total science," as the essential topic at stake. Quine compares such total theory to a field of force whose boundary conditions are experience.[39] Such fields are connected at innumerable places to experiences of innumerable sorts. Empirical pressures on one part of the field have consequences, but these are often indirect and time-lagged. We represent the longest "lines of force" by universal concepts depicting the pervasive features of things, connecting and providing structure within a theory as a whole, regardless of fluctuations in the boundary conditions. Superimposed on these categorical features of a theory as a whole are more specific local perturbations needing representation by models of lesser scope but greater imaginative vividness. The features of any theoretical model help direct our thoughts as we depict how things are, but models will always have important negative as well as positive analogies to their subject-matter referents.[40]

39. See W. V. O. Quine, "Two Dogmas of Empiricism," in Quine, *From a Logical Point of View: Logico-Philosophical Essays*, 2d ed., rev. (New York: Harper Torchbooks, 1963), 42–43.

40. See Mary Hesse, "Models and Analogy in Science," *The Encyclopedia of Philosophy*, ed. Paul Edwards (New York: Macmillan, 1967), vol. 5, 354–359. See also my "Mapping

The rational acceptability of any model will be dependent upon the congruence between at least some of its important formal features and the supporting categorical features of the total theory, as that total theory relates more or less robustly to the empirical boundary conditions of experience as a whole.

Natural theologians are theologians who must also be philosophers. That means that certain features of a natural theologian's "total theory" will be authoritatively provided by the religious community within which reflection is being attempted. The natural theologian, *qua* theologian, is not free to begin absolutely from scratch. As Maimonides put it, "if we were left only to our intellects," as unaffiliated metaphysicians might (in principle, at least) be, some things might not need to be said. Given certain fundamental features of a general theistic theory, however, through which all particular experience needs to be articulated, and given, as well, certain vivid images through which to interpret the theory's categorical features, the natural theologian has the task of using theoretical intelligence in the philosopher's (or the highly theoretical scientist's) way to sort out which are the positive and which the negative analogies.

Natural theologians are no less philosophers who work on comprehensive topics important to theology. This means that, quite apart from the mandates of any special community, the general criteria of theoretical consistency, coherence, and adequacy require them to warn religious believers of pitfalls that may be implicit in certain unwary interpretations of belief. Maimonides, as philosopher and as theologian, was poignantly aware of the logical and valuational gap between the limited models available to human minds and the incomparably great and valuable reality to which they attempt to point. He was convinced on positive Aristotelian grounds that God exists, that He exists necessarily, that His existence is entirely outside the categories of materiality and its forces, and that His existence is radically simple. This required him to oppose all "associations," if implied by positive attributes predicated directly of God. On those positive theoretical grounds he attempted to find a way between allowing ignorant and demeaning associations for God, on the one hand, and falling into sheer nescience, on the other. Contemporary natural theologians, similarly, on the basis of a positive theoretical understanding of the inevitable logical gap between metaphysical models-cum-theories and the reality they importantly but (always) inadequately interpret to human

---

the Logic of Models in Science and Theology," *The Christian Scholar,* XLVI, no. 1 (Spring 1963), 9–39.

minds, would be wise to make the same move, eschewing both literalism of attribution and mere agnosticism at the same time. Even as they work to show the robust connections between theories articulating a theistic model of reality and experience as a whole, contemporary natural theologians need to foster caution about the component imagery and concepts that make up the texture of global theories of reality as a whole. They can also serve by reminding other comprehensive theorizers, metaphysicians, cosmologists, and philosophically adventuresome scientists, as well, of the need for similar caution and humility.

To summarize: Negative theology needs a positive context and motivation if it is to escape the intellectual and spiritual emptiness of sheer nescience. That positive context is supplied from two sources.

The first, religious context, is provided by the authorized imagery of the committed tradition. For Maimonides this was a minimum set of positive attributions for God drawn from Torah and from canonical prayers. For other natural theologians, now as much as then, the sources will vary, depending upon the specific community. Scripture, ecclesiastical tradition, authoritative pronouncements of Councils or Popes, charismatic figures, quiet consensus within a gathered community—these are some of the ways of authorizing the valuationally charged positive predicates that make up the vivid religious models that need to be articulated and connected to wider domains of experience as a whole.

The second, philosophical context, is provided by the best theories available to the natural theologians of a time about how one may most responsibly think at the outer boundaries of comprehensiveness. For Maimonides, this was the corpus of Aristotelian thought, inherited through high Arabic civilization. For us, whatever our specific persuasions on this matter, the positive context is given through these theories within which logical warnings and permissions are intelligible.

Positive predicates are not optional, then, if theology—natural or revealed—is to be possible at all. Given some positive theoretical framework in which to think about God's many exceedingly important differences from the world of ordinary experience, it might even be possible to praise anthropomorphism,[41] as (within its proper limits) giving us vital and otherwise unavailable content for directing our minds, without at the same time falling victim to anthropocentrism and to "unintended obloquy and vituperation." Doubtless this last pro-

41. See my "In Praise of Anthropomorphism," *International Journal for Philosophy of Religion*, 16 (1984), 203–12.

posal would stretch Maimonides' tolerance beyond its breaking point. Perhaps here he would resign as guide. But, whatever happens at the end, Maimonides has brought us a long way and continues to remind us that all our positive predicates need to be tempered with an adequate understanding of the limitations of our farthest intellectual reach—and even of our highest human values.

The University of Georgia

6   How to Avoid Speaking of God: The Violence of Natural Theology

JOHN D. CAPUTO

Is it not already too late?[1] Have we not already succumbed to violence? By reason of our title, by reason of this opening sentence, have we not already shattered the silence, already said too much about God? Are we not already speaking about God?

How to avoid *speaking* of God, how not to say a thing. How to *avoid* speaking, what to avoid when we speak of God. You hear the oscillation between two different intonations. First: how not to *speak* of God, how to respect the absoluteness of God absolutely, by silencing language, both written and spoken. How to loosen and absolve the absolute from any linguistic ties that would turn God into something relative. That is the harder saying, the saying that wants to say nothing, the more absolutist saying. But short of that, or en route to that, there is another intonation. How to *avoid* speaking of God? How to avoid saying anything inappropriate, ungodlike; how to say nothing wrong; how to delay, to put off, saying what God is.

Two pleas to avoid violence: how to avoid the violence of speaking; how to avoid speaking violently. The first pursues a more radical a-theology, a desert silence; the second pursues a negative or apophatic theology. Perhaps not two pleas at all, but only one. Do they not say the same thing? Does not the first plea speak up vociferously in favor of not speaking, thereby adding to all the talk? Correspondingly, does not silence function in the second plea like a regulative ideal? Would it not like to board up the house of language altogether? Either way, the issue is to avoid violence.[2] But the desire to avoid violence runs

---

1. I have adapted the title of this paper from Derrida's "Comment ne pas parler. Dénegations," in his *Psyché* (Paris: Galilée, 1987), 535–95; see p. 561. Eng. trans. "How to Avoid Speaking: Denials," trans. Ken Frieden in *Languages of the Unsayable* (New York: Columbia University Press, 1989). See also his *Of Spirit* (Chicago: The University of Chicago Press, 1989) on the whole problem of "avoiding" (*ne pas parler, eviter*).

2. I have adapted the subtitle of this paper from Derrida's "Violence and Meta-

into an aporia, an impasse. On the one hand, we must not do violence to God; we must respect God's transcendence. We must take every means to avoid compromising God, reducing God to something less than God is. We do not want to turn the creator into a human creation; to make God the image and likeness of man; to worship an idol, a graven image. We must not violate the absoluteness of the absolute. That is what Meister Eckhart had in mind when he preached of the truly divine God (*der göttliche Gott*), the Godhead beyond God, the God of whom he said "I pray to God to make me free of God."[3] I pray to God to rid me of my violence.

But on the other hand there is the necessity, the inescapability of language, mediation, conditionality, interpretation, signs, horizons of understanding, conditions of possibility. For it is already too late. We are always already speaking, always already delivered over to language. Do we not say yes to language before we say anything at all? Do we not say yes to language even when we say no—to language, to God, to one another—with a primordial yes, let us say with an ontological yes, which antedates every particular, ontic yes or no, spoken or written, which antedates everything cataphatic or apophatic?[4] Is not linguisticality a kind of ontological constraint under which we necessarily labor? Is not the violence of language inscribed in our being? Language is the condition of our having a world, a theology, even a negative theology that asks how to avoid speaking of God.

Here, too, the idea is to avoid violence, not this time the human violation of God, but the violence of the wholly or absolutely other; not the violation of the divine order by the human, but the violation of the human order by a kind of otherness or transcendence that just comes crashing in upon it. By conceding the inevitability of a certain ontological violence, we avoid a greater violence. For to follow the path of the absolutely unconditioned is not only an impossible demand, an illusion, it is a dangerous illusion. To start with an absolutely absolute, something absolutely unconditioned, is to abandon philosophy, thinking, all responsibility. Not to submit God—or the categorical imperative, or Levinas's Other—to a linguistic or historical conditioning is dangerous. For what we always get—it never fails—in the name of the

---

physics: An Essay on the Thought of Emmanuel Levinas," in *Writing and Difference*, trans. Alan Bass (Chicago: The University of Chicago Press, 1978), 79ff. The parallel between my critique of Marion and Derrida's critique of Levinas (and of Marion) will become clear in the course of this study.

3. *Meister Eckhart: Sermons and Treatises*, ed. and trans. M. O'C. Walshe, 3 vols. (London: Element Books, 1987), vol. II, 202.

4. On this ontological yes to language, see Derrida, *De l'esprit*, 147–54, n.1; *Psyché*, cited above, 547, 561.

Unmediated is someone's highly mediated Absolute: their jealous Jahweh, their righteous Allah, their infallible church, their absolute Geist that inevitably speaks German. In the name of the Unmediated we are buried by an avalanche of mediations, and sometimes just buried, period.[5] Somehow this absolutely absolute always ends up with a particular attachment to some historical, natural language, a particular nation, a particular religion. To disagree with someone who speaks in the name of God always means disagreeing with God. Be prepared to beat a hasty retreat. The unmediated is never delivered without massive mediation.

You see the trouble we are in. Violence on either side, the violence of theology, in a double-genitival sense: the violence theology perpetrates on God; the violence it perpetrates on us in the name of God. There is always already violence; nothing is ever innocent—theology included. Is natural theology violent? Is there a natural violence in theology? Can there be a violent nature? What, then, is being violated? What is nature?

GOD WITHOUT BEING

I want to put this aporia to the test in the paper that follows by taking up a most remarkable contemporary attempt to deal with it, Jean-Luc Marion's *Dieu sans l'être*.[6] Marion wants to avoid the "idolatrous violence" of Being (79), the violence of submitting God to an anterior condition, an anterior conceptuality, borrowed from the Greek philosophy St. Paul chided in his first letter to the church at Corinth. Marion does not want us to speak about God in ungodly terms but to speak of God *à partir de lui* (75), or in God's own terms (57), in the terms God has given us. Marion tells us how not to speak of God: do not speak of Being; do not pass an ontological screen over His face; do not make the Unconditioned into something conditioned.

I want to track the movements of Marion's quite interesting argument and to show in the process how he does not escape the violence

5. I derive the heart of my argument in this paper from Derrida's criticism of those who "on the pretext of delivering you from the chains of writing and reading" proceed to "lock you in a supposed outside of the text, the pre-text of perception, of living speech . . . of real history . . . . And it's also with supposed nontext, naked pre-text, the immediate, that they try to intimidate you, to subject you to the older, most dogmatic, most sinisterly authoritarian of programs, to the most massive mediatizing machines." Jacques Derrida, *The Truth in Painting*, trans. G. Bennington and I. MacLeod (Chicago: The University of Chicago Press, 1987), 326–27.

6. Jean-Luc Marion, *Dieu sans l'être* (Paris: Fayard, Communio, 1982). All page references in parentheses in the text will be to this work.

he wants to avoid, indeed how he provokes an even greater violence; how in the name of avoiding mediation he visits upon us a massive mediation. I will intervene upon his text repeatedly, annoyingly, insolently. I will buzz around him like a gnat or a gadfly, like a brazen, deconstructive pest.

Marion's position turns on a distinction between the "idol" and the "icon," which are alternately the pagan and the Christian ways to make the divine visible (18–26).[7] In the idol the divine is embodied in wood or stone but in a movement that is arrested. Here the divine is in a sense too visible, for it holds our look captive, so that we cannot look beyond it into the "distance." The idol is always a mirror in which we behold ourselves and one that sends our look bounding back on ourselves. While the idol arises from authentic religious experience, it is embedded in a limited, historical embodiment that condemns it to pass from the historical scene. Without the Greeks, Greek statues lose their religious power; idols always have their twilight.

In the icon, on the other hand, there is something surpassing, an excess, an infinity (26–35). There are invisible depths to its visibility, so that the look is not caught by the object but is carried off into the distance. Thus to venerate an icon is to venerate what is depicted in it, not to stop short with the visible thing itself. Furthermore, the icon is not a blind mirror, not a statue deprived of eyes, but a face that envisages us with its invisible powers. The icon exceeds the domain of aesthetics and human creation, exceeds its own embodiment, speaks to us from an infinite distance. (You can hear a lot of Levinas in Marion's distinction, the invisible infinity of the face of God, which opens up invisible depths in something finite and visible.)

But suppose we objected to Marion that the distinction between icon and idol is strictly historical, that one man's (or woman's!) icon is another man's idol? He will only admit half of this: the Greeks were able to experience the divine in their statues, but we are not; their religious art was authentic for them, but it has lost its power for us (41–44). Then are we to understand that Christian icons do not suffer from the same limitations? If Christian icons are touched by the beyond (41–44), do they have a power that rises above their historical embodiment, and so have an infinite depth (32) that allows them to retain their effectiveness without regard to time or place? Does that mean that they would retain their power even without Christians? Do Christian icons have a power that persists, per impossible, even without Christianity? Would that not be magic and a loss of distance?

7. *L'idole et la distance* (Paris: Graesset, 1967). Idolatry abolishes "distance." It is always necessary to choose between them (See *Dieu sans l'être*, cited above, 239).

It also follows from what Marion is saying that while idols are man-made creations, there is some sense in which the icons are not. To be sure, icons do not drop from the sky, they are works of Christian art, products of human hands—but that is not all. They are more than just man-made; someone or something else is cooperating in their production (33), so that this human opus is also an *opus dei*. In the idol, man is revisited by his own ghost (*revenant, Gespenst,* 33). That must mean that the icon has an inspired status for Marion, a kind of *Begeisterung* that fills it with a true and infinite spirit, Geist (but evidently a universal Geist with a particular attachment to Roman Catholicism, which has no time for Latin American theology or the Dutch catechism). But I am getting ahead of myself. I should stop interrupting.[8]

Marion thinks that metaphysics is the peculiar form of idolatry that we Westerners have devised (26–27). "Being" is our most treasured idol. Having lost the capacity both to create and to appreciate pagan art we have instead devised a paganism of our own and have created the idol of philosophical conceptuality. (This is a lot like Hegel's saying that art is past, in the sense that art no longer serves the West as the primary depository of its truth.[9]) You see the idolatrous functioning of the metaphysical concept: the concept seizes God round about, measures the divine by humanly comprehensible standards, holds the look of the mind's eye captive, and cuts off the infinite, incomprehensible depths of God. Lacking infinite depths, the metaphysical look is accordingly not sent off into the distance but is reflected back onto itself. A metaphysical concept of God, let us say that of the *causa sui,* is an image of the metaphysician. It is not inspired but constructed, not infinite but finite, not an excess but an incision into the divine. So Westerners are just as prone to idolatry as anybody else, but ours is the idolatry of the concept. The God of metaphysics, of what Heidegger calls onto-theo-logic, is an idol that, like all idols, has its twilight—in Nietzsche's metaphysical nihilism. That god is dead and good riddance. Thank God for getting rid of that god (45). The dispute between classical metaphysical theology and Nietzschean atheism is a lover's quarrel about an idol (49–51).

Thus far, Marion offers us a sensitive religious application of Heidegger's critique of the violence of the God of onto-theo-logic, of

8. In *De l'esprit,* Derrida plays up the ghostly *revenant* in every *Geist,* particularly the *Geist* that gives itself absolute airs.

9. Gadamer offers a commentary on this remark of Hegel's in *The Relevance of the Beautiful and Other Essays,* ed. Robert Bernasconi (Cambridge: Cambridge University Press, 1986), 4–6.

natural theology. But now he moves against, or beyond, Heidegger, criticizing what he calls a "double idolatry," idolatry revisited on a higher level, the idolatry even of Heidegger's post-metaphysical, truly divine God. This is the theoretical heart of Marion's position, and everything stands or falls with this move.

But perhaps I should speak more cautiously, be careful not to say too much. Does Marion even have a position? Does he not write a man-made book? Is not the idea here that this is nothing merely man-made, no linguistic artifact of Marion's, but something touched with the divine truth itself, straight from the heart of God? We are trying to avoid idolatry—so this must be an icon; this must be inspired. If that is so, I must be more careful; I intervene at my own peril. Or perhaps Marion is only mediating something about icons to us, giving us a little conceptual supplement (cf. 35–37). But is that not pagan, idolatrous, anterior to the divine? Then I need not worry, for I am performing a service, criticizing an idol, for which the faithful everywhere will be grateful.

For Marion, Heidegger's "thought of Being" represents a second and more insidious idolatry (58). Heidegger has taught us that to get to the truly divine God, we need to think the ontological difference, that is, make the step back from the horizon of metaphysics, which does not give God enough space, to that Open which *permits* (*lassen*) the appearance of the God before whom we can dance and sing.[10] But you see the trouble Heidegger is causing; you see how his God needs Being's "permission," Being's letting-be, in order to make an appearance! Instead of stepping back from the God of metaphysics to *God* (we will have to reach an agreement about how to write that), Heidegger takes the step back to an intermediary, to the thought of Being, to the Open (or *Ereignis*, *Sprache*, etc.), and thereby erects another obstacle, another barrier, or what Marion calls a "screen of Being" (*écrivan de l'être*, 58) between us and . . . .

How are we to finish this sentence? We must at all costs avoid violence; we must not let God fall victim to any anterior conditions. Shall we just say: God? But that is an English word—and so another screen. *Dieu* just ties us up in a French connection; *Gott*, *theos*, and so on are just more linguistic screens. Well, for the time being (for being and time? *Being and Time*?), let us provisionally write "Dieu" with scare quotes when something idolatrous is afoot, and just write God (while

10. See Heidegger's *Gesamtausgabe*, vol. 9, *Wegmarken* (Frankfurt: Klostermann, 1976), 338–39, 351; Eng. trans. "Letter on Humanism" in *Basic Writings*, ed. David Krell (New York: Harper and Row, 1977), 218, 230. See also his *Nietzsche*, 2 vols. (Pfullingen: Neske, 1962), vol. 2, 394.

Marion writes *Dieu*), erasing the quotation marks, when what we have in mind is the real thing, the unscreened *Sache selbst, même chose.*

Heideggerian idolatry is centered on Heidegger's onto-centrism, that is, on the priority of Being over any being, God included, with the result that Heidegger's "God" is always screened, a "being" who must always wear a halo of scare quotes. The God who is thought in terms of Being is really no more than a reflection of our projection of Being. Now if this second form of idolatry consists in setting up something anterior to God (65), then clearly the only way to escape from idolatry altogether is, as Marion writes, "To think God without any condition, not even that of Being; thus to think God without pretending to inscribe or describe him as a being." (70).

Now if it is the same thing to think and to be (Parmenides), if the soul is in a certain way all beings (Aristotle), if being is the first thing that is conceived by the mind (Aquinas), then it might be objected to Marion that to abandon the conditionality of Being is to abandon thought itself. So be it, Marion responds; so much the worse for thinking (71), for St. Paul says that wisdom of God makes foolishness of the wisdom of men—and that includes Parmenides, Aristotle, Aquinas, and Heidegger. It is hard to imagine what Marion means by this, by what seems like a hyperbolic effort to remove himself from every human conditioning. Is he not thinking now? And even if it is a different kind of thinking, one tied to prayer and praise[11]—that is all right, I do not object to prayerful thought—is that not still thinking? Would Marion not be angry if we said that his book was thoughtless, that he should think about all this more carefully?

To get beyond the God of Being, or the Being of God, is to heed what is revealed to us in the *ego sum qui sum* (but that's Latin) of *Exodus* 3:14, which on Marion's rendering runs, "I am what I want to be" (71). But that is English and "Je suis celui que je veux être"—that is French. Perhaps it is inspired French; after all, we do speak of inspired translations. In any case, we should be grateful to Marion for this excellent rendering, this very fine mediation of this passage to us. The sacred writer means—we have Marion's word for it—that there is nothing that Being can say of God that God cannot challenge, nothing that the *Seinsgeschick* can send God's way that God cannot return to sender. God is saying to us—we must be grateful for Marion's help with what God is saying here—that he can do without Being's help (11, 71). At that point, we have pushed ourselves up to the edge of

---

11. See *Psyché*, cited above, 572–74, n.1, where Derrida criticizes the effort made by Marion in his final chapter (259ff.) to play down the predication and to play up the element of praise in proclaiming Jesus as Lord.

the unthinkable, and it is under this figure of unthinkability that we are able to "think" God. Now the idolatrous God, pinned between quotation marks, can be rewritten, not as God, but under erasure, as G̶o̶d̶, where the cross signifies unthinkability (and ultimately the cru-cifixion; this is excellent writing, although writing is dangerous). It is not so much that we erase God with our thought, as that God erases (*rature*) our thought by saturating (*sature*) and overwhelming us with his excess (72).

GOD IS LOVE

If Marion were telling us how to avoid *speaking*, then this would be the end, the last sentence in the book, for by crossing out God and Being, we have crossed beyond the line of Being and thought, wan-dered off the Parmenidean path of what can be or can be thought, outside of which, sheltered by this nothingness and silence, lies the truly divine God. But it turns out that Marion's desire to tell us how *not* to speak—speak *without* Being, God does not need it—means that he has a lot to say about how *to* speak and furthermore *who* should do the speaking. (Will God need this speaking? And these privileged speakers?)

For by breaking the idol of Being, we allow the Gospels to speak. God is love, St. John tells us—and love is beyond Being, Marion sup-plements. How so? Because love is unconditional; it does not offer itself conditionally, only when certain terms are met in advance.

But is this the same thing? Does the unconditionality of love mean the same thing as moving beyond the Heideggerian thought of Being? Did not Heidegger, following Angelus Silesius, say that the rose is without why? Did he not claim that this was possible only because the mystical poet has entered that realm outside the sphere of the strict accounting system of the principle of sufficient reason? Did he not describe this as a leap into the groundlessness of Being, of the play of Being, of Being's refusal of ground and thought's refusal to seek after ground? And do not Eckhart and Silesius say that love is without why? And does not Heideggerian *Gelassenheit* belong to this same realm? Are not *Dichten* and *Denken* marked precisely by their irredu-cibility to thinking in terms of grounds, reasons, accounting?[12] Do they not belong to a general economy, to expenditure without reserve?

Love, Marion continues, does not try to encompass or reduce some-

12. See Martin Heidegger, *Der Satz vom Grund* (Pfullingen: Neske, 1957), chaps. 5–6, 185–88; for a full account of these matters see my *The Mystical Element in Heidegger's Thought*, rev. ed. (New York: Fordham University Press, 1986).

one to its own terms; it does not cling to itself, but rather is a self-giving that advances without imposing conditions. The upshot of this is that the second idolatry is surpassed by love because love alone lets God be thought (*laissant Dieu se pense*) in terms of a demand that is purely, solely his own (*à partir de sa seule et pure exigence*), namely, as pure generosity, pure self-donation. And that does away with the prior screening by any concept (metaphysics) or any other higher condition (the ontological difference). "God can give himself to thought without idolatry only on his own terms" (*à partir de lui seul*), namely, as love, as giving, as gift (75).

I thus run the risk of angering the gods, maybe even God, by raising another objection here. Suppose I just said that Marion does not attain God "without condition" (*sans condition*, 106) but that he is merely switching to *another condition*, love? He does not take a step back from an idolic God to God in Himself, but he shifts the hermeneutic horizon from Greek ontology to biblical *agape*, from Athens to Jerusalem, and claims that this hermeneutic fore-conception—love—is better than the philosophical one. The God without Being is the God with (of) love, and so it is love that provides the mediation, the condition of possibility, the horizonality, within which God can be thought and experienced properly as God. It is love that lets God be God (*laissant Dieu*), that thus grants God permission to be God. Is that not to reproduce the gesture that submits God to an anteriority, but this time a more adequate anteriority?

After all—I realize this is bold, to make love give an accounting of itself in this way—how does love acquire such an exceptional status, such unconditionality, such extratextuality, such extraterrestriality? Does it drop from the sky? Does it not belong as much to our human vocabulary as does Being? In fact, is it not a lot more anthropomorphic than Being? Do we not know of it first and foremost from human relationships and do we not then apply it to God, *mutatis mutandis*, because it is one of our better words, one of our finer human moments? What would possess Marion to say that it is a word that describes God *à partir de lui* and not, like everything else we say about God, *à partir de nous*, which we then, by a kind of theological effort, transfer to God?

Marion's answer to this objection is that the notion that God is love—as opposed to the metaphysical conception that God is Being—is a biblical idea, that it has been revealed to us, that this is God's own word. But—again I risk angering the gods, or at least Marion—that only raises the problem up a notch, or switches the terrain on which it is to be worked out, to the Scriptures. First of all, a good negative theologian like Marion cannot seriously believe that God uses words, that he speaks, that he expresses his thoughts, that he lets himself get tangled up in a chain of signifiers, that he needs the discourse of love (the way he does not need ontological discourse). Is not the whole idea of God's words, spoken or written, already stretching things a little, stretching the screen of language itself over God?

Furthermore, even if we admit that biblical language has a special place amidst human discourse generally, still is it not the case that the Scriptures are mediation through and through? Are they not *conditioned* in various and multiple ways? What is the New Testament except the way a human community gives voice to the impact that the man Jesus made in its life, to the way he transfixed and transformed them? And upon what were these writers to draw in order to say what they had to say, other than the places and things of their everyday life, the human relationships that bound them together as a community? Is not their voice through and through that of a specific time and place? When Jesus taught us to call God *abba* (202, n.1), father, he took a familiar word from the patriarchal tradition he grew up in that expressed a warm human relationship and transferred it to God with the idea that this was the most adequate discourse that human prayer could adopt, not that it named God *quoad se*. (Was Jesus a negative theologian? Did he prefer a language of familiarity or of distance?)

So, too, the *agape* in terms of which John speaks about God is drawn from the love that the Christians bore one another. Is his Gospel not written in a natural language, whose terms and meanings are drawn from a human and finite matrix? Is he not just using the best discourse he has available to get something across? Is not John, is not the whole New Testament already itself a *hermeneusis*, written down somewhat later, filled with the debates of the day, with issues in local churches, with formulas that arose from later liturgical celebrations, marked by a plurality of interpretations and competing theologies, all of which is a translation—into Greek—of something that happened in Aramaic? Do we not have to worry about establishing good texts and learning how to read Greek, and measuring up to a host of other limiting conditions? Do we not have to admit that this discourse is conditioned through and through, all of which is propaedeutic to explaining the sense in which it is inspired?

But I am talking too much, not letting Marion get a word in edgewise. Let us give him a chance to explain himself.

Heidegger, Marion says (91ff.), at one point actually recognized the incommensurability between metaphysics and faith, that each belongs to a different domain, and that the God of faith cannot be expressed in the discourse of Being. In a seminar at Zurich in 1951, Heidegger said:

Being and God are not identical, and I would never try to think the essence of God in terms of Being . . . . Were I yet to write a theology, something to which I am at times attracted, the word Being would not be permitted to occur in it. Faith has no need of the thought of Being. If it [faith] uses that, it is already no more faith. Luther understood that.[13]

But Heidegger does go on to say that the experience of God and his revelation is nonetheless subject to a prior conditionality, to the "dimension of Being," so that even if Being does not enter "into" theology, as one of the divine predicates, it remains "over" theology, regulating it as an anterior condition of possibility, laying down the parameters within which theology can function. Heidegger's God is always a "divine prisoner of Being" (106).

In fact, when it comes to Being, according to Marion, Heidegger is in the same boat as Aquinas, both of whom subject God to the anteriority of Being with equal violence. Marion criticizes Thomas for overturning the traditional Neo-Platonic thesis that the good is beyond being, which Thomas found in Pseudo-Dionysius, by turning it into a thesis about the supereminence of God's being. Because of his commitment to Aristotle's doctrine of the four causes, Aquinas failed to see that the primacy of Being arises only from a human point of view intent on scientific understanding (*ens* is the first thing understood by the intellect), whereas, from God's point of view, it is the good, that is, nonbeing, which has the primacy (119–22).

This is interesting. God sides with Neo-Platonism over Thomism. An unprecedented case of divine intervention in a metaphysical dispute. This is bad news for the Thomists, who always thought they had the inside line on Exodus 3:14.[14] You see how people who disagree with Marion keep discovering that they are in fact falling out of God's point of view? Still, if Dionysius was faking it about being Dionysius, faking it even about having St. Paul's point of view (*Acts* 17:34)—was he not known as Pseudo-Dionysius, Dionysius the phony? Was he not a dangerous supplement?—how can we be sure he has God's point of view? One would have thought that Dionysius simply had Plotinus's point of view and that he was using the categories of fifth-century

13. Martin Heidegger, *Gesamtausgabe*, vol. 15, *Seminare* (Frankfurt: Klostermann, 1986), 436–37 ("Zürcher Seminar"). See Derrida's commentary on this text in *Psyché*, 590–92.
14. I have worked out the Thomistic thesis on Being (*esse*) vis-a-vis Heidegger's critique of onto-theo-logic in my *Heidegger and Aquinas: An Essay on Overcoming Metaphysics* (New York: Fordham University Press, 1982).

Neo-Platonic metaphysics. But perhaps Plotinus had God's ear, too. To put it plainly: Is not the Neo-Platonic metaphysics of the good beyond being an intermediary condition, an intellectual artifact, a conceptual anteriority, no less than Thomas's *ipsum esse subsistens* or Heidegger's *Geviert*? Are we not just trying to find the right conditions rather than the unconditioned, to get into the circle in the right way and not to escape from the circle?

Still, I have promised to let Marion have his (very considerable) say. We do not see what Marion is after until we actually follow his very suggestive readings, his very excellent supplements, of the Scriptures, which are as it were actual case studies of what it means to think God without Being and to do theology without violence. In the Scriptures, Marion says, we will find an economy that operates without, or that is indifferent to, Being, that does move along the Being/beings axis, that moves outside the idolatrous enclosure of Being and beings, that is indifferent to the ontological difference (126–28).

In *I Cor.* 1:28, for example, St. Paul says that God chose "those who are nothing (*me onta*) in order to show up those who are (*onta*)." The men of Corinth are nothing in the eyes of the world, for they have nothing worldly to glory in. Clearly what the world calls Being could not matter less to Paul. Paul annuls, or is indifferent to, the world's distinction between beings and nonbeings. It is in quite the same sense that Paul says to the Romans that God is free to treat the things that are not as if they are (*Rom.* 4:17), for God shows the same indifference to the world's distinctions. Paul would rather be nothing in the eyes of the world and glory only in God. He does not adopt Being as the ground of his discourse (*fond du discours*, 138); he is interested only in how one stands with respect to God. What counts is not a difference with respect to Being but with respect to "glorying" (139). Beings thus are set by Paul into a different play, where the difference between what is and what is not, according to the world's standards, is cast into indifference in favor of the difference between glorying in God or in oneself. A similar reading that breaks the rule of Being, of worldly *ousia*, can be given to the story of the prodigal son. The two sons are both at fault for they can think only in terms of *ousia*, of possessions and goods, the father only in terms of love. For the sons, the father's money is an idol they can't see beyond; for the father it is an icon of his love.

Now, I do not wish to take anything away from Marion's felicitous readings of the Scriptures, to treat them as if they were nothing, for there is much of substance in them. I am just baffled that he thinks any of this contradicts Heidegger (let alone Derrida). If anything, Marion has confirmed what Heidegger held from his earliest days, that there is a difference between understanding the world—or Being—in terms of *ousia* or *Vorhandensein* and understanding it in terms of *Existenz*. What Paul says depends entirely upon the fact that he switched the understanding of Being from what is merely factually present (*Vorhandensein*) to what has worldly standing, a sense that is picked up by the Greek *ousia* and by English expressions like "men of substance" or "powers that be." It is to Being understood thus, understood differently, that the Christians at Corinth profess their indifference. Implicit in Paul's claim is its inversion, that from God's point of view those who glory in themselves are *me onta*, whereas Christians live and move and have their being in Christ Jesus.

Far from refuting the role of the ontological difference, Marion gives a rich and textured application of it. For—let us give Heidegger a word here—it is only because metaphysics fails to think the difference between Being and beings, that is, fails to see that beings can be projected differently in their Being, that metaphysics ends up painting a monochromatic world of factual presence at hand, which world is confounded by Paul's discourse. What Paul is saying makes sense only if one takes the step back from Being as presence to Being itself, Being, the truth of Being, difference, and so on. What Paul does, from Heidegger's point of view, is to set the distinction between beings and nonbeings on a different axis, reframe it on a different ground of discourse, one toward which the church at Corinth may adopt indifference. But what is that if not to recognize what at first was called the "ontological difference," and later on just "difference" (*Unter-Schied, Austrag*), or the languaging of language (*Sprache*)? If the meaning of Being is worldly prestige, Paul will take his stand with the *me onta*, for he would rather have his being in Christ Jesus. It is this capacity to switch horizons, to differentiate Being from its ousiological or entitative constraints, that makes Paul's discourse possible.

It is not an exaggeration to say that Heidegger's single, lifelong thought is that Being cannot be reduced to presence, that the difference between Being and beings opens up the possibility of alternate understandings of world and Being. It is a high irony to me that it is precisely to illustrate the fecundity of the ontological difference that Heidegger cites exactly the same text from St. Paul, that God has chosen the things that are not to annul the things that are, to show that "world" means not simple cosmic or entitative presence but the "how" of being-in-the-world—that is, whether Dasein is turned toward or away from God.[15] This "how" of Being regulates how to speak and how to avoid speaking about Being, God, and world.

In other words, by turning to the Scriptures, Marion does not find a God without Being, but only a God without Being taken as mere presence or Vorhandensein. Marion has not discovered an understanding *without* Being but the possibility of understanding Being *differently*.[16] Above all, he has not found an understanding without mediation and anteriority, but an understanding where everything depends upon what sort of anterior conditions of possibility one deploys. The economies of the New Testament elude the horizons of ousiology, so one should keep one's hermeneutic guard up and be prepared to shift one's forestructures, for there are more things under heaven and earth than are dreamt of in ousiology. In the Scriptures, we do indeed encounter another world, another understanding of Being, man, and time. That is not only not an objection to the ontological difference, it was Heidegger's first example of the difference and arguably his original point of departure. For it is only in virtue of marking the ontological difference that one liberates Being from a narrow ousiology, thereby opening up the play or open space within which the biblical "world" of "love" and "giving" Marion invokes can appear. That means that it is only by opening up the ontological difference that one can avoid violence, for one would do violence to the world of the New Testament were one to understand St. Paul's words ousiologically and so deny the distinction between *onta* and *me onta* the space within which it is playing in this text. The "indifference" of the Christians at Corinth to "being" and "not being" is a function of the worldly understanding of Being and depends upon it.[17]

Still, none of this explains why, in the Zurich seminar in 1951, Heidegger said that if he wrote a theology he would not use the word Being, although any possible theology would remain within the dimension of Being. Why did he not just say that he would use the word Being differently? The reason for this is that later on in his life Hei-

15. Martin Heidegger, *The Metaphysical Foundations of Logic*, trans. Michael Heim (Bloomington, In.: Indiana University Press, 1984), 173.

16. A major thrust of Derrida's rebuttal of Marion has been that even Neo-Platonic discourse about a God "beyond being" has been mainly in the service of establishing a *hyperousion*, supereminent being. Cf. *Psyché*, 540–44. Derrida thus agrees with Aquinas's reading of Pseudo-Dionysius.

17. Furthermore, Marion himself calls upon the ontological difference, upon its capacity to transform the temporal matrix, in order to rethink the Eucharist in terms of a futural, eschatological gift, and to loosen it from the constraints of now-time. Cf. 239ff.

degger gave up on the word "Being" and handed it over to ousiology, which has tended to corner its use. (He also gave up on the word truth!) Being means (has come to mean and we can't reverse the process) presence, and so it is not a word he would use for poetry or "thought"—or theology. So it is necessary to step back from the Being of metaphysics to what he calls here the "dimension of Being"; elsewhere he calls it the "truth of Being" and later on just *Ereignis*. Even in the Marburg period, Heidegger was describing his attempt to step back from Greek ousiology as a matter of getting "beyond Being."[18] He also described it as thinking Being "differently," as thinking *Seyn*, or Being. He tried a lot of things to twist free of ousiology. But any way you look at it, he had already marked off what Marion means by getting along "without Being."

My point is that even when you speak of God without Being, or beyond Being, you have not extricated God from all anterior conditionality. You have not gotten something unconditioned but something better conditioned to a religious sensibility. Such a God is nothing unmediated or unconditioned, and we cannot rightly claim that this is God's point of view. What Marion offers us is an argument for the higher religious adequacy of biblical discourse (mediation, conditionality) over that of metaphysical ousiology, an argument that does not rebut but depends upon the ontological difference, that transcends the idolatry of the *causa sui* but not of the "second idolatry." He has not found a world beyond human mediation that speaks God's own language—for God does not have a language—but he simply shows us why we ought to prefer the biblical vocabulary. He has managed to occupy not God's point of view but that of a certain human religious experience that is from one end to the other expressed in the thoroughly human terms of loving, giving, and earthly glory, and that is, if anything, a good deal more anthropomorphic than anything to be found in Heidegger or, a fortiori, Derrida. The terms of "giving" and "donation" need first to be given (*es gibt*) in order then to elaborate a discourse about God's loving gift of himself.

That means that Marion has not found anything nonviolent, anything that is innocent of the originary, ontological violence of which I spoke in the beginning, the violence that belongs structurally to, indeed that constitutes, language itself. The "word of God" is a metaphor. To call upon a revealed, nonviolent language, upon words that are the words of God himself, is already to submit God to the violence

18. Martin Heidegger, *Basic Problems of Phenomenology*, trans. Albert Hofstadter (Bloomington, In.: Indiana University Press, 1982), 284–86.

of a metaphor, to the language of metaphor, and to the metaphor of language. It is to bring God within the sphere of influence of the primordial ontological yes to language that precedes every particular yes or no, every particular vocabulary or natural language. For God does not speak at all; he does not have a tongue or vocal chords or make use of writing instruments. He does not favor Hebrew or Aramaic, Greek or Latin; he does not favor one vocabulary over another. He is not a father because he is not even a "he." Love is no less a creature than being (159); both are linguistic creations, creaturely languages. Being and love are equally linguistic, mediating, conditioning. Whatever revelation is, it is not something unmediated, unconditioned, dropped from the sky—which is why Heidegger said that what you think about revelation (*Offenbarkeit*) depends upon the dimension of Being, that is, the Open (*das Offene*).[19] To have sacred books is to subject God to the anteriority of writing, textuality, language. It is to confess that there is nothing outside the text, not in the sense in which that notorious statement is often (mis)understood, that texts lack reference, but in the more sensible sense that there is no reference that can escape the influence of texts, textuality, language.

Anything else—shall I say it? Will Marion forgive me if I say it?—is idolatrous. It is to fail to preserve the distance between revealer and revelation, God and the word of God, Jesus and the New Testament.[20]

ECCLESIOLOGY WITHOUT VIOLENCE

Up to now I have been arguing that the ideal of nonviolence Marion pursues is illusory, that there really is nothing we can say about God that is not violent in the sense that it does not cast God in certain terms, that it does not subject God to a certain horizonality, and so set up something *anterior* to God, with a kind of ontological violence. It is not that we are putting something ahead of God, as if we were consigning him to an entitative second place, but we are conceding that our understanding of God operates under certain constraints. From our point of view, then, Marion is arguing that the horizons of

19. *Gesamtausgabe*, cited above, vol. 15, 437.
20. Only once (159–60) does Marion explicitly address the question of how such unconditionality is possible for us finite beings. His answer is that we move from the paganism of Being to the iconism of love through the intermediary experience of vanity, the *vanitas vanitatum* of the *Book of Ecclesiastes*. But of course, from my point of view, that is only to describe the movement not from the conditioned to the unconditioned, but from inappropriate to appropriate conditions via a connecting or intermediate condition or horizon, in short, from Greek experience to Christian experience through Hebrew experience. See the brilliant analyses of chap. 4.

biblical experience are better than the parameters of Greek ousiology and not, as Marion understands himself, that the biblical understanding is unconditioned, God's own point of view. We can never clear away the screen without the screen going blank; we can never make unmediated contact without eliminating the means of contact altogether; we can never eliminate the conditioning to which we subject God without knocking out the conditions in terms of which it is possible to think or speak about God.

But now I want to take my argument one step further. Not only is the ideal of unconditioned understanding an illusion, it is a dangerous illusion. Marion's desire for the unmediated is ethically and politically dangerous, and, let us say, it brushes with violence in the worst sense, in the ethico-political sense.

From his opening pages Marion (9–10), in resolute opposition to "postmodernism," is intent upon establishing the *hors texte*. He wants to see to it that theological *verba* make way for and so give way to the extra-textual *Verbum*. Theo*logy* must always counter its *logos* with its *theos*, which is the Divine Logos. Theo*logy* must constantly be monitored by *theo*logy. It would be blasphemous were any human *logos* to precede the Logos of God. Theology must move in docile abandon to, and allow itself to be regulated by, its own divine Logos. For Jesus is the *Logos* of the father, the Word he has been speaking through all eternity. He is the perfect unity of word and Word, speaker and spoken about, proclaimer and proclaimed, sign and referent (197–203).

You see the top-down character of Marion's theology. He does not allow that calling Jesus the *logos* of the father, his eternal wisdom (which is not anything Jesus ever did himself), is a practice that arose among Greek-speaking gentile Christians, who took this word and extended it to Jesus because, given their linguistic, cultural, and historical horizons, they found it a felicitous way of expressing their faith in him. I am insisting that the anteriority, the horizonality, this very Greek horizonality, is already there in John. Calling Jesus the *logos*, and saying that he is the "word" "spoken" by the father from all eternity, that is all anterior to Jesus, a horizon that is called upon in order to bring their experience of Jesus to words. It is also to reinscribe Jesus's very Hebraic *abba* spirituality within Greek logocentric horizons. The divine Logos cannot regulate human logos from above, because speaking of the divine Logos is an extension of human logos and starts from below in the first place.

Marion's problem is that the New Testament is only a text, and that is dangerous. Like the veil of Veronica (*verum-icon*), it contains only the trace of the Verbum, of the life, death, and resurrection of Jesus.

There is a dangerous gap between the event and the text, between the *Verbum* and the *verba*. So what Marion wants to do is to reconstitute the originary unity of sign and referent found in Jesus himself, to put it to work again now, in the church, to make this the model of reading the text, so that the gap between text and *hors texte* can be closed (204–10). Texts bear the mark of absence; they yield to more than one meaning; their referents are in dispute; they are mediation through and through. That is why Marion wants to diminish the textuality of the New Testament, to put this text under maximal constraints, to arrest its flux of meaning, to fix its reference once and for all. He wants a hermeneutics free of the limits of the hermeneutic situation, of hermeneutic conditioning. He wants a hermeneutics that is no hermeneutics at all, because the interpretation is not an interpretation but a kind of absolute deliverance that delivers us from the conflict of interpretation that arises if you admit that you really have a text on your hands.[21]

That model of assured hermeneutics, of what he calls "absolute" or "Eucharistic" hermeneutics (210–11), is given to us by the New Testament itself, in the story of Jesus on the road to Emmaus, instructing the disciples on the meaning of the Scriptures, giving them a *hermeneuein* whose truth the disciples instantly recognize when Jesus breaks bread with them (207–8, 211–12). In this story, Jesus, the one who is proclaimed, explicates the proclamation; the unity of subject and object, *interpretans* and *interpretandum,* is absolute. From this we learn, Marion suggests, that all interpretation of the Scriptures undertaken by theology must reinstate that primal hermeneutic ideal. Christians thus do not have to submit to the limitations of textuality that others do, for the reference of their texts is ever present to them—in the Eucharist (206). What is outside the text, their *hors texte,* is made present daily in the Eucharistic celebration (12), which is neither idol nor icon but substantial, sacramental presence (235, n.1). Hence, every interpretation is to be done in the context of the Eucharistic celebration.

Now, if Marion simply meant that understanding occurs in the context of a prayerful, Eucharistic faith, *ratio et oratio,* one could take no exception to him. But for Marion, all of this has a darker, onto-theopolitical sense. Theological police are beginning to move in and take

21. It is with a concession of the textuality of the text of the New Testament in mind, and to avoid absolutizing cultural, linguistic, and historical features of the text, that Elizabeth Schüssler Fiorenza calls the New Testament a "historical prototype" rather than a "mythical archetype" in *Bread Not Stone: The Challenge of Feminist Biblical Interpretation* (Boston: Beacon Press, 1984), 10–15.

up their position. It means that the priest who stands in for Jesus controls the reading while the congregation listens like the disciples. But the priest himself stands in for the bishop, who is the theologian par excellence (214); only the bishop merits the title of theologian in the full sense (215). True, the bishop can delegate his privilege, but there's a string attached:

> In the same way that the priest who breaks his communion with the bishop is not able to enter into ecclesiastical communion, so a teacher who speaks without, indeed against, the Symbol [capitalized] of the apostles, without, indeed against, his bishop, is no longer able absolutely to conduct his discourse in an authentically *theo*logical site. (215)

Priests who break with their bishop have lost the right to offer the Eucharist, and theologians who break with the bishop have lost the site from which to interpret. That, presumably, is why the Vatican can silence them, or remove their official theological credentials. Marion does not say this. He is silent about this silencing. But do we not hear it? That is also why theology cannot be a science and must monitor the growth and the character of its own *logos*. That is also why the multiplicity of meanings that do in fact emerge from reading the text are regulated by a deeper unity, a kind of central spiritual control, which sees to it that the multiplicity is kept within manageable limits. All talk about "progress" in theology must be regarded with suspicion, for there can be only a kind of unfolding of what we already knew. So beware of theological innovation (221–22). Beware in particular of the "deviant" Dutch Catechism and liberation theology (235, n.1; 253), which are the primary targets of Marion's Eucharistic theology (Part Two, *"Hors Texte"*).

You see now why I take to heart Derrida's warning against those who "on the pretext of delivering you from the chains of writing" proceed to "lock you up in a supposed *hors texte*." It's the *hors texte*, the thing itself, the unconditioned, that locks you up! Derrida continues: "it's also with supposed nontext, naked pre-text, the immediate, that they try to intimidate you, to subject you to the older, most dogmatic, most sinisterly authoritarian of programs, to the most massive mediatizing machines" (*supra*, n.5). You see too how the celestial hierarchy laid out by the false Dionysius, he who assumes heavenly airs/heirs, reproduces itself on a terrestrial scale, and how the desire for silence results in an order of privileged speakers.[22]

Theology is either for liberation or against it. Everything is always, already political. There are no pure, apolitical theologies. Theo*logy*—

22. *Psyché*, 552–54, n.1.

even and especially when it congratulates itself for having become *theo*logy, for having played down its *logos* in favor of *theos*—theo*logy*, no less than *theo*logy, is always already housed within an institutional power. Now if onto-theo-logic is always also onto-theo-politics, if metaphysics always implies a metaphysical power structure, a seat and site of power and authority, if metaphysical binarity has always meant rigorous hierarchical distinctions and massive powers of exclusion, then Marion has done very little to overcome paganism and metaphysics in *Dieu sans L'être*. Indeed, I would say that he has done a great deal to reinstate it, that this theology of docile abandon to the *Logos* lends onto-theo-political power a helping hand in its most violent form. It does indeed have a great deal to do with how not to speak, with theological silence, namely, with silencing Dutch and Latin American theologians; it has a great deal to say about how not to speak about God, namely, in disagreement with the bishop. God may evidently do without being, but not without the bishop. (What does Marion do when bishops disagree and will not keep silent?)

You see the massive mediation in this talk of the unmediated, the unconditioned, in removing finite, human conditions of anteriority. Is this what Jesus was getting at when he looked around at the theological powers that be in Jerusalem and called them a brood of vipers? Is this what he had on his mind when he systematically took the side of the outcast, the poor, the sinners, the prostitutes, the Samaritans, the lepers, of everyone who was excluded by the powers that be? Is this what it means to be *me onta* in the eyes of worldly power?

Of course Marion's attempt to get absolute extra-textual footing here is futile, for it is pinned entirely to a piece of the text. The story of the disciples on the road to Emmaus is as thoroughly textual as any other part of the text. And Marion's mediation of it to us depends minimally upon having a text that is not corrupt, one whose grammar and vocabulary is understood, and finally and above all upon having an interpretation *of that text*, an interpretation whose authority clearly cannot depend *upon that text*. For example, there is Schillebeeckx's interpretation, that all such post-Easter appearance stories are not records of actual events that serve as the basis of resurrection faith, but rather are preceded by and give expression to resurrection faith, to a faith that Jesus lives still in the power of his father.[23] This is a reading of the text that scarcely permits the exorbitant theological, or onto-theo-political, power play, let us say the massive ecclesiastical violence, that Marion wants to perpetrate. It must be Dutch!

---

23. Edward Schillebeeckx, *Jesus: An Experiment in Christology*, trans. H. Hoskins (New York: Crossroads, 1979), 379–97.

ON GIVING IN TO VIOLENCE

Marion's attempt to lift the veil, to remove the screen, to erase the mediation, to remove the conditions, is an illusion that is at once impossible—for it just cannot be carried out—and dangerous, for it gives one divine airs (heirs), invests one's own finite, mediated views with a pretended absolute authority, lends support to absolute violence. The attempt to eliminate ontological violence, to extricate God from any anterior conditions of possibility, is both misguided and hell-bent on producing a worse violence, ethico-ontical violence, violence of the meanest sort.

I will now conclude these remarks by offering a certain generalization of the point that I have been arguing one way or another throughout this confrontation with Marion. One might say that it is a deconstructionist point and one of the more important implications of deconstruction for theology. The point is that nothing is ever unmediated—a point that ought not to be so hard to swallow for Christianity, which has always been a religion of mediation, where the father has mediated himself to us in Jesus. We do not make naked contact. We are always already immersed in historical and linguistic horizons, always conditioned by them. But such conditions do not only limit us, they enable us to think and speak, to put things in a meaningful perspective, to gain access to such things as we are wont to call from time to time the things themselves.

That is a more timid, "hermeneutic" way of saying there is nothing outside the text, which is a bold, "deconstructionist" way of saying something similar but stronger. This rather notorious declaration of deconstruction does not mean that there are only texts, which would be absurd, but that we never gain access to things by leaving the text behind. Furthermore, it does not mean text in the narrow sense of what we ordinarily call texts, but the "general" text, textuality, écriture, the trace, supplementarity, and so on (the sort of thing Marion keeps supplying everytime he wants to get his point across).

To put it in the Saussurean terms of early Derrida, there is nothing without the chain of signifiers; that is, meaning is not constituted, reference is not made, apart from an enabling code of repeatable signs. Meaning and reference are not inwardly constituted, are not self-constituting, without means and mediation, and then merely outwardly expressed. Meaning and reference arise from below, from within preconstituted chains, from within communities of discourse that in slow and complex ways weave a world. The world is a textured product, and what we are inclined to call the things themselves are things with which, having dwelled for a lifetime among them, we have become exceedingly familiar. The deconstructionist claim is not that there are no such things, but that there are no such things without the enabling chains by means of which they are constituted, no such things without signs. *Kein Ding sei wo das Wort gebricht*: Without the signifier, the thing itself always steals away.[24]

What Marion wants to do is extricate religious discourse and Christian theology in particular from the conditions of textuality, to say that in Christian revelation we have come upon Godtalk in the strong sense of God's own words, that the revealed Word operates as a control on the words of revelation, that the *hors texte* keeps the text in line. That is to make a play for the transcendental signified, to escape the chain of signifiers, to shed the limits of textuality, and to situate ourselves outside the textual site. Marion's Eucharistic, theological site, understood as he understands it, is the view from nowhere, a utopic demand to shed our own textual skin.

The life and death of Jesus was a historico-linguistic event. It transpired in a moment of historical time, and it was expressed and remembered in a language marked by its historical and linguistic horizons. It was mediated from the start, which is why Jesus asked Simon who Simon took him to be, and why Jesus evidently asked himself the same question. No Christologist today seriously entertains the idea that Jesus knew what Thomas Aquinas said he knew about himself. The Mediator was mediated even to himself. Jesus was rabbi and teacher, but he taught about his father; he did not teach the unity of proclaimer and proclaimed that began to take shape in the early churches shortly after his death. The history of the church is the history of the elaboration, the constitution of its theology, within the linguistic and historical horizons of its Hebraic and Greek beginnings, its Latin middle, and its European modernity. It has been mediated ever since, as generations of Christians have let themselves be addressed by the same question.

How not to speak of God? Not without being—for someone may deny that he is (11)—and not without love—for someone may try to reduce him to pure being. Not without metonymy or metaphor,[25] praise or predication, singing or dancing. It is not a question of finding

24. I relate Heidegger's reading of this line from Stefan George to the concluding lines of Derrida's *Speech and Phenomena* in my "The Economy of Signs in Husserl and Derrida," in *Deconstruction and Philosophy*, ed. John Sallis (Chicago: The University of Chicago Press, 1987), 99–113; see especially 109–111.

25. Negative theology, as Derrida points out in *Psyché*, 535, constitutes a complex textual practice with its own economy—of metaphors, metonymies, rhetorical and grammatical devices, etc., with which all who know this "literature" become familiar.

a pure nonviolent discourse, but of giving in to the violence of discourse, the violence that discourse is, of letting words fly up like sparks from hearth fires everywhere, even those of the base communities—and even from The Netherlands—and anywhere else where there is the hope that something may catch on. And when someone tells us that he has the pure discourse, let us beware of this immaculate conception, for along with that go judgments of impurity, contamination, and exclusion.

God does not speak. He is not *Logos*. So there can be no question of claiming access to the language God himself favors. The primordial yes we say to language is a human necessity, is always already violent. But let us say yes to this archi-violence, which is nothing more than the constraint imposed upon us by our human condition, in order to avoid the violence that excludes, excommunicates, silences. For that silence is more violent than speech.

Villanova University

7   Is a Natural Theology Still Viable Today?*

W. NORRIS CLARKE, S.J.

The enterprise of natural theology (or philosophy of God) is a particularly difficult one to carry out in our day. Philosophically, it has come under heavy attack from empiricists and Neo-Kantians, from analytic philosophers tinged with both of the above, from historical and linguistic relativists, appealing to hermeneutics, and more recently from Deconstructionists and Post-Modernists in general. On the other hand, its relationships with contemporary science, in particular theoretical physics and cosmology, have warmed up considerably in recent times. Let us begin with a brief look at these varied relationships.

RELATION TO SCIENCE

In relation to contemporary science, natural theology is, from one point of view, on better terms with it than it has been for a long time. The notion that mind has a place in nature, that nature points to mind as its completion, is much more acceptable, even plausible, to many scientists today, especially theoretical physicists and cosmologists. A cosmologist like Fred Hoyle, for example, once a self-proclaimed atheist, now speaks of *The Intelligent Universe*. Many are favorably impressed by the now famous Anthropic Principle, which seems to point to an extremely precise fine-tuning of the four basic forces of the material universe, with its enormous statistical improbability, as a sign that the universe was planned from the beginning in view of the presence of conscious observers like ourselves in it. Very significant is the recent text of the physicist Arthur Dyson:

I conclude from the existence of these accidents of physics and astronomy that the universe is an unexpectedly hospitable place for living creatures to

*This paper is a heavily revised version of one published in the Symposium sponsored by the Vatican Observatory: *Physics, Philosophy, Theology: A Common Quest for Understanding*, ed. Robert Russell, William Stoeger, George Coyne (Rome: Vatican Observatory, 1988—distributed by the University of Notre Dame Press).

make their home in. Being a scientist, trained in the habits of thought and language of the twentieth century rather than the eighteenth, I do not claim that the architecture of the universe proves the existence of God. I claim only that the architecture of the universe is consistent with the hypothesis that mind plays an essential role in its functioning.[1]

Two points are noteworthy here. The first is the openness or "compatibility" of the scientific picture with the theistic hypothesis, rather than the closedness that used to predominate. But the second is the warning that from within the scientific outlook this hypothesis is only *compatible* with the results of contemporary science, not authorized or established by them. As Ernan McMullin's fine recent paper has shown us, theistic philosophers in the past have persistently tried to argue to the existence of God from some gap in the existing scientific picture of the universe, from some need discovered within the web of scientific explanation for a further grounding that the scientific explanation itself could not supply. Thus, Newton believed that God's intervention was necessary to keep going the constant motion of the heavenly bodies. Paley and others argued from the marvelous adaptation of the various species of living organisms to their environment—given the common pre-Darwinian acceptance of the fixity of species—to a Cosmic Planning Mind that had thus ordered them; and so on. But in each case science eventually closed the gap in its web of explanation, and in so doing closed out the argument to the existence of God based on this gap. The "God of the gaps" has been progressively put out of a job.[2]

The same kind of process seems to be at work again today. Despite the initial plausibility and strong suggestiveness of arguments for the need of a world-ordering Mind from unfilled gaps in the current scientific picture, especially those based on the statistical improbability of our present world order,[3] this foundation does not seem to me a secure one for building a cogent natural theology. The figures are indeed impressive: for example a Princeton scientist, Don Page,[4] recently calculated that the odds against our present universe are something like one in $10,000,000,000^{124}$. But opinions continue to vary as

1. Arthur Dyson, *Disturbing the Universe* (New York: Harper and Row, 1979), chap. on "The Argument from Design," 251.
2. "Natural Science and Belief in a Creator," in the Symposium mentioned in the initial note.
3. A valuable survey of details on this can be found in L. S. Betty and B. Cordell, "God and Modern Science: New Life for the Teleological Argument," *International Philosophical Quarterly,* 27 (1987), 409–35.
4. See D. E. Thomsen, "The Quantum Universe: A Zero-point Fluctuation?" *Science News,* 128 (Aug. 3, 1985), 73.

to the basis for making such calculations, given the unique situation or "singularity" of the earliest stages of the cosmic system. Others have put forward ingenious hypotheses, such as that no choice is needed for the peculiar initial conditions of our universe, since an infinite number of *all possible* universes actually exist, so that ours is bound to turn up somewhere without the need for any calculus of probabilities or selective agent. Others try to argue that ours is in fact the only possible universe that can be actualized (given in quantum physics that many of the conjugate properties of subatomic particles can only be actualized by conscious observers like ourselves). Others weaken the base of the impressive argument from the fine tuning of the four basic forces and other precisely balanced constants of the universe, by reducing the four forces first to three, then to two, then hopefully, in the light of some highly controversial hypotheses like superstring theory, to one simple, all-embracing one from which all else can be deduced. Some suggest tracing the beginning to a mere chance fluctuation of a primordial quantum field, emerging out of a pure, formless, high-energy vacuum state or pre-space-time "foam," which they ambiguously identify as "nothing."[5] In view of the intense ferment of speculation going on at this time in high-level theoretical physics, it does not seem to me possible yet to find any secure foundation within the exigencies of scientific explanation for the postulation of a Transcendent Mind as the only adequate cause of the origin and structure of our cosmos.

Others from within the biological community, or philosophizing on its data, suggest there is even stronger evidence for the need of a Cosmic Planning Mind to explain the origin of life and the large jumps to new species in the course of evolution. They argue from the huge statistical improbability of the passage from a nonliving molecule to a living cell—Fred Hoyle and his associate have calculated it to be 1 in $10^{40,000}$—the failure thus far of all attempts (despite some initial apparent successes) to reproduce successfully the conditions of such a passage, and the now widely conceded breakdown of Darwinian chance selection as an adequate explanation for the passage from one species to another of a higher order.[6] But again, such gaps in current explanations might possibly be filled in by some future hypothesis.

---

5. It would be more accurate to describe it as a nothingness of *form*, not of *energy*, which is still very much in the real order. See, in the Symposium mentioned above in the initial note, John Leslie, "How to Draw Conclusions from a Fine-Tuned Cosmos"; C. J. Isham, "Creation of the Universe as a Quantum Process"; Frank Tipler, "The Omega Point Theory: A Model of an Evolving God."

6. Cf. the article cited in n. 3, and C. Thaxton, W. Bradley, R. Olsen, *The Mystery of Life's Origins: Reassessing Current Theories* (New York: Philosophical Library, 1984).

And I might add that reductionist materialism still seems to have strong support in the biological sciences, more so than in physics today.

So, somewhat reluctantly, and without denying the powerful suggestiveness of inferences from the apparent enormous improbability of our present universe, both in its origins and in the evolution of life within it, I think it wiser to agree with Ernan McMullin in the paper just mentioned, that natural theology today should avoid any attempt to build its foundations on apparently unfillable gaps in the scientific picture of the universe. The "God of the gaps" has so often been put out of a job in the past that I think he should be, for the time being if not permanently, retired. Only a radically metaphysical argument, from the very existence of any determinate world at all, or from the existence of any dynamic order at all, has a fair chance of succeeding, as I see it.

PHILOSOPHICAL OBSTACLES

There have been many attempts in modern and contemporary philosophy to block any project of constructing valid philosophical arguments for the existence of a Transcendental Reality. There are, of course, both older and newer more sophisticated forms of *empiricism* and *Kantianism,* whether in scientific, linguistic, or phenomenological versions, that are still tenaciously pervasive in contemporary thought. All these are fundamentally anti-metaphysical, in the sense that it is impossible to move, by philosophical reason, beyond the world of human experience, inner or outer, to affirm legitimately the existence of some reality transcending this experience. Then there are the newer movements of historical, cultural, linguistic, or hermeneutical *relativism,* together with the latest "demolition squads," known as *Post-Modernists* and *Deconstructionists.*

For the relativists, all our expressed knowledge claims are history-, culture-, and language-bound, meaningful only within a given historical and linguistic framework of inquiry and expression, but never allowing any unconditional truth statements which, with appropriate translation, are capable of transcending the limitations of such frameworks. This at least seems to cripple any attempt to construct a natural theology with any cogency outside its own narrow tradition—if it can be done there.

For the *Post-Modernist,* there is "no meta-narrative legitimation of first-order narratives." You have your story; I have mine (or my group and your group). But there is no norm beyond the individual stories by which to judge their truth or value. We must allow neither political nor conceptual tyranny: both are functions of the will to power, not truth. "Let all flowers bloom."[7]

The *Deconstructionist* calls on us to resist—and sabotage—the arrogant "logocentrism" of the West, with its pretensions to capture reality adequately in all-inclusive, totalizing conceptual systems, transparently reflecting the nonlinguistic real, à la Hegel. They propose a "heterology" (championing the Other, the different, the exception, the marginalized) in opposition to a "henology" (the reduction of the many, the different, the unique to some all-inclusive, all-explanatory One), as has been customary in Western metaphysics. The more radical versions, which Jacques Derrida, the most visible "father" of the movement, often makes gestures of repudiating, maintain that no expressed signifiers ever connect up unambiguously with the truth, or nonlinguistic reality, that there is no unambiguous dividing line between metaphor and objective concept, literature and philosophy, that all signifiers trail off into an endless labyrinth of reference to other signifiers and these to others, into traces of traces of traces . . . . In place of so-called truth claims, they unveil the hidden pretensions of the philosophers to impose their metaphorical schemas on others by the "will to power" (the influence of Nietzsche is clear here, and often explicitly avowed). In addition, all texts can be cracked open to reveal a hidden subtext that works against the surface text to undermine it. The radical Deconstructionist is a "double-agent and a nomad," who infiltrates one system to blow it up from within, then, with no "home" (or position) of his own, moves on to blow up another. It is obvious that an effective natural theology—or any kind of theology, it turns out—is, in such a context, a logocentric illusion.[8]

CLEARING THE OBSTACLES

Let me indicate briefly how I would go about removing or circumventing the above philosophical roadblocks to the positive construction of a natural theology. First, as to the contemporary relativists, Post-

7. For typical examples, see *After Philosophy: End or Transformation?* ed. K. Baynes, J. Bohman, T. McCarthy (Cambridge, Mass.: MIT Press, 1987), in particular the essay by J. F. Lyotard, leading French Post-Modernist, entitled "The Postmodern Condition," 67–94.
8. On Deconstructionism, see the essay by Derrida in the collection cited in n. 7; also John Caputo, *Radical Hermeneutics, Repetition, Deconstruction, and the Hermeneutical Project* (Bloomington, In.: Indiana University Press, 1987); John Sallis, ed., *Deconstruction and Philosophy* (Chicago: The University of Chicago Press, 1986); Hugh Silverman and Don Ihde, eds., *Hermeneutics and Deconstruction* (Albany: SUNY Press, 1985); Christopher Norris, *Deconstruction: Theory and Practice* (London: Methuen, 1982).

Modernists, and Deconstructionists. I think it would be a serious mistake—an intellectual loss of nerve—to allow ourselves to be intimidated by these movements, with their often strident proclamations of the end of Western logocentric reason. My reason is this: Whenever these positions move to a really radical stance, blocking all access to objective truth, they promptly self-destruct and become inoperative as a critique. For either they are claiming to be informing us of some truth—what is the case—about all linguistically expressed human thought, and then their assertive performance contradicts the content of their assertions, namely, that all such assertions are culture- and language-bound so that they cannot connect up unambiguously with the truth; or, if they are not really claiming to tell us some significant truth about all of us, then their own position immediately becomes relativized and turns into just another late-twentieth-century culture-bound opinion, perhaps even localized to a small group of thinkers in a few large cities, and there is no reason for the rest of us to bother our heads about it; we are free to go on in our own contexts happily asserting our objective truth claims.

In short, the natural, spontaneous, and, in the last analysis, inextinguishable drive of the human mind to discover and give recognizable expression to the truth, to what is the case in reality, cannot tolerate for long any attempt at systematic self-sabotage of its own natural drive and innate cognitive structure of experience-insight-judgment as to what is the case about ourselves and the world we live in. As Derrida himself has well said somewhere, understanding this as a pragmatic necessity of actual human living, "Il faut la vérité" (There must be truth).

If the above movements are taken in moderation, however, they can lead us to an important, more realistic understanding of what in fact is the case about our human reason. There is no going back to a pre-hermeneutic understanding of human thought and language. What has really been demolished is the old and indeed arrogant Cartesian and Enlightenment ideal of human reason as pure, impersonal, autonomous, self-sufficient Reason, independent of any tradition, culture, historical perspective or authority, that will in principle be able to gather into itself unaided and with perfect transparency all the real, knowable, or worth knowing, with special priority given to *the* scientific method, specifiable according to rules, as the ideal method of reaching any truth available to us.

Accordingly, a self-aware contemporary thinker in any field should be willing to admit (1) that our human reason must always see the world from some limited (incomplete) historical perspective or vantage point; (2) that what is seen from other vantage points is—if we have done our work carefully—complementary, not contradictory; (3) that we cannot come intellectually naked to understand the texts of man and his world, but must go through some apprenticeship in a living hermeneutical tradition; (4) that the reliable knowledge we can indeed attain about the real is not the Cartesian ideal of absolute certitude such that the opposite can be shown to be a logical contradiction— this is attainable only in mathematics and logic—but is "reasonable affirmation," as Bernard Lonergan puts it, achieved not by impersonal, automatic, clearly specifiable rules for correct thinking, but by personalized responsible thinking (taking possession of oneself and one's drive to know and committing oneself to it), striving for intelligent insight into the meaning latent in the data and for personally responsible judgment based on evidence recognized as sufficient for its purposes; (5) finally, that all of our perception, concepts, and understanding are, as Polanyi has shown so well, a synthesis of focal and peripheral (or background) knowledge, such that it is neither possible nor necessary to make formal and explicit all that is in this background knowledge (for it is a mode of existential lived knowledge, acquired by sharing in a practical "form of life" never fully susceptible of explicit conceptual formulation), and that this is not, as Deconstructionists so often overlook, crippling to our capacity to understand, but positively enabling.

On the other side of the picture, however, it should always be remembered that no matter how limited or incomplete a perspective may be, it is still an opening onto something beyond the viewer. A perspective that opens onto nothing, or only inward into the viewer, is not a perspective at all, but a hall of mirrors. Similarly, no matter how much one may have to start within a hermeneutical tradition to learn a tradition and skills of inquiry and interpretation, a hermeneutics that effectively does its job is one that enables us to understand a situation or text that needs interpretation and, by a sensitively intelligent "fusion of horizons," come to understand significantly—though never totally—a different or older tradition. A hermeneutical viewpoint is a vantage point from which to discover and understand something—although not all that is to be seen, to be sure; it is not a labyrinth or prison in which one gets to know only the prisoners.

As for the *Deconstructionists*, Polanyi's theory of focal and peripheral knowledge, appropriately amplified for the study of texts, already takes care of many of their significant warnings—without the skeptical consequences. As for the claim of the Other, the absent, and so on, to deserve equal status with the One, being, presence, and so forth, it is my impression that Deconstructionists often exhibit a systematic blind-spot to what St. Thomas was so well aware of, namely, the distinction between the mode of discovery of a concept as explicitly distinct from others and the content signified by it. Thus, in a realistic metaphysics like that of St. Thomas, the metaphysical notion of being, like most metaphysical concepts, is intrinsically analogous, that is, pregnant with one and many, sameness and difference, remaining systematically vague, so that all that is in it can never be made fully explicit; fur-thermore, the notion itself is indeed brought to explicit possession by contrast with partial absences, particular instances of nonbeing, etc. But all these differences, absences, partial nonbeings, and so on are always enveloped within the overall horizon of being, differences within being, not outside of it in a radical or unqualified sense. There is no warrant to argue, as it seems to me Deconstructionists persis-tently tend to do, from the mode of discovery of our concepts to the conclusion that in the real order nonbeing and absence can claim independent equality, much less priority, with respect to being, pres-ence, unity, and so forth. All truly analogous concepts contain the many within the womb of the one from the outset.

As for *empiricism,* even in its various diluted contemporary forms, our basic response to it is that it cannot make stick its claims to block any ascent of rational human intelligence to transcendent reality, either within us or above us. It is in essence an arbitrarily restrictive theory of knowledge, attempting to constrict the natural dynamism of the mind to know and understand the real in all its fullness, attempt-ing to tie it down merely to the realm of experience. It would allow description and correlation of the data of experience, with a privilege given to sensory data, but no explanations reaching beyond experi-ence to fill the gaps of intelligibility found within experience. As many metaphysicians in the analytic tradition, like Strawson—who do not, by the way, consider themselves card-carrying empiricists of the Humean type—have put it succinctly: Descriptive metaphysics (description of the basic linguistic categories of our experience) is in. Explanatory metaphysics is out.[9]

But, in addition to an impoverished theory of efficient causality, the radical weakness in this procedure is that the knower itself cannot be

9. Similarly Anthony Quinton, definitely a metaphysician in the analytic mode, main-tains this stricture on the use of causal inference: "For a causal inference is only legit-imate if it is at least possible to obtain evidence for the existence of the cause which is independent of the events it is said to explain." "The Problem of Perception," in G. Warnock, ed., *The Philosophy of Percpetion* (New York: Oxford University Press, 1967), 62. All the classical metaphysicians in their ascent to God through causal inference have systematically violated this restrictive rule.

caught adequately in the empiricist's net of all that is knowable. The intelligent knower who is looking at the data attentively, striving to gain insight into its meaning, interpreting and judging it, discerning value or disvalue within it, is not out there among the sensory data. The knower cannot "look" at itself as self-conscious, self-possessing, responsibly judging, self-governing "I," if empiricism is true. But, in fact, we do just this all the time in our conscious rational life. The knower transcends all its empirical data, is not reducible without remainder to all or any part of its empirically given data. This surplus between the knower in all its depth and its empirical data opens the way to a nonempirical (i.e., metaphysical) ascent of the mind through the exigencies of intelligibility to whatever transcendent reality is needed to fill the gaps in intelligibility found in the empirical data taken by themselves alone.

But there is one principle of explanation that must be explicitly rescued from the straightjacket of empiricism, if our ascent is to be viable. That is the principle of efficient causality. The empiricist would have us believe that the foundational and only legitimate meaning of causality is simply the regularly observed succession in time of empirically observable antecedent and consequent events, such that from the first one can predict the second according to some law. Any further intrinsic link between cause and effect, such as the active production or bringing into being of the second by the first, the fact that the cause is responsible for the effect, which therefore has an ontological—though clearly not sensibly observable—link of dependence on its cause—all this is declared to be later, unnecessary, and unjustifiable baggage added on by the metaphysicians.

The opposite is in fact the case. Our modern natural sciences have indeed good reason, for methodological purposes, to restrict the meaning of efficient causality in practice to "predictability according to law," whether deterministic or, more often today, statistical. But the original meaning of the term, deriving from the Greek law courts, and its flourishing continued use today in ordinary life situations for explaining why things happen, is the notion of "that which is responsible (originally "guilty," in court room use) for" the given occurrence of some event, the presence of some entity, and so on, that of itself needs explanation, is judged (not empirically observed) not to make sense by itself alone.[10]

10. For the origin of the term "cause" in the Greek law courts, see H. Boeder, "Origine et préhistoire de la notion philosophique de l'AITION," *Revue des sciences philosophiques et théologiques*, 40 (1956), 421–43. For a defense of the common-sense notion of efficient causality as active causal efficacy, see R. Harré and E. Madden, *Causal Powers*

The principle of efficient causality, thus understood in ordinary life and more self-consciously and abstractly in realist metaphysics, is really, in the last analysis, simply a function of the inquiring mind at work, with a flexible analogous application just as wide as the reach of the mind itself. It is nothing more, but nothing less, than the reaffirmation of the basic commitment of the inquiring human mind to the unrestricted intelligibility of the real, tailored to fit a particular situation. When allowed to operate without arbitrary restrictions, the search for the efficient cause (or causes) is simply the search for whatever is needed to fill a discerned gap of intelligibility in the data of our experience. Wherever this search leads, to whatever is shown to be indispensable to fill this gap, whether a cause in the empirically given world or beyond, this can be affirmed legitimately under pain of allowing the initial data we are trying to explain to remain with a declared unfillable hole or "wound" in its intelligibility. In its wide-open scope, as wide as being itself, this principle contains no restrictions such as empiricism would force upon it. Realist metaphysicians should reclaim without intimidation the principle of efficient causality as the natural birthright of the innate drive of the mind to know and the indispensable instrument for carrying out the mind's natural commitment to the intelligibility of being—a commitment of "natural faith," as Einstein and other great scientists have put it, that is really the inner dynamism and soul of all serious intellectual inquiry, scientific or otherwise.

As to the last of our roadblocks, *Kantianism*, two brief remarks will have to suffice. Kant is indeed a great thinker, especially in ethical matters. But we have been too long intimidated by his long shadow in epistemology, in particular his anti-realist and anti-metaphysical stance, which claims to bar the way to a rational affirmation of anything beyond empirical appearances. In the first place, his refutation of the so-called "Cosmological Argument" for God is flawed by a serious misreading of the traditional argument as presented by realist meta-

---

(Totowa, N.J.: Rowman Allenfeld, 1975); Dorothy Emmet, *The Effectiveness of Causes* (Albany: SUNY Press, 1984); Galen Strawson, "Realism, Causal Efficacy, and Causation," *Philosophical Quarterly*, 37 (1987), 253–77; John Wild, "A Realistic Defence of Causal Efficacy," *Review of Metaphysics*, 2 (1948–49), 1–14. For a fuller treatment of efficient causality as applied to arguing to the existence of God, see my book, *The Philosophical Approach to God: A Neothomist Perspective* (Winston-Salem: Wake Forest University Philosophy Department, 1979), chap. 2: "The Metaphysical Ascent to God through Participation." For another robust defense of active efficient causality and its application to proving the existence of God, see the important new book by David Braine, *The Reality of Time: The Project of Proving God's Existence* (Oxford: Clarendon Press, 1988), chap. 3

physicians like St. Thomas. In the last crucial step of the argument, Kant distorts it to become an attempted deduction of the existence of a Necessary Being (I would prefer to call it a Self-Sufficient Being) from the idea of the *Ens Realissimum* (or infinitely perfect being). St. Thomas would indignantly repudiate such a procedure, all too easily refuted by Kant. The traditional procedure is precisely the opposite. Once the reality of a Self-Sufficient Being has been established from causal arguments, it is then argued that such a being could not be at once self-sufficient and finite, for the latter by nature requires a cause of its being as finite. Therefore the Self-Sufficient Being must be infinite, and so, by an easy step, only one. There is no deduction from the idea of perfection or from any idea in itself, although some such procedure may have been invoked by some of the rationalist metaphysicians of the Wolffian type just before Kant.

As to Kant's attempt to bar access to any valid affirmation about a real world beyond the knower, it suffers from a fatal flaw, a massive blind spot that has also plagued most of modern Western epistemology since Descartes, as pointed out insightfully by John Dewey, as well as by Thomists: namely, overlooking the key role of action as the self-revelation of being in our human knowing—an absolutely central theme in the epistemology of Aristotle, St. Thomas, and Dewey himself. For, on the one hand, Kant must admit action coming from the real world of things-in-themselves into the human knower, since he insists that he is not an idealist, that we do not create by thought the objects of our knowledge. On the other hand, he will not admit that this action is revelatory of anything objective in real things, anything true of them—not even their real existence, since "being" itself represents only the positing by the mind of its own synthesis of the unordered appearances in the sense-manifold and the innate, a priori forms of sense and intellect. But action that is totally non-revelatory of the nature of the agent-source from which it comes is itself unintelligible, cannot be truly action.[11]

Kant cannot have it both ways. Either there is no real action of the real world upon us—and he is forced into idealism, which he rejects vehemently—or he accepts the fact of real action of the real world

11. For the philosophical significance of action in St. Thomas's metaphysics and epistemology, and its relevance to Kant and modern epistemology, see my essay "Action as the Self-Revelation of Being: A Central Theme in the Thought of St. Thomas," in L. Thro, ed., *History of Philosophy in the Making* (Lanham, Md.: University Press of America, 1982), 63–81. For John Dewey's reference to action as the key to epistemology and its neglect in modern philosophy, see his 1897 Lecture, "The Significance of the Problem of Knowledge," *Early Works of John Dewey* (Carbondale: Southern Illinois University Press, 1972), 295, 297.

upon us—and then this action is necessarily revelatory, a manifestation—incomplete indeed, but authentic in what it does manifest—of
its real agent-source. As a thing acts, so must it be—*agere sequitur esse*,
as the ancient Scholastic adage goes.

The root of the trouble lies, I suspect, in Kant's implicit rationalist
ideal of knowing the real as knowledge, by a detached, uninvolved
pure knower, of a real being as it is in itself independent of any action
upon others, including the knower himself. Of course, such a knowledge is impossible save for a purely creative knower, which we are not.
But the whole key to an action-based realist epistemology is that our
knowledge, involving incoming action from the thing known, received
according to the mode of receptivity of the knower, is through and
through relational; but this relation itself is thoroughly real, what is
the case, necessarily revealing something real about the other end of
the relation. For it reveals the known as actor, as in itself this kind of
actor—which is precisely, in the last analysis, just what an essence (i.e.,
a nature, an abiding center of action) should really mean in a realist
epistemology, I would maintain. Thus, St. Thomas himself is not in
the least reluctant to admit—in a text that astonishes many contemporary epistemologists—that "[t]he substantial forms of things as they
are in themselves are unknown to us, but they shine forth to us
through their accidents [i.e., their operations] . . . as through doors
surrounding them," so that our mind points back to their hidden
natures through their manifestations in "a kind of discursive movement"[12]—which I interpret as the intentionality of judgment, as opposed to a direct intuition.

Such a relational knowledge through action is necessarily perspec-
tival and incomplete, proportional to the limitations and conditions of
the receiver, but it is a genuine perspective on the known as agent—
and in the last analysis isn't that what we most want to know about
other real beings, what characteristic actions we can expect of them?
Given this umbilical cord to the real world through action on us, we
can follow up any gaps in the intelligibility of the world thus revealed
to us to affirm as real whatever is needed to fill these gaps, empirical
or transempirical, as the case may be. This is precisely the path of
efficient causality, of causal explanation, freed of arbitrary empiricist
shackles.

To sum up now what has gone before, all attempts to lay mines that
will definitively block the modest but real access of the human mind

---

12. I have joined together two texts, one from *Summa Theologiae*, I, q. 77, art. 1, ad
obj. 7, the other from *Expositio in Libros Sententiarum*, III, dist. 35, q. 2, art. 2, sol. 1.

to the real and to whatever is needed to fill the gaps in its intelligibility succeed finally only in blowing up the mine-layers with their mines, leaving the rest of us free to navigate with critical care between the rocks and through the rapids. The metaphysical hypotheses worked out along the way, including arguments for the existence of God such as I will present presently, are not Cartesian absolute certitudes, but explanatory hypotheses that recommend themselves as worthy of reasonable affirmation because they fill the gaps in the intelligibility of the real world we experience in a more illuminating and adequate way than other, competing hypotheses—or lack of them—which either leave out something significant from our experience or leave gaps in its intelligibility unfillable in principle from their perspective. Now to our positive task.

CONSTRUCTING A NATURAL THEOLOGY

From all contemporary philosophical discussion has taught us, it should be clear that it is not realistically possible to construct a purely objective philosophical argument for the existence of God—or for anything else, indeed—floating free from all personal roots, one that is capable of convincing by its pure impersonal cogency any intelligent hearer whatever, irrespective of all predispositions and presuppositions, moral and intellectual, of all cultural and conceptual frameworks—all hermeneutical traditions, if you will. As Polanyi, Gadamer, and others have shown, there is no presuppositionless thought, in any field. We do presuppose, therefore, in anyone who is willing to give sympathetic consideration to the arguments we are going to propose, a certain familiarity with—or at least willingness to enter into—what I would call a metaphysical type of thinking, that is, one that is open to asking radical questions about the very existence and intelligibility of the world we live in, following out the discovered exigencies of intelligibility (of making good sense), wherever they may lead, and not cutting short, a priori or arbitrarily, the innate drive of the mind to understand the real as fully as possible.

Our metaphysical procedure will be, first, to identify significant gaps in the intelligibility of our universe as a whole, if we can find them, then to propose in a kind of branching technique the main options for filling these gaps, and to try to eliminate all of these options, or explanatory hypotheses, save one. By "gap in intelligibility" I do not mean merely something I do not yet understand, some mystery; I mean that one must show positively that given the nature of the data there is something in them that excludes any adequate explanation of them—or rendering of any sufficient reason for their existence—if taken by themselves alone; in a word, that they just cannot, because of some built-in deficiency of their being, be self-explanatory, but demand the help of some further real being, which fulfills the role of efficient cause, that is, that which is *responsible* for their actual being or their coming into existence. In a metaphysical type of inquiry, because of its vast generality—and therefore elimination of details—it is possible to reduce the relevant options for explanation to a very few at one step, then move onto the next and do likewise— something that is rarely possible in the natural sciences because of the complex details to be explained and the wide range of hypotheses open. The elimination of all options but one can rarely be done by purely logical means, but usually requires metaphysical insight into intrinsic idea-connections, which cannot be commanded but which can afford, if carefully checked, sufficient grounds for reasonable affirmation of what it reveals.

I agree with Charles Hartshorne in his later works that it is more accurate these days to speak of "arguments" rather than "proofs" for the existence of God, since "proof " as understood today has become so rigorous in its requirements that it is impossible, properly speaking, to prove the existence of any real being (outside the knowing "I"), let alone the existence of a transcendent reality like God. Secondly, I agree with him that such arguments (or "reasonable ascents of the mind to God") exhibit a certain cumulative effect, one argument opening one side of the intelligibility needed; another, another side, or perhaps one argument for one type of mind, another for another. I believe, too, that a well-rounded and effective natural theology should proceed in a two-pronged approach: one that I would call the "Inner Path," through the exigencies of the inner life of man as intellect, will, and moral person; and the other the "Outer Path," through the exigencies of the entire cosmos (including man). The Inner Path would proceed from reflection on the innate drive of the human spirit toward the unlimited horizon of being as truth and goodness, such that one is faced with the option that either an Infinite Fullness of Being as truth and goodness actually exists as the only adequate goal of this innate drive, a drive that is constitutive of the human—hence not capable of being substituted for by any finite goal or set of them—or our human spirit is radically absurd, oriented toward what does not and cannot exist. And since there is no good reason for opting for the absurd, the unintelligible, and every good reason for opting for the existence of the Infinite as closing the gap in intelligibility in us— with room to spare!—it is uniquely reasonable to opt for the latter, though the opposite can never be shown to be a logical contradiction (it may be a "lived" one, however). I fear we will have no further space to develop the Inner Path argument in the present paper.[13] The reason I choose the Outer or Cosmic Path for fuller development here is that the Inner Path can indeed reach an Infinite Good as *my* final good, *my* God, but not as the Ultimate Source of *all* being, which is necessary for an adequate notion of God. I have also chosen this path because the original context for this paper was a discussion with scientists.

I. Argument from Any Caused Being to a Single Infinite Source of All Being

Let me start with my own adaptation of a classical argument of St. Thomas, combining three essential steps, which he stretches out over some nine questions in his *Summa Theologica*, Part I (beginning at question 2, article 3, and finishing at question 11—a point too often overlooked by those who look only to the Five Ways in question 2 for his complete proof). This argument, the longest one I shall give, will at least serve the purpose of initiating the reader into a metaphysical type of inquiry, even if it does not convince him.

It is important to note the question we are asking as we begin this "ascent of the mind to God." The basic question we are raising about the beings of our experience is not: What are they? What are their properties? How do they operate? It is rather the radical question about their very existence: Why do they exist at all in this way that they do exist? What is the ultimate intelligibility, or sufficient reason, why they in fact exist at all? It is important not to short-circuit this question from the start, as Bertrand Russell and many empiricists have done. "Explanation," for them, as one told me, "means to relate the parts of the universe to each other *within* the system as a whole. But one can't raise questions about the system itself *as a whole*." As Russell put it in a nutshell in his famous BBC debate with Father Copleston some years ago, when the latter pushed him on this point: "The world as a whole just is, that's all. We start there." Scientific explanation, it is true, must start there; a science can use its methods only on some subject matter already given to it in existence and cannot answer questions about the very existence of its own subject matter. But philosophically speaking it is an intellectual cop-out, an arbitrary restriction of the natural drive of the mind to know, to refuse to raise the most radical of all questions, the question of the very existence of our uni-

13. I have developed this path at greater length in my book *The Philosophical Approach to God* (n. 10 above), chap. 1, "The Turn to the Inner Path in Contemporary Neo-thomism."

verse and ourselves as knowers within it. The primary theme song of all metaphysical inquiry, we might say, is, "Don't fence me in!"

The argument unfolds in three steps: (1) Given any conditioned being, there must exist at least one absolutely unconditioned, or self-sufficient, being; (2) No being can be self-sufficient unless it is qualitatively infinite or unlimited in perfection; (3) There can be only one such being infinite in all perfections—which therefore must be the unique Ultimate Source of all being. Such a being we can appropriately call "God."

Step one: There must exist at least one self-sufficient being. Let us begin with the beings around us. All of these manifest themselves to us as *conditioned existents.* That is to say, they are not self-sufficient, but depend on other beings outside them as conditions for their own existence, either to bring them into existence or to maintain them in existence, or both. Thus all human beings depend on their parents for initiating their existence, and on the air, temperature, nourishment, and many other factors around them to maintain themselves. The same is true of all living things, down through animals, plants, and whatever other intermediaries there may be. The same is also true of all molecules, which depend on the atoms composing them and on many other conditions of space-time, fields of force, temperature, and so on, without which they could not hold together with their specific properties. The same now appears to be true of the whole domain of atoms themselves. All depend on external conditions; for example, they could not hold together until the initial temperature of the cosmos cooled enough to allow it. The same seems to be true also of the primordial particles making up atoms, although we cannot directly corroborate this yet scientifically. Thus what many believe to be the most elementary particles, quarks, cannot exist alone but need always to be joined with two or three others. Everywhere around us, then, as far as our experience can reach, is a vast web of conditioned existents, none of which is self-sufficient for its own existence.

Now the question arises: Can all the entities of our universe be thus conditioned, non-self-sufficient, dependent on others for their existence? On reflection the answer must be "no." Take any conditioned being A. It must depend on another entity B in order that its own conditions for existence be fulfilled. But now in our search for intelligibility we must ask the same question of entity B: Is it conditioned or not? If so, we must look further to entity C in order to explain B. And the same question will arise for C, D, and all other members of this causal chain. Can there be an infinite regress in this chain, so that the causal chain of dependency would extend endlessly, with all its members having the same existential status of conditioned existents, none of them self-sufficient for its own existence? Whether the chain extend backwards in time or simultaneously across the universe makes no difference; the problem is the same. Again, the answer must be "no." For if all the beings in the chain remain conditioned, dependent on another, then nowhere will the conditions for the existence of any member be adequately fulfilled. The search for the necessary fulfilling conditions will endlessly go on and in principle be impossible of completion. For in principle the necessary conditions can never be fulfilled. Hence the entire chain remains suspended without a sufficient reason, or adequate grounding, for any of them to exist. But the original beings we started with do in fact actually exist here and now—which means that in fact all their necessary conditions must be already fulfilled. Hence, under pain of the entire chain of conditioned existents remaining unintelligible in their actual existence, there must be somewhere in existence at least one absolutely unconditioned being, completely self-sufficient for its own existence, either at the beginning of the causal chain or outside of it, supporting the whole. There can be no conditioned beings unless there is at least one unconditioned one, which is the initiator (not necessarily in time) of the causal flow of existence into all the others in the series. (As far as we know at present, there may be many such series.)

Nor can it be objected that, even though all the parts of the world system may be conditioned, the system as a whole may be unconditioned, self-sufficient. Once the system is actually there, with its energy within it, it might be self-maintaining—that is another question we need not go into at present. But it cannot be the self-sufficient reason for its being there in the first place. For such a system that is made up of parts, even though a higher mode of being may emerge from the union of the parts, still depends on its parts, presupposes them as that out of which it emerges. It cannot operate as a whole at all unless the parts are already there. If it is the final source that generates its own parts, then it must be ontologically prior to and independent of them for its own existence. The question then must be raised whether it is self-sufficient or not, as before.

Nor can it be argued that the causal dependence might be circular: A depends upon B, B upon C, and C in turn upon A. For C must then be prior to A and B ontologically (not necessarily temporally), in the order of existential dependence, and yet must be posterior to A as depending on it. But it is contradictory for the same entity to be at once prior and posterior to another being in the same order of dependence. Such a circular system can be placed there all at once as a unity by an independent cause, and then might maintain itself by reciprocal support. But none of the parts can generate their own mutual togetherness as an existing whole.

The rejection of an infinite regress might be put in another, perhaps more austerely logical, way. Given that being A here and now exists, categorically and unconditionally. Now suppose one tries to explain A thus: A exists only if B, and B only if C, C only if D, and so on to infinity. In this case, since each one depends upon the conditions of its cause being fulfilled, and these conditions remain endlessly unfulfilled, the entire series remains conditional in its existence. Unless somewhere along the line one of the members exists unconditionally, that is, with no more conditions to be fulfilled, then the original existence of A itself becomes only conditional. There can never be a categorical affirmation of anything at all (nothing but "only ifs"). But the original A does categorically and unconditionally exist, as a fact, not "iffily." Hence we have failed in our search for the intelligibility of its existence—unless we go on to posit the unconditional existence somewhere along the line of a real cause that is self-sufficient, self-explanatory of its own existence, uncaused.

Many arguments stop here—as for example do three of St. Thomas' Five Ways (four in fact, since the third gives no reason for its final step). But there is much more to be done. What sort of being will qualify for being self-sufficient? And how many such can there be? The great Aristotle himself thought finally that there must be 55 unmoved, uncaused Prime Movers. So we must put an appropriate question to the self-sufficient being we have discovered that will smoke out its significant attributes further. The crucial one is this: Is it finite or infinite in perfection?

Step two: Any being self-sufficient for its own existence must be infinite in perfection, that is, unlimited in its qualitative fullness of all perfections. Or: *No self-sufficient being can be finite.* Why? Let us suppose it were finite. This means it would be one determinate, limited mode of being (limited in qualitative intensity of perfection) among at least several other modes possible, such that at least one higher mode were possible (i.e., this one does not exhaust all possible fullness of perfection). Otherwise it would not be finite or limited. Now there must be some sufficient reason why the being in question exists in this particular limited and determinate mode of being and not in some other possible. Why this being, or this whole finite world-system, in fact, and not some other? A principle of selection is needed to select this mode of being from the range of possibilities and give actual existence (energy-filled existence) to it according to this limited mode (or "essence," as the metaphysician would say). But no finite being can do this selection of its own essence and conferral of existence on itself. For then it would have to preexist its own determinate actual existence (in some indeterminate state), pick out what it wills to be, and confer this upon itself. All of this is obviously absurd, unintelligible. It follows that no determinate finite being can be the self-sufficient reason for its existence as this determinate being. Therefore it requires an efficient cause for its actual existence as this being. But since we cannot go on to infinity in caused causes, we must eventually come to some Infinite Cause of these finite beings.

The same conclusion can be reached through a slightly different approach. Suppose that a finite being were self-sufficient. This would mean that it would have to be the total, ultimate source of all the positive attributes within it, including the central, all-embracing perfection of actual existence, energy-filled existence itself. Now it does not make sense that the ultimate source of a perfection should possess this perfection in some limited, imperfect way, less than the full plenitude possible of the perfection in question, when it is the very source of this perfection itself. Nor does it make sense that it should deliberately restrict its own possession of this perfection of which it is the ultimate source to some limited degree when it could enjoy the full plenitude of it. The notions of ultimate, self-sufficient source of a perfection and limited possession of it clash irreconcilably and cancel each other out. No being self-sufficient for its own existence, therefore, can possess existence only in some limited, incomplete, imperfect way.

Conclusion so far: every finite being, not only each one in particular, but any system as a whole that is finite and determinate in its mode of existence, as ours clearly is, needs a self-sufficient infinite being to draw it out of the range of possibilities and make it to *be* in this particular way and no other. It does not matter, in fact, how many other modes actually exist, or even whether all possible ones exist. Each one needs to be given actual existence according to its determinate mode, and no one can do it for itself.

Step three: There can be only one such infinite being. This is a quick and easy one, admitted by just about all metaphysicians, I believe, once the existence of an absolutely infinite being is granted. For suppose there were two such. Then one would not be the other. But this is impossible unless at least one of the two lacks something the other one has. Otherwise they would coincide into total indistinguishable identity. But if one lacked some positive perfection, it could not also be absolutely infinite in all perfections. Also, as Duns Scotus has pointed out, at least one would be unable to know the other—a great imperfection; for either one would have to create the other or be acted on by the other; and in either case one of the two would have to be dependent on the other, hence not self-sufficient—which we already established.

Conclusion of whole argument: If anything at all exists, then there must exist one and only one Infinite Source of all being. This we may call an apt philosophical definition of "God."

II. Argument from Any Finite Being to a Single Infinite Source of All Being

It may have occurred to the alert reader that it is possible to condense the above long argument into a much simpler and more elegant one beginning with Step Two and proceeding directly from any finite being to the necessity of a single Infinite Source of all being. This is perfectly true. One has only to find a limited being in our experience—and God knows there are all too many around us, including ourselves—and immediately proceed from finitude itself as the ground for the need of a cause, as the gap in intelligibility needing to be filled by another. To avoid an infinite regress of finite causes one would have to bring in again the elimination of this possibility outlined in Step One. Step Three—that there can be only one Infinite in perfection—follows immediately as above to cap off the argument. This is a classic Neo-Platonic procedure, often used by St. Thomas himself (as in *De Potentia*, q. 3, art. 6), and echoed in his Fourth Way (though the order of parts is inverted—unfortunately, to my mind). Every finite being, St. Thomas says, by the very fact that it is limited, indicates that it is a participated perfection, and points beyond itself to an unparticipated infinite Source.[14]

Instead of starting from some particular finite being, one can also make this into a more powerful and impressive argument, simply by stepping back and taking as our starting point the entire system of our material cosmos as a whole. This is clearly a determinate limited system, whose basic constants are precisely limited—for example, the four basic forces, the speed of light, Planck's constant h, and so on (whether or not there is some infinity on the purely quantitative level can be left open for settlement either way). Therefore the entire system as a limited whole can provide no sufficient reason why it actually exists as this determinate system and no other. Physicists have been able to show that it is possible to vary the values of the basic

14. *Summa Theologiae*, I, q. 93, art. 6; q. 44, art. 1, ad obj. 1.

constants of our universe (e.g., the speed of light, the force of gravity, etc.) and still get a consistent system. Why, then, this determinate one rather than some other? The system itself can provide no answer. The only conceivable way one could do so would be if one could show that this particular material universe was absolutely and in every respect the only one possible—that is to say, there could be not only no other material universe, but no other universe of any kind at all, including all possible modes of higher spiritual beings (for, although something would always have to have existed, there is no way of showing that a material universe must exist, if other modes of being exist). It is clearly impossible to make any such all-inclusive claims, particularly from the point of view of any natural science, or science of any kind we know.

The argument holds firm, I believe. There is no way for the system itself to fill the gap in its own intelligibility, to illuminate the sheer brute fact of its own limited existing thisness. Note, too, that this argument is a purely metaphysical one, quite independent of any changes or progress in the content of the sciences. For the natural sciences by their very nature must always be dealing with new patterns and systems of determinate, finite—and probably measurable—entities, of whatever sort. Science and the determinate finitude of its objects are by necessity always linked together.

It is noteworthy, too, that the whole process of scientific inquiry implicitly reaffirms the philosophical claim that our finite universe as it manifests itself to us does not contain within it the sufficient reason for its own existence in this particular way, is not self-explanatory. For at each stage of explanation, science keeps raising new questions why the system should be such—which is an implicit admission that it is not self-explanatory. It keeps seeking for the ideal goal of a single ultimate unifying principle from which all else may be derived, and a principle that is as simple as possible. But is not this an implicit admission that, as long as we remain with some determinate complexity, we have not yet reached the end of the line in intelligibility? No finite determinate mode of being, that is *this* and not *that,* can ever be ultimately self-explanatory. Only an unqualifiedly infinite fullness of existence can ever be the final resting place of the search for intelligibility. Science itself cannot formulate this last step of its search, for there is no scientific way of giving meaning to it or solving it in terms of scientific data or empirical verification. This is precisely where science points the way toward metaphysics as the next stage of the journey toward the fullness of meaning of our always question-laden universe.

III. Further Reflections on the Contingent Existence of Our Universe

I would be reluctant to describe this reflection as another independent "argument" for the existence of God in the strict sense. It is rather a deeper reflection on the profound gap in intelligibility that lies between the possible existence and the actual existence-with-energy of our universe, in short, a reflection on its radical contingency in the order of existence. It would thus be in the order of a metaphysical insight, or "musement," in Peirce's sense. It was stimulated by some of the highly theoretical—and still very controversial—speculations of some cosmologists about the Big Bang origins of our material universe. Some have speculated—and tried to work out mathematical hypotheses expressing this—that ours might be, in some significant sense, the only possible universe (in its large lines of course, not in all the details of its evolution). In the Vatican observatory Symposium that was the original context of this paper, Frank J. Tipler has in fact formulated a hypothesis along these lines and drawn the implications for a natural theology:

> In this paper I shall discuss two recent developments in physics which have important implications for religion . . . . The second development is the possibility of a Theory of Everything (TOE). A TOE might imply that there is only one logically possible universe. This would refute the Cosmological Argument and, more importantly, its premise that God had some freedom of choice in creating the universe. The traditional God would be made superfluous, but an evolving God might be made necessary.[15]

That such an objection should even be formulated reveals a profound metaphysical insensitivity to the abyss between mere possibility and actual existence. Even if it were proved—which it certainly has not been—that this was the only possible material universe (nothing, of course, could be said by science about other higher levels of spiritual existence), this would still leave our universe a merely possible plan, or model for a real universe. It would in no way necessarily entail that such a universe actually existed, endowed with power and energy, that the model or "essence" was *actually* instantiated in the real order. Actual existence is a wholly different order from mere possibility, no matter how beautifully intelligible the latter may be in itself. The essential insight here is that there is nothing in the intelligible plan, model, or "essence" (essential structure) of our universe that demands or prescribes its own actual existence-with-energy. There is nothing

15. Frank J. Tipler, "The Omega Point Theory: A Model of an Evolving God," in the Symposium *Physics, Philosophy, and Theology* (see initial note), 313–14.

in its laws that prescribes that they must be instantiated. In fact, no determinate model, especially a mathematical one, can ever specify its own instantiation. It is merely a formal structure of relations of laws, properties, and so on, which of itself is timeless and unmoving. It cannot *do* anything actually, cannot deploy the energy its laws regulate. In short, our universe is radically contingent: it can exist (because it does) but cannot ground or explain its own actual active presence. Stephen Hawking, the great British physicist, seems to have a keen sense of this point in his best-selling book, *A Brief History of Time*, when he remarks:

Even if there is only one possible unified theory, it is just a set of rules and equations. What is it that breathes fire into the equations and makes a universe for them to describe? The usual approach of science of constructing a mathematical model cannot answer the questions of why there should be a universe for them to describe. Why does the universe go to all the bother of existing? Is the unified field theory so compelling that it brings about its own existence? Or does it need a creator, and if so, does he have any other effect on the universe? And who created him?[16]

Well said! (except for the last question, which we have already taken care of). What is needed to close this gap between possibility and actuality is some cause that is already firmly planted in actual existence and can confer it on others, in fact—to avoid an infinite regress—one that does not just *have* existence as a sheer brute fact but one for whom actual existence is a part of its very essence, whose very essence *is* the fontal plenitude of actual power-filled existence itself, an existent self-explanatory of its own existence. But this is precisely for St. Thomas the proper philosophical name of God, Subsistent Existence itself (*Ipsum Esse Subsistens*), interpreting the biblical name of God given to Moses, "I am Who am." This must be ultimately the actualizing-energizing cause of all whose essence is not identical with existence

16. Stephen Hawking, *A Brief History of Time* (New York: Bantam, 1988), 174. In the light of this text I find it a step backward and hardly consistent to read his earlier enigmatic statement: ". . . the quantum theory of gravity has opened up a new possibility, in which there would be no boundary to space-time . . . no singularities at which the laws of science broke down and no edge of space-time at which one would have to appeal to God or some new law to set the boundary conditions for space-time. One could say, 'The boundary condition of the universe is that it has no boundary.' The universe would be completely self-contained and not affected by anything outside itself. It would neither be created nor destroyed. It would just BE" (136). If he means only that the universe need not have had a beginning in space-time, this, though controversial, can be acceptable philosophically. But if he means that our material universe, determinate in structure and energy though it be, is totally self-sufficient for its own existence in this mode, this does not follow from the scientific hypothesis at all and stops short of the radical question of why it should exist at all.

itself. And such a cause, since it is the very source of all possible modes of real perfection, cannot but be unique and beyond all limitation.

The same argument would hold against the other leading claim, inspired by scientific speculation, that no higher cause is needed to choose this universe out of other possible ones. According to this hypothesis, at the moment of the Big Bang, an infinite number of *all possible* universes blew out like bubbles from the initial energy point, each independent of and not communicating with the others. Since *all* possible universes actually exist, there is no need of any higher cause to choose between them, hence no God is needed. But here again the objection starts too late, with all the universes *already existing.* The question still arises, Why should any of them at all actually exist? Just because they are possible in no way grounds or necessitates that they are actually present with built-in energy. They cannot of themselves cross the abyss between possibility and actuality. A self-existent, actualizing-energizing source transcending them all is needed. In a word, our universe is contingent in its very being, and can never be self-explanatory.

Note that none of our arguments above is built on the supposition of a beginning of our universe in space and time, but only on the actual existence of some limited determinate system of active beings. Contrary to common belief, a beginning in time is not the only reason—in fact not even the principal one—why our material universe needs a transcendent, self-existent Ultimate Cause. The question whether something is self-explanatory of its own existence is not answered by asserting that it has always existed. An eternally dependent universe is no less dependent just because it has always been around.

IV. Argument from Order in the World

This ancient argument from order or design in the world, now more commonly known as the teleological argument (teleology = activity ordered towards an end), St. Thomas calls the most widespread and most efficacious path to God (*via efficacissima*) for all peoples, in all times and all cultures. And I think he is right. Such an argument, however, needs special adaptation to be effective in the light of contemporary science, both evolutionary and cosmological. In the brief space at my disposal let me indicate how I think it can be adapted.

One classic form of the argument, sketched by St. Thomas in his Fifth Way, argues from the regular action of natural agents producing their effects (unless hindered) to a dynamic orientation built in to their natures.[17] The reason is that such regularly repeated action cannot

---

17. *Summa Theologiae*, I, q. 2, art. 3.

be the result of mere chance. All chance, in fact, must be built upon some matrix of built-in, regularly acting natural properties, or nothing will happen at all. But such a built-in dynamic orientation toward a not-yet-existent future effect requires making this not-yet-existing future present as a guide or focus in the very structuring of the nature toward action. And such making the future present, or taking into account a not-yet-existing future, can only be the work of a mind ordering means to a possible future effect through a creative idea. Hence the ordered activity of nonrational nature must at least ultimately be the work of a creative Ordering Mind transcending nature itself.

This argument, I believe, is a sound one in itself. But it runs into complications when applied to the evolutionary development of living organisms (a fact unknown to the originators of the argument), because of the large interweaving of chance involved, as we see the process today—although it is now well known that the original Darwinian hypothesis of evolution by pure random selection and survival of the fittest has proved to be seriously, if not irretrievably, flawed. It is wiser today to restrict the argument to the great underlying physico-chemical laws of the universe that in fact remain stable throughout all the evolutionary development of living organisms, as the necessary permanent matrix of order upon which the latter build. For unless there were some basic ordering of the fundamental active elements of the universe to interact with each other in some definite ways, nothing would ever happen; they would simply pass by or through each other like ships in the night, uncommunicating, with no interactions at all. There would be no foundation for chance itself to work on, since chance is always parasitic on some stable properties of several different items in order to start off its calculus of probable interactions. Furthermore, unless this basic matrix of physico-chemical laws were stable, it would be impossible for living organisms to learn from experience. They must lean on the stable to build the new.

I would like now to present what I think is a more powerful adaptation of the argument, fitting more closely the way we understand nature today. (St. Thomas himself did indeed lay down the basic principle, namely, that when many nonrational agents cooperate together to form a single world order, some unifying mind must be the source of this ordered system. But he developed it differently in detail, applying it only to the relations between species and levels of being [e.g., plants and animals, not the basic physical elements themselves]).[18] My form of the argument runs thus:

18. Some samples are *Summa contra Gentes,* bk. I, ch. 13, no. 35; ch. 42, no. 7; *De*

Take any dynamically ordered system of active elements, such as our own material cosmos, such that the various constitutive elements are ordered toward regular reciprocal interaction with each other. For example, all hydrogen atoms are ordered towards combination with all oxygen atoms in the fixed proportion of 2 to 1, whereas all oxygen atoms are in turn ordered towards all hydrogen atoms in the reciprocal proportion of 1 to 2, to form water (H_2O); the same holds for the fixed chemical valences of all atoms, the mutual gravitational attraction of all particles in the universe with mass, the strong force holding together the particles in the nucleus of atoms, electromagnetic laws, and so on—all of these laws combining to form a unified cosmos-wide order. Now in such a system, where each active element's basic properties (their natures, in metaphysical terms) are defined by relation to the others in the system, no one element can explain its own nature, be the sufficient reason for its own active nature as existing and operating, unless it is also the sufficient reason for all the others reciprocally related to it. But this is impossible. For then this element would have to be both prior (in causal, not necessarily temporal priority) in its activity to the others and responsible for them, and at the same time presuppose them, since its active properties are all ordered to interaction with them according to law. It would thus in its very nature as active presuppose the others as reciprocally constituted in relation to itself, and yet be independent of and responsible for these correlated properties in others by which its own active nature is defined. Clearly this will not work.

Such a cosmos-wide order, therefore, is one in which many are brought together under the unity of great overarching laws of mutual interaction. But such cosmos-wide order, which is a form of unity, can have its ultimate sufficient reason, its intelligible grounding, only in some cosmos-wide unifying cause, capable of thus ordering many active agents into the unity of one order. Such a unifying, ordering agent, which is needed to set up the system-wide unity of reciprocal interactions of the multiple elements of the system, can only be a Mind.[19]

There are two reasons for this, closely intertwined but helpful to

---

Potentia, q. 3, art. 6. For an analysis of all Aquinas's arguments to God from finality and order, see Leszek Figurski, *Finality and Intelligence* (Lanham, Md.: University Press of America, 1979), chap. 6.

19. Charles Hartshorne develops well a similar argument, using the felicitous phrase, "a cosmic-wide order needs a cosmic-wide orderer," *A Natural Theology for Our Time* (LaSalle, Ill.: Open Court, 1967), 58–62, and in other later versions of the same—for which cf. Donald Viner, *Charles Hartshorne and the Existence of God* (Albany: SUNY Press, 1985), chap. 6, "The Design Argument."

distinguish. (1) These overarching laws of reciprocal interaction are each a one-over-many, gathering many different elements into an intelligible unity that is system-wide, yet without collapsing together the real distinctness and separation in space and time of each element. This is a space-and-time-transcending unity that can only be constituted by an idea—which in turn can only be generated by a mind. Such a unity of many in one, leaving intact the distinction of each, is almost a definition of an idea.

(2) The ordering of the natural properties of these elements towards dynamic interaction must be constituted prior (priority of causal dependence, not necessarily temporal priority) to their actual operations of interacting, since they interact according to their (already constituted) natures. But this means that they must be ordered toward, constituted in view of, not yet existing future actions, or possible future actions. Now only a mind can constitute out of possibility a future order, can "order means to an end," as St. Thomas likes to put it. Only a mind can thus make present in its field of consciousness the future and the possible, which do not exist in themselves and can have only a mental presence. A purely material being without consciousness is locked into the here and now of its place in space and time. To order possibilities with a view to future action is again almost a definition of mind, or certainly one of its most characteristic functions. Thus the cosmos-wide dynamic order of our world system necessarily requires a cosmos-ordering Mind to constitute its order.

It follows by immediate inference that such a Mind must transcend the system that it has constituted, that is, not be dependent on the system itself for its own existence and operation. For if it did thus depend, it could not exist or operate unless the system were already set up and operating, whereas in fact the system itself cannot exist or operate unless the ordering Mind has already set it up. Both the Mind and the system, then, would have to be both prior and posterior (in the order of dependence) to each other at the same time. This is obviously a contradiction. Hence the world-ordering Mind must be outside of, or transcending, this cosmos of ours that it has constituted. To sum it up, the last word about this or any cosmos must always be (to paraphrase philosophically the beginning of St. John's Gospel): "In the beginning was the Word." Before all action, there must always be the inner word, the creative thought, the *Logos*.

Theoretically speaking, of course, to complete the search for the intelligibility of the universe, we must raise the further question whether the Mind we have discovered as the ground of the universe's order is one or many, finite or infinite. Recourse must be had here once again to the earlier—and, in the last analysis, indispensable—argument from finitude to one Infinite Source of all being (second and third steps of Argument I). But it should be noted that even without taking this last step explicitly, we have already reached a Transcendent Reality upon which our whole cosmos and ourselves within it depend for our very natures. This already gives a sufficient basis for a basic religious attitude of gratitude, reverence, love, and obedience toward the Author of our nature and destiny. This is enough for the ordinary nonphilosophical person, who probably makes the leap to a single Infinite Source implicitly and spontaneously. At any rate, we are already out of the world of the secularist and the materialist into the religious.

The beauty of this argument is that it works for any basic dynamic order in our or any universe whatever. For without some primal ordering of the basic elements in a system to mutual interaction, prior to their actual operation, nothing would happen at all, not even by chance. There simply would not be a world at all.

Does this argument lose its power when set in the context of current discussions of theoretical physics and cosmology, all of which are attempting to reduce the present complex order to an original simpler order, or possibly to some absolutely simple primal state? Thus some speculate that our present cosmos came about as a chance fluctuation in a primal quantum energy field or high energy "vacuum." This does shift the ground of the argument significantly, and one must think hard about its implications.

But it seems to me that the argument still holds firm. For no matter how simple the original energy state may be, it does evolve into, or give rise to, a system of determinate active elements that exhibit a built-in dynamic orientation to combine together in mutual interaction in regular determinate ways to form an ordered system. Some prior dynamic orientation must have existed within the original energy state to thus evolve into determinate dynamic order. Otherwise the latter would arise with no intelligible grounding in anything prior at all, as a sheer brute fact in total discontinuity with what precedes it, as totally unintelligible, with no sufficient reason whatever. This is not an explanation at all, but an intellectual cop-out. Note, too, that even if the particular cosmic order that emerges from the original simple energy state emerges purely by chance—which is highly controversial—it still remains that any ordered system whatever would have to be internally ordered within itself if any reciprocal interaction is to take place within it, if it is to be a determinate cosmic order at all. And therefore an ordering Mind would have to be somewhere at the origin of the unity of its order. It seems, then, that the principle of the Argument from Order holds firm: any determinate dynamic order at all, whether primal in itself or originating from some previous physical energy state, must be grounded ultimately in an ordering Mind transcending the system itself.

With regard to the evolutionary development of living organisms, let me add: No matter how much chance there may be in the external conditions of the environment that these organisms exploit to evolve, what remains as the essential prior condition for the whole process is the built-in *inner dynamism*, the unflagging *dynamic drive* of the organisms toward interacting in determinate ways with the other agents in the universe around it, toward actively exploiting the opportunities offered them by chance. This innate positive drive to survive, to act, to interact, cannot be supplied by any chance exterior conditions. It must be built in to the active potentialities (or dispositional properties) of the very natures of the organisms, prestructured from the beginning to interact with other natural agents in some basic determinate ways. It is this innate drive that is not supplied by evolutionary theory, but must ultimately be predetermined by some creative ordering Mind, the only power that can transpose intelligible possibilities from creative idea into actual entities endowed with focused energy.[20]

V. Derivation of the Divine Attributes

Since it is impossible to condense a whole course in natural theology into this one paper,[21] let me sketch out with extreme brevity the general procedure for determining which attributes (or predicates) can legitimately be applied to the God we have discovered at the term of our quest for the intelligibility of our universe: one single, self-existent Source of all being, endowed with the infinite qualitative fullness of all possible perfection.

Two basic principles are involved. One is a corollary of the nature of efficient causality—understood, of course, in its active productive ontological sense, not as mere Humean succession with predictability.

20. For some recent attempts to build on the enormous statistical improbability of the passage from a nonliving molecule to a living cell as a basis for an argument to the need of an outside cause, see L. J. Betty and B. Cordell, "God and Modern Science: New Life for the Teleological Argument" (cited in note 3), and *The Mystery of Life's Origins* (cited in note 6). Despite their suasiveness, however, I am reluctant to recognize this as a cogent argument in view of the new Chaos theories of Prigogine and others, according to which conditions of apparently chaotic high turbulence can give rise to unpredictable new forms on a higher level. See Arthur Peacocke, *God and the New Biology* (New York: Harper and Row, 1986), 63–64.

21. I develop this whole theme of the divine attributes at greater length in chap. 2 of my *The Philosophical Approach to God.*

This is the similitude that must exist in at least some analogous way between an effect and its cause. For, since the effect as effect receives its being from its cause, and the cause cannot give what it does not possess at least in some higher equivalent way, there must be some bond of real similitude between them. This can then serve as the bridge by which we can link our knowledge of the effect with what we can affirm of the cause.

The second principle is that we cannot without further analysis transfer any attribute found in the effect directly and literally to its cause. In the case of God, for example, any attribute (or predicate) containing in its very meaning some limit or imperfection must be winnowed out as implying some contradiction if literally applied to God—this is what St. Thomas calls "the negative moment" in the process. The attribute in question must be reduced to some broader, more universal one that is purely positive in its meaning, containing no limits or imperfections in the core meaning of the term, including the lower limited attribute as only one of its limited modes or degrees, and calling for our unqualified approval, such that were God to lack it, He-She would be less perfect than we are. Thus visual power in a creature would be transposed into knowledge in God, and so on. A small number of basic attributes survive this purification process and can be applied literally, though analogously, to God, with the index of infinity added.

Such viable attributes turn out to be a small number of basic ones, like existence, unity, activity-power, goodness, intelligence, will, love, and a few others derived from these. A central one would be God as supremely personal being, although we could not philosophically derive the intersubjectivity within God (God as Triune). This derivation procedure is not a simple logical, deductive one, but a very delicate one, requiring careful reflection as to what we truly value with unqualified approval. We can and must affirm these as necessarily true of God, that is, we must affirm that He-She possesses them in an infinite way, while at the same time we recognize that just *how* God possesses them (His own proper essence or mode of being) is totally beyond the grasp of our abstract concepts. As St. Thomas tells us, constantly insisting on the unknowability of the divine essence in itself, we know "*that* God is intelligent, but not *how.*" Our own natural dynamism of intellect and will toward the Infinite must be brought into the process here; for it illumines obscurely but richly this mystery-shrouded essence of God by a certain "connatural affinity" with Him (St. Thomas) as His lovingly created images, that is, by a "knowledge of the heart" (Pascal) through longing and love, as magnetized in the depths of our being by this Infinite Good that is our final End—a "knowledge" through longing and love, I repeat, not through vision—at least in this life.

Let me point out, finally—a point too often overlooked in discussions of the divine attributes and the difficulty of knowing the divine essence—that there is one thing that we do know with absolute precision about this mysterious Ultimate Reality: that it is Number One on the scale of value of any and all positive attributes, and alone there, the unique supremely perfect one in any line of perfection. But is not this all we really need to know in order to give it, without reservation, the fullness of our religious adoration, reverence, love, trusting commitment, and so forth? As long as we know this being is the Number One in wisdom, power, love, and so on, and therefore uniquely worthy of our religious worship, do we really need to know just how our God exercises his various attributes? Do we really need a do-it-yourself kit for the divine attributes? What we do know is something of supreme importance for the meaning of our lives, something we do not know of any other being in the universe (in fact, we know it cannot be true of any other). It seems to me this is to have found the pearl of great price, which is more than enough for the truly religious person in quest of final meaning for his or her life.

Let me conclude by suggesting as a fascinating task-challenge-opportunity for natural theology today to speculate creatively and imaginatively as to what the "personality" or "character" must be like of a Creator in whose image this astonishing universe of ours is made, with its prodigal abundance of energy, its mind-boggling complexity yet simplicity, its fecundity of creative spontaneity, its ever-surprising fluid interweaving of order and chance, law and apparent chaos, and so forth. Must not the "personality" of such a Creator be charged not only with unfathomable wisdom, power, and exuberant generosity, but also with dazzling "imaginative" creativity—might we say a daring Cosmic Gambler who delights in working out his providence by a creative synthesis of both law and order, on the one hand, and chance, risk, spontaneity, on the other—a "coincidence of opposites," as St. Bonaventure put it long ago?[22]

22. See the very suggestive essay of Robert Russell, "Quantum Physics in Philosophical and Theological Perspective," in the collection *Physics, Philosophy, Theology: A Common Quest* (initial note above), 343–74, and also the considerably more daring essay in the same collection by Sally McFague, "Models of God for an Ecological, Evolutionary Era: God as Mother of the Universe," 249–710, based on her books, *Metaphorical Theology: Models of God in Religious Language* (Philadelphia: Fortress, 1982), and *Models of God: Theology for an Ecological, Nuclear Age* (same press, 1987). I think she goes too far,

To return now to the question with which we began: "Is a Natural Theology Still Viable Today?" I am prepared to answer with modest conviction that it certainly is, if one asks the right questions, the most radical ones about existence itself, and does not short-circuit the process by an arbitrarily restrictive epistemology or metaphysics, and gives full rein to the deep dynamism of the human mind in its quest for total intelligibility of the real.

Fordham University

---

however, in her metaphor of the universe as the "body" of God as Mother, where God combines in her one nature both matter and spirit, thus "overturning the dualism of body and mind, flesh and spirit . . . . an explicit rejection of Christianity's long and dangerous alliance with spirit against body, an alliance out of step with a holistic evolutionary sensibility, as well as with Christianity's Hebraic background" (260). The dispersal of parts outside of parts across space that seems essential to the notion of body as material seems to me incompatible with the infinite intensive unity and perfection proper to God as Infinite Spirit.

8   In Defense of a Kind of Natural Theology
BOWMAN CLARKE

That natural theology has been on something of a hopeless defensive since Hume's *Dialogues Concerning Natural Religion* and Kant's *Critique of Pure Reason* is something of a truism for most philosophers and theologians today. There are usually, I think, two assumptions made here by these philosophers and theologians. The first assumption is that the task of natural theology is to provide a demonstration for the existence of God, and the second assumption is that Hume and Kant have provided us with sound arguments that it is logically impossible to construct such a demonstration. If both of these assumptions are true, then natural theology simply becomes an impossible task. I want to look at the second assumption concerning Hume and Kant and then discuss the task of, at least, a kind of natural theology and the place of proofs for the existence of God. Later, I shall consider certain more contemporary attacks on natural theology and discuss them.

In the *Dialogues*, Hume puts into the mouth of Cleanthes what I take to be a Humean argument for the impossibility of a demonstration of the existence of God. The argument is actually stronger than that; the conclusion of the argument is that there is no conceivable being whose existence is demonstrable. The existence of God is only one possible application of the general argument. The argument rests on three premises:

(C1) "Nothing is demonstrable unless the contrary implies a contradiction."

(C2) "Nothing that is distinctly conceivable implies a contradiction."

(C3) "Whatever we conceive as existent, we can also conceive as nonexistent."[1]

From these three premises, it does follow that if we can conceive of

---

1. David Hume, *Dialogues Concerning Natural Religion*, ed. Henry D. Aiken (New York: Hafner, 1984), 58.

God, then we cannot demonstrate God's existence, or the existence of anything else for that matter. So, if Cleanthes's three premises are true, and if the task of natural theology is to demonstrate the existence of God, then natural theology is simply an impossible task.

Here I think it should be emphasized that the *Dialogues* is presenting an argument against any possible demonstration for the existence of God. After all, Hume and, as we shall see, his German cohort are philosophers, and philosophers tend to go for broke and concern themselves with all possible so and so's. I think we often overemphasize the attack on the design argument in the *Dialogues* and tend to push into the background the overall picture. The treatment of the design argument is designed to show that it is not a demonstration for the existence of God; in fact, Hume has the very proponent of the design argument himself, Cleanthes, be the one to present the argument that no demonstration for the existence of God is possible. The design argument, as such, gives us only a vague conjecture, or hypothesis, as a conclusion; as an argument, it is no more than what Peirce called an abduction. Thus, as Philo can conclude at the end of the dialogue, ". . . the whole of natural theology . . . resolves itself into one simple, though somewhat ambiguous, at least undefined proposition, *That the cause or causes of order in the universe probably bear some remote analogy to human intelligence.*"[2] It is significant, I think, that Philo goes on to say that if this proposition is "not capable of extension, variation, or more particular explication, and if it affords no inference that affects human life," then natural theology is really rather useless and we might as well flee to revelation.[3]

Returning to Cleanthes's three premises upon which the impossibility of demonstrating the existence of God rests, it is interesting to note here that he offers no justification whatsoever of any one of these three premises of his argument; they are simply asserted, I would guess, as obviously true. His premise (C2) appears harmless enough and appears to be no more than a way of giving a necessary condition for conceivability; that is, as lack of contradiction. Its purpose is to provide Hume with a way of connecting demonstrability in the first premise with conceivability in the third.

The first premise, (C1), however, is not quite so harmless. It results in an extremely limiting concept of demonstration. To illustrate what I have in mind, take a rather simple arithmetic sentence, 'If a is greater than b and b is greater than c, then a is greater than c,' where 'a,' 'b,' and 'c' refer to three unspecified natural numbers. I think most of us

---

2. Ibid., 94.   3. Ibid., 94.

would take this sentence to be demonstrable in arithmetic no matter to what natural numbers 'a,' 'b,' and 'c' referred, but negate that sentence and show wherein lies the contradiction. If we negate the sentence, we merely have, 'a is greater than b and b is greater than c and it is not the case that a is greater than c.' What is the p and not-p implied by this sentence? One can get a contradiction here only if one takes the negation of our sentence in conjunction with the accepted axioms of arithmetic. The sentence implies a contradiction only within a theoretical context of which certain axioms are a component.

This situation is due to the fact that "is greater than" is a relation, and the demonstrability of the above sentence rests on the properties of that relation. Relational properties in a system ultimately rest on axioms and, it is relatively safe to say, the negation of no mathematical axiom will produce a contradiction. If it would, that axiom would be demonstrable by the sentential logic and would not need to be taken as an axiom. If we accept Hume's narrow necessary condition for demonstration at face value and unqualified—and one can use the term *demonstration* anyway one wishes—we must face the fact that we have eliminated demonstration from most of mathematics, particularly the more useful and interesting parts.

It is the third of Cleanthes's premises, (C3), however, that turns out to be an extremely strong and limiting statement. Let us think of conceivability in terms of the modal notion of possibility; this certainly appears safe enough in the light of premise (C2), where the necessary condition for conceivability is not implying a contradiction. Using this modal translation, we have for number three, 'P $(\exists x)Qx \supset$ P $\sim (\exists x)Qx$,' where 'Q' can be any predicate whatsoever. Now, given the standard modal definitions, that sentence is logically equivalent to 'N$(\exists x)Qx \supset$ I $(\exists x)Qx$,' which is merely the bold assertion that no individual necessarily exists. And if one reads Cleanthes's third premise carefully, one can see that it simply asserts that there is no such thing as a necessarily existing individual. In short, all individuals are contingent individuals; it is a principle of universal contingency. Given the standard definition for 'It is contingent that . . . ,' Cleanthes's third premise is also logically equivalent to 'P$(\exists x)Qx \supset$ C$(\exists x)Qx$,' in short, it limits all possible existing individuals to contingently existing individuals. As we have seen, all the first and second premises in Cleanthes's argument do is to connect the conceivability of the nonexistence of an individual, as asserted in the third, to the impossibility of demonstration, in the narrow sense of demonstration that is characterized in the first premise. Before we consider the questionable nature of Cleanthes's first and third premises, let us first examine

Kant's argument for the impossibility of demonstrating the existence of God, for I think we have the same principle of universal contingency there and the same narrow notion of demonstration.

Kant, being a German rather than a Scotsman, does not give us as nice and neat an argument as Hume does for the impossibility of demonstrating or, in his case, proving the existence of God. Kant's argument is far more elaborate, but I think that it boils down to essentially the same argument as the one presented so tersely by Cleanthes. Kant begins by arguing that there are only three possible kinds of proofs for the existence of God, a physico-theological, a cosmological, and an ontological. "There are, and there can be no others,"[4] he writes. He then argues that a physico-theological proof depends upon a cosmological, which in turn depends upon an ontological proof. The reason for this dependence is that only a being "the non-existence of which is impossible,"[5] the being of the ontological proof, could serve as the being that the other two kinds of proofs seek. Now, he asserts, "in the absence of contradiction I have . . . no criterion of impossibility."[6] Thus, analogous to Cleanthes's first premise taken in application to God, we can paraphrase Kant in this way:

(K1) The existence of God is provable, only if the nonexistence of God implies a contradiction.

This is merely an instantiation of Cleanthes, (C1), to God.

Kant has an analog for Cleanthes's principle of universal contingency, or (C3), also. He, for example, writes, "whatever it may be that exists, nothing prevents me from thinking its non-existence."[7] His counterpart of Cleanthes's (C2) is, ". . . in the absence of contradiction I have . . . no criterion of impossibility."[8] Usually, however, Kant combines both Cleanthes's premises (C2) and (C3), connecting the principles of contingency directly to the principle of contradiction. We have him telling us, for example, "If its (the concept of a thing's) existence is rejected, we reject the thing itself with all its predicates; and no question of contradiction can then arise."[9] Again, he writes, "I cannot form the least concept of a thing which, should it be rejected with all its predicates, leaves behind a contradiction."[10] Let us then formulate a premise, (K2), that is an analogue of Cleanthes's (C2) and (C3):

4. Immanuel Kant, *Critique of Pure Reason,* trans. Norman Kemp Smith (London: Macmillan, 1963), 500.

5. Ibid., 501.   6. Ibid., 503.

7. Ibid., 515.   8. Ibid., 503.

9. Ibid., 502.   10. Ibid., 503.

(K2) I cannot form the concept of a thing the nonexistence of which implies a contradiction.

Kant's premises (K1) and (K2) give us the same conclusion as (C1)–(C3). Both arguments rest on the principle of universal contingency and the narrow sense of demonstration or provability.

I do not think Kant gives any more of an argument in justification of his premises, (K1) and (K2), than does Cleanthes his (C1)–(C3). In fact, in speaking of his (K2), Kant says such things as "every one must concur"[11] or "as every reasonable person must admit."[12] Kant does, however, attempt to help you see that it is true. For example, he writes, "If in an identical proposition, I reject the predicate while retaining the subject, contradiction results."[13] Suppose, for example, we define 'x is a bachelor' as 'x is an adult, unmarried male,' then we have something like 'Bx $= (Ax \cdot Ux \cdot Mx).$' If we reject the predicate, 'Ax $\cdot Ux \cdot Mx,$' and keep the subject, 'Bx,' we get, he says, a contradiction, something like 'Bx $=$ not Bx.' "But," Kant continues, "if we reject subject and predicate alike, there is no contradiction; for nothing is then left that can be contradicted."[14] In other words, we merely have 'not Bx $=$ not $(Ax \cdot Ux \cdot Mx),$' which is no more than 'not Bx $=$ not Bx.' This Kant then ties into the positing and rejecting of existence, "If its existence is rejected," he tells us, "we reject the thing itself with all its predicates; and no question of contradiction can then arise."[15] In short, this would be analogous to 'not Bx $=$ not $(Ax \cdot Ux \cdot Mx)$' above, which we saw is no more than 'not Bx $=$ not Bx.' In short, to say 'There are no bachelors' is merely to say 'There are no adult, unmarried males.' There is no contradiction here.

Although Kant's logical machinery here is somewhat primitive, given contemporary advances, and his discussion somewhat clumsy, it is relatively easy, I think, to see what he is doing. All concepts (or ideas) can be analyzed into components, much as I suggested for 'bachelor' above, and these, again, ultimately into simples. Now since all ideas, or concepts, are so analyzable, Kant's above treatment of concepts and contradiction should be universally applicable to all possible concepts, and once we see this, we see the truth of his (K2) and Cleanthes's third premise, (C3).

This notion of the analysis into simples, which has been the subject of such widespread attack in more recent years, appears to have been shared with him by Hume, Locke, Descartes, and Leibniz. It was a

11. Ibid., 503. 12. Ibid., 504.
13. Ibid., 502. 14. Ibid., 502.
15. Ibid., 502.

belief that spread across the great empiricist/rationalist divide; their differences here lay primarily in the nature of the simples, not in the fact of the analysis into simples. It is easy for us now to see why both Hume and Kant readily accept Cleanthes's third premise. Had Hume felt called upon to give a justification of Cleanthes's third premise, no doubt he would have said somewhat the same thing as Kant did above. The "intuitive" pull of Cleanthes's third premise, (C3), and Kant's (K2) apparently lies in the acceptance of the analysis of all ideas, or concepts, into simple components.

So far I have not even mentioned the problem as to whether or not existence is a determining predicate, which usually gets the brunt of attention in most of the discussions of the proofs for the existence of God in the first *Critique*. I so far have tried to avoid mentioning this discussion, for I feel that the emphasis usually given to these few pages in the chapter on "The Ideal of Pure Reason" tends to push into the background what is really going on in that chapter.

It is interesting to note how Kant introduces this problem. He has just stated his principle, which I quoted earlier, "I cannot form the least concept of a thing which, should it be rejected with all its predicates, leaves behind a contradiction." He then writes, "Notwithstanding all these general conditions, in which everyone must concur, we may be challenged with a case which is brought forward as proof that in actual fact the contrary holds."[16] In short, even though (K2) is something "in which everyone must concur," there is a possible counterexample. This challenging possible counterexample to Kant's general principle, (K2), is, to use his own term, the *ens realissimum,* a term that is his definite description for the ideal of pure reason and that he takes to be a definite description for God. The concept of this particular individual is fully determined in this way, "if all the possible predicates of things be taken together with their contradictory opposites, then one of each pair of contradictory opposites must belong to it."[17] As he goes on to explain, of course, negative predicates are "derivative" of some positive predicate, and it is all the possible positive predicates that are taken in the determination of the concept of the *ens realissimum,* which becomes "the sum total of all possibility."[18]

The proof for the existence of the *ens realissimum* goes, Kant tells us, something like this:

It is declared that it possesses all reality, and that we are justified in assuming that such a being is possible . . . . Now [the argument proceeds] 'all reality'

16. Ibid., 503.   17. Ibid., 488.
18. Ibid., 488.

includes existence; existence is therefore contained in the concept of a thing that is possible. If, then, this thing is rejected, the internal possibility of the thing is rejected—which is self-contradictory.[19]

In the light of the kind of analysis Kant used to justify his general principle, (K2), it is difficult to know exactly wherein lies the self-contradiction here. The proposer of this counterexample of the *ens realissimum* seems to be saying something like this: 'x is God = (x is omnipotent. x is good . . . . . x exists).' Now Kant could not be talking about the contradiction resulting from holding to the subject and rejecting the predicate as before. When he says in the above quote, "If, then, this thing is rejected," he must mean "If, then, the *existence* of this thing is rejected, the internal possibility of the thing is rejected." It is the nonexistence of the thing that is supposed to produce the contradiction anyway. Accepting this alteration in Kant's above statement, the rejection of the existence of the thing would be the rejection of one of its determining predicates and thus make it an impossible thing. Kant goes out of his way in granting that the counterexample, the *ens realissimum,* is a possible thing. The contradiction must consist in making it both a possible and an impossible thing. And this appears to fit what Kant says in the above quote about the contradiction resulting from rejecting the internal possibility of a possible thing.

Whatever it is that constitutes the contradiction here, from Kant's remark at the end of his discussion about "the famous ontological argument of Descartes,"[20] one is safe in assuming that this is Kant's interpretation of what Descartes was saying in his Fourth Meditation. Every philosophy major, of course, knows Kant's response to this apparent exception to his general principle, (K2): it is an "illusion caused by the confusion of a logical with a real predicate."[21] Existence is a "logical" predicate and not a "real" predicate, "that is, a predicate which determines a thing."[22] Consequently, "x exists" cannot not occur alongside "x is omnipotent," "x is good," and so forth in the determining concept of "x is God" as above. In terms of the determination of the concept of the *ens realissimum,* 'existence' and its negation cannot be among the pairs of contradictory predicates from which we can choose in determining it. With that, the contradiction vanishes and this possible counterexample to Kant's principle, (K2), and Cleanthes's third premise, disappears.

I have labored Cleanthes's short argument and Kant's discussion at some length in an effort to see exactly what Hume in the *Dialogues*

19. Ibid., 503.
21. Ibid., 504.
20. Ibid., 507.
22. Ibid., 504.

and Kant in the first *Critique* have done. They have shown no more than this: If you accept (1) their limited necessary condition for a demonstration, or proof, in connection with the existence of God and (2) their principle of the universal contingency of existence, either (C3) or (K2), then a demonstration or a proof for the existence of God is impossible. If then you accept (3) that the primary task of natural theology is to provide a demonstration, or proof, of the existence of God in their sense, then natural theology is impossible. But this, I think, is all that we can say that Hume and Kant have shown. I have mentioned that Hume's and Kant's notion of a demonstration, or proof, is a very narrow one, and that the "intuitive" basis for universal contingency lies in the analysis of ideas, or concepts, into simples, a most questionable notion and one which, I think, serves also as the basis for the narrow notion of demonstration. I want now to consider the primary task of natural theology.

I seriously think that very few, if any philosophers or theologians, who considered themselves doing natural, or philosophical, theology, ever thought of their primary task as that of showing that the negation of the sentence, 'God exists,' produces a contradiction. There are, though, different interpretations of the task of natural theology, or philosophical theology if one prefers the term, and that is why I have entitled this paper, "A Defense of a Kind of Natural Theology." It is a kind of a natural theology that sees as its primary task, first, the task of providing a definite description in order to answer the question "Who is God?" and, second, to provide that definite description within a particular philosophical framework. In short, it is to face the question Moses faced in the presence of the burning bush, "Whom shall I say sent me?" and to answer that question within a particular philosophical framework.

Let me spell out better what I mean by a philosophical framework. Whitehead begins *Process and Reality* with this: "Speculative Philosophy is the endeavor to frame a coherent, logical, necessary system of general ideas in terms of which every element of our experience can be interpreted."[23] You may call this 'speculative philosophy,' 'metaphysics,' 'revisionary metaphysics,' 'systematic philosophy' in contrast to 'edifying philosophy,' or what you will; it is the task and its goal in which I am interested, and by a philosophical framework, I mean such a general scheme of ideas.

Whitehead spells out this philosophic task further by explaining what he means by the phrase, "in terms of which every element of

23. A. N. Whitehead, *Process and Reality* (New York: Macmillan, 1929), 4.

our experience can be interpreted." He writes, "I mean that everything of which we are conscious, as enjoyed, perceived, willed, or thought shall have the character of a particular instance of the general scheme."[24] This all-comprehensive and universal character of the general scheme, or framework, of ideas gives rise to two more important adjectives, 'applicable,' it applies to something, and 'adequate,' there is nothing in experience that does not find its niche in the framework or is not a particular instance of the general scheme. In the scheme's comprehensiveness, or applicability and adequacy, is also found its necessity. The necessity characterizing this sought-for scheme is not a logical necessity; it is its universal applicability. "The metaphysical first principles can never fail of exemplification," he writes. "We can never catch the actual world taking a holiday from their sway."[25]

Let us now return to the theological problem. Now it is an obvious fact that the same individual can be known under, or referred to by, many different definite descriptions, as well as different names. As for names, God tells Moses that he has been known as Elohim, El Shaddai, and Yahweh. Also, as for definite descriptions, he has been referred to with 'the maker of heaven and earth,' 'the god of Abraham, Isaac, and Jacob,' 'the father of our Lord Jesus Christ,' 'the unknowable,' and 'the *ens realissimum*,' all of which are definite descriptions. If one is doing natural, or philosophical, theology, however, the task is to provide an answer to the question, "Who is God?" within a philosophical framework. It is not to prove that God exists, as such, but to say who God is within that philosophical framework by providing a definite description for God in the language of that philosophical framework. Now insofar as a proof of existence is given, it is no more than a demonstration that the framework requires the individual characterized by the definite description. In the history of western philosophy and theology the list of such definite descriptions is legion. They begin with 'the world soul' and 'the prime mover' and go through 'the One,' 'that than which nothing greater can be conceived,' or 'the greatest conceivable,' and 'the first efficient cause' and on up to 'the ground of being,' and including 'the *ens realissimum*.' In all cases, though, these definite descriptions belong to a particular philosophical framework and, I would argue, cannot be torn out of that framework.

Let me go to the history of natural, or philosophical, theology in order to illustrate what I am suggesting here and also to show that my proposed notion of natural theology is not something radically new or nontraditional. In his first way of demonstrating the existence

24. Ibid., 4.   25. Ibid., 9.

of God, St. Thomas in the *Summa Theologica* (I, q. 2, a. 3) tells us that "It is certain, and evident to our senses, that in this world some things are in motion."[26] And by 'motion,' or perhaps better, 'change'—since motion today usually means locomotion—the saint tells us that he means "the reduction of something from potency to act." He then goes on to characterize that relation: x is moved by y, as irreflexive, that is, nothing is moved by itself, and as transitive, and the field of the relation as finite, that is, given any sequence of movers and things moved, there is a first. St. Thomas then tells us that, due to these characteristics of that relation, x is moved by y, "it is necessary to arrive at a first mover which is moved by no other." In short, it is the Aristotelian characteristics of the relation, x is moved by y, that Thomas spells out and maintains demand that there be a first unmoved mover. Take the definite description 'the unmoved mover' outside that context and the meaning of the description changes and the demonstration may fail.

The situation here is perfectly analogous to the point I attempted to make with the sentence, "If a is greater than b and b is greater than c, then a is greater than c." The necessity and the demonstrability of it requires the context of its mathematical framework, and it cannot be taken outside that framework and negated and produce a contradiction. The same applies here. The medieval saint was quite aware of this. Plato, for example, had characterized motion quite differently from the way it is described above. Souls, for example, are characterized as self-movers, a denial that the relation, x is moved by y, is irreflexive as it is described above. Listen to what St. Thomas himself says in the *Summa Contra Gentiles* (I, 13, 10), when he gives a more detailed version of his demonstration from motion:

It is to be noted, however, that Plato, who held that every mover is moved, understood the name *motion* in a wider sense than Aristotle. For Aristotle understood motion strictly, according as it is the act of what exists in potency in as much as it is such. So understood, motion belongs only to divisible bodies, as it is proved in the *Physics*. According to Plato, however, that which moves itself is not a body. Plato understood by motion any given operation, so that *to understand* and *to judge* are a kind of motion.[27]

This is, I think, one of the more perceptive quotes in the history of natural theology. It is extremely contemporary and its implications are tremendous. Take the definite description, 'the first efficient cause.'

26. All quotations from the *Summa Theologica* come from the Anton C. Pegis edition (New York: Modern Library, 1948).
27. All quotations from the *Summa Contra Gentiles* come from the Anton C. Pegis edition, *On the Truth of the Catholic Faith* (Garden City, N.J.: Doubleday, 1958).

Unless 'efficient cause' is understood in Aristotle's and St. Thomas's sense, the definite description, 'the first efficient cause,' changes and the proof very likely collapses. The situation here is precisely analogous to the one I pointed out with mathematics in discussing Hume's notion of demonstration.

This problem of taking definite descriptions for God and proofs for the existence of God outside their philosophical frameworks plagues most seventeenth-century philosophy. In Part IX of his *Dialogues,* for example, Hume has Cleanthes say, in speaking of the notion of a cause and its use in a proof for God: "that relation implies a priority in time and a beginning in existence."[28] In other words, temporal priority and a beginning of its existence is a necessary condition for something's being a cause. Now there is nothing in St. Thomas's use of the term 'efficient cause' that entails priority in time to the effect or contingency. Hume, and probably most modern and contemporary philosophers, are simply not using the term 'cause' in the sense in which St. Thomas used it.

This emphasis upon the context of a philosophical framework that I have used to argue against the supposedly mortal blow Hume and Kant struck to destroy natural theology has brought forth another, far more contemporary, criticism of the task of natural theology. The Humean and Kantian notion of the analysis of concepts, or ideas, into simples culminated in Wittgenstein's *Tractatus,*[29] and their tie to simples of sensation in Carnap's *Logical Structure of the World.*[30] These together became the early backbone of Logical Positivism and culminated, in the early half of this century, in a charge of meaninglessness for all discourse about the divinity, a position popularized by A. J. Ayer's *Language, Truth and Logic.*[31] The early attack upon this tradition in Quine's *Two Dogmas of Empiricism*[32] and its softening by Carnap's Principle of Tolerance and Wittgenstein's Language Games have resulted, in the later half of this century, in talk of "a web of belief," "holism," "conceptual frameworks," "contextualism," "theory-ladenness," and the like. In short, the view of natural theology, as I have explicated it, ought to be not only a possible but a very acceptable task. The new criticism not only essentially accepts the fact that natural

28. Hume, cited above, 59.
29. Ludwig Wittgenstein, *The Tractatus-Logico Philosophicus,* trans. D. F. Pears and B. F. McGuinness (London: Routledge, 1961).
30. Rudolph Carnap, *The Logical Structure of the World and Pseudoproblems in Philosophy,* trans. Rolf A. George (Berkeley, Cal.: University of California Press, 1967).
31. A. J. Ayer, *Language, Truth and Logic,* 2d ed. (London: Gollancz, 1946).
32. Willard Van Orman Quine, "Two Dogmas of Empiricism," *Philosophical Review,* LX (1951), 20–43.

theology, as I have characterized it, is a logically possible task and one that could result in meaningful talk, but it asserts that natural theology simply becomes a far too easy task.

This criticism I have in mind focuses on precisely what we saw St. Thomas doing in our quote from the *Summa Contra Gentiles*. These critics see history as a parade of philosophical frameworks in which we might do natural theology, provide our definite descriptions, construct our demonstrations, and what else we wish. The question that arises, though, is, On what basis does St. Thomas, or do we for that matter, choose Aristotle's framework over Plato's, or any one of the plethora of possible frameworks over the others. They would argue that we have no "objective" or "trans-historical" position from which we can view this historical parade and choose one over the others. It was once thought by some that what we can and cannot say in ordinary language could serve as a canon, but ordinary language has come to be seen as a somewhat elastic ruler and, too, most of these historical frameworks have influenced the state of ordinary language. We appear to be left with no place to stand and no canon with which to judge.

I used Whitehead's characterization of speculative philosophy in my explication of the task of natural theology for a specific purpose. His characterization of the task of speculative philosophy provides within its characterization of its task the canons of its success: it must be logical, coherent, applicable, and adequate. And this is, I think, true of any task. The degree to which we are clear about a task is the degree to which we would know what it would be like to succeed in the task. If we are clear about what we are doing, the criteria of success are right there. And it is a common task that creates and holds together a community of investigators.

I did not argue for Whitehead's four criteria for judging philosophical frameworks, or his four canons of success; I merely wanted to show that they grow out of the conception of the task. I'm not sure what sorts of justifications could be given for the criteria. But it must be noted I am not focusing on any particular framework, but on the task of constructing a certain kind of framework, and I take the criteria to be a part of the definition of that task. What does someone say to a person who presents a different conception of a task? Merely that it is another task. The above criteria are used for judging alternative frameworks presented as fulfilling that particular task of philosophy.

I think that it is historically inaccurate to present the history of philosophy as a series of attempts to answer a set of everlastingly recurring questions, or problems, according to some transcendent view of rationality that pervades its history, as too many introductory texts do. Likewise, I do not see the task of what Whitehead called "speculative philosophy" as what Rorty might call "the essence of the task of systematic philosophy,"[33] that is, running throughout its history. On the other hand, I do not see the history of philosophy as a passing parade of possible incommensurable philosophical frameworks, each with its own criteria of evaluation. The truth, I take to lie between these two extreme alternatives. There are no trans-historical criteria for evaluating all historical philosophic systems; the criteria themselves have a history. On the other hand, the criteria are not limited to each system, making them incommensurable. The vision of the task and the criteria of success change, but they evolve out of the past and impose limitations on the future.

Take, for example, Whitehead's criterion of logicality. Logicality was, likewise, the criterion of a metaphysical system for Aristotle, but that term means something a little different for Whitehead, the co-author of *Principia Mathematica,* than it did for Aristotle. Logic itself has a history, but it is a history that can be traced with stages evolving from earlier stages. The same is true for the task of speculative philosophy. Whitehead's vision is likewise not Aristotle's, but Whitehead's vision has a history and that history can be traced back to Aristotle in much the same way as the history of the logic of *Principia Mathematica* can be traced back to Aristotle. In fact, I rather think it is true of any historical task that its vision and its criteria of success change as they become more spelled out in practice.

As another example, take Whitehead's criterion of coherence. Even though I consider myself to be a member of the community of investigators engaged in the Whiteheadian task of speculative philosophy, I am not quite clear exactly what it means. I think, from his examples, that it is a type of simplicity; but that, as we know today, is a many-splendored thing. The criterion is in need of a great deal of spelling out in practice, and this means more precise redefining of the task. There is no such thing as absolute clarity, rather we can only become clearer. That we all know clearly what we are engaged in and what our criteria of success would be is an assumption that has little evidence to support it. Spelling out further what coherence is will change the criteria of success, and it might split into two distinct criteria upon which there is disagreement. Members in a community of practitio-

---

33. See *ad passim* Richard Rorty, *Philosophy and the Mirror of Nature* (Princeton: Princeton University Press, 1979).

ners, for example, might move in different directions as the vision of the task and the criteria evolve, and when the strain over the criteria of success within the community reaches a certain point, it might be better to conceive of the group as engaged in two distinct tasks. Historically this does, I think, happen. There is nothing to stop people who want to be engaged in two distinct tasks; some people want to do philosophy, some people want to do physics and some people want to write poems.

There is another contemporary, and far more subtle, criticism of the task of natural theology as I have defined it, that is, the task of formulating a definite description for God in a philosophical framework as Whitehead has envisioned. These critics may even feel warmly toward my view of the historical nature of the task of speculative philosophy and its criteria, yet they would look at me, frown, and say, "But why do you want to do something like that?" Strangely enough, I have gotten this criticism more frequently than any other when I have outlined the task of natural theology as I have above.

The way the question is usually uttered, it sounds as though they are questioning the importance of doing natural theology. Look, for example, at Richard Rorty's "pragmatists," who do not say that God does not exist. They just think that "research concerning the nature or the will of God does not get us anywhere," he writes.[34] In short, it is not an impossible task, more a pointless one; it "does not get us anywhere," they say. So, according to Rorty, these "pragmatists," who should not be identified with the historical pragmatists, "just doubt that the vocabulary is one that we ought to be using," and they "want to change the subject."[35]

I think that if religion is important, then natural theology is important. If religion is not important, then I personally see no reason for doing natural theology either. Let us assume, then, that religion is important, then natural theology becomes that connection, of which Whitehead spoke, of "the rational generality of philosophy with the emotions and purposes springing out of existence in a particular society, in a particular epoch, and conditioned by particular antecedents."[36] To attempt to do natural theology goes some distance in salvaging religion from a bondage solely to the intensity of feeling. Natural theology is religion seeking understanding. Rorty's "pragmatists," I fear, are western intellectuals who have isolated themselves

34. Richard Rorty, *Consequences of Pragmatism* (Minneapolis: University of Minnesota Press, 1982), iv.
35. Ibid.
36. Whitehead, cited above, 23.

in their offices with their tattered copies of the writings of August Comte, oblivious of what is happening on television, much less in the rest of the world near the end of this twentieth century. This position of these isolation "pragmatists," who prefer not to talk about God and to change the subject, is dangerous. Religion is felt as intensely important by the vast majority of the people in this world.

University of Georgia

Soft Natural Theology
NINIAN SMART

Since I wrote, many years ago, that natural theology is the sick man of Europe, there have been signs of his recovery.[1] But the logic of the situation requires that the recovery can never be complete, save perhaps in heaven. I think it is salutary to spell out the reasons why natural theology—if we go on using the phrase—must at best be soft. I wish to sketch these reasons, and then add some points for future reflection.

Maybe, of course, we are only judging natural theology to be sick by reference to a concept of health that was always inappropriate. Since natural theology's meaning arises from the implied contrast with revealed theology, and since revealed theology springs from faith, there is already a pious ambience to the very idea of natural theology. It was perhaps always *fides quaerens intellectum*. Nevertheless, it has often seemed to belie this, for it seems to contain the claim that rational proofs of certain truths are a possibility: and insofar as these alleged proofs point to God there remain profound problems about them. And these profound problems relate to the reasons why natural theology remains the sick man of Europe. But I do want to say that there are more modest ways of reasoning that are relevant to religious truth, and if these constitute natural theology, it is still very relevant to our condition, and indeed growingly so.

It is obviously necessary for us to look at natural theology in the context of the real world. Despite the fact that philosophy, that is Western philosophy, has more or less completely ignored alternative points of view from Eastern and other cultures, it is more than an open secret that in matters of religion the old blinkers cannot be retained. There was a time, in the 1930s, say, when the urgencies of European conflict meant that religious debate in the West was carried

---

1. Ian Ramsey, ed., *Prospect for Metaphysics* (London: George Allen and Unwin, 1961), 81.

on as if the alternatives were variants of Christian theism and Western atheism; such a perspective has been diffracted by the growing awareness in the last forty years of such religions as Buddhism and Hinduism. It was indeed against that background that I placed my original discussion of natural theology's sickness. (The wider vision that I and a handful of others had was before its time[2]: now, that more cross-cultural purview is more commonplace.) Now it might be asked what essential difference the cross-cultural milieu makes to the project of natural theology. Does it not simply expand the variety of theisms? For already medieval thinkers had been aware of Islam and Judaism as alternative kinds of theism. What difference does throwing in Rāmānuja and Madhva and Shinran make?

One of the most important differences made by a global and cross-cultural perspective hinges upon a startling discovery. Not everyone yet realizes the nature of that discovery, but to anyone with a proper grasp of the history of religions it is—for Westerners—an amazement. It is the finding of religions that are not only nontheistic, but even non-absolutistic. That is, they are traditions whose focus is upon an ultimate that is not some personal or impersonal Substance. Such religions as Theravada Buddhism and Jainism represent a radical challenge to many of our assumptions about religion. Thus the Theravada does not wield the idea of Being: there could thus be no talk of a necessary being. The whole ontology, not just of Aquinas, but of Swinburne's *The Coherence of Theism*,[3] would be swept aside as misleading. The project of showing such notions to be coherent would be thought a little naive. After the Theravada, and in parallel with certain trajectories out of early Theravadin thinking, the Madhyamika school is even more radical in its challenges.

In one way, these schools can be seen as merely adding extra voices to the debate. After all, there are plenty of critics of natural theology in the West, from Hume to Flew. But from another point of view, these schools call radically into question a whole major tradition—the mainstream of Western thinking about God and religion. But this is not a question of some incommensurable challenge, since for a very long period the debate between differing schools in India included both non-substantialist Buddhists and Hindus who argued for a substantial God in a mode not unlike their unknowing and unknown Western counterparts.

The existence of spiritual systems that do not include a serious God

2. Ninian Smart, *Reasons and Faiths* (London: Routledge, 1958), the first cross-cultural philosophy of religion in the analytic tradition.

3. Richard Swinburne, *The Coherence of Theism* (Oxford: Clarendon Press, 1977).

or even a serious Absolute doing duty for a personal God calls for deeper thoughts than that here we have a very different pattern of thinking from what we are used to in the West. It raises the issue of what the difference means in religious experience and practice. For one thing, worship becomes unimportant or at least secondary in such a system.[4] All that cluster of ideas entangled with worship seem to be of little moment: ideas such as obedience, law, grace, devotion, love, and so on. So many of the key ideas of the Jewish and Christian and Islamic traditions fade in meaning. This does not mean that there are not others that overlap with some key concepts in parts at least of the Western traditions, such as meditation, trust, compassion, ignorance, insight, wisdom, for instance. There are convergences between Christian and Buddhist mysticism that have been well elaborated by such writers as D. T. Suzuki[5] and Heinrich Dumoulin.[6] Yet—and especially if we are looking to the Theravada—there are tantalizing differences, too. The Christian mystic may enter a dark night of the soul, and lose herself in a cloud of unknowing or a dazzling obscurity, and here we feel affinities with some images in the Buddhist tradition; but she also feels herself merged with Love and bathed in God, and any sense of union here with a personal Being cannot hold in the Buddhist case, where there is no such Person to merge with—no significant Other with which to become One.

One can, if one likes, do a simple thought experiment. Take a number of predicates ordinarily used of God, such as "is loving," "creates the world," "knows everything," "is awe-inspiring," and so on. Imagine they are applied to nirvana.[7] They do not make sense then. (But, incidentally, we can well imagine them applied to Brahman or to Ultimate Reality.) There is, then, something highly different about Theravada Buddhism, and Buddhists of this tradition have long felt their deep divergence from theistic traditions in a way in which, of course, Hindus have not.

Incidentally, there is a political side to this. It happens that in modern time Hinduism has been interpreted by many Western-educated intellectuals as all-embracing. The new Advaita Vedanta of Swami Vivekananda or Sarvepalli Radhakrishnan has thought of all religions pointing to the one Truth. They are so many symbolic systems leading humans upward to the Light. If Hinduism has any advantage over

---

4. Ninian Smart, *The Concept of Worship* (London: Macmillan, 1972).

5. D. T. Suzuki, *Mysticism, Christian and Buddhist* (London: George Allen and Unwin, 1979).

6. Heinrich Dumoulin, *A History of Zen Buddhism* (London: Routledge, 1963).

7. Donald Wiebe, ed., *Concept and Empathy* (New York: New York University Press, 1986), "Numen, Nirvana and the Deposition of Religion."

other systems, it is merely that it has recognized this unity of faiths from ancient times and has not fallen into the intolerance of certain kinds of Christianity, Islam, and so on. This doctrine of the unity of all religions has been more than a philosophical or theological one: it has been the main underpinning of India's federal pluralism and of her constitutional system of religious toleration. It was recently declared by Gandhi to be an essential feature of the Indian State. But the Buddhists of Sri Lanka never produced such a theory. Their religious ultimate was not of the right sort. Because they had no notion of the fundamental unity of all religions, they supplied no meaningful theory of the role of Christianity and Hinduism and Islam in the world or in society. At best such theisms are delusions. So Sri Lanka created no overarching ideology of toleration, and this is one of the political problems of the alienation of the Tamil minority and the consequent civil war. These observations about the political significance of the modern Hindu ideology indicate why it has enduring appeal in the contemporary world (a variant formulation occurs in John Hick's recent Gifford Lectures, for instance).[8] It is well fitted to the needs of a pluralistic world culture. But Buddhists and historians of religion may well ask whether it be *true*. Here we come back to the deeper challenges posed by the Theravada, which have not been sufficiently presented in the West, even now.

One of the predicates in my thought experiments was "is awe-inspiring." The fact is that Otto's famous notion of the numinous experience as being central to religions fails to apply in the case of the Theravada. There may be numinous elements in the religion: the cult of images, though mostly very serene in spirit rather than awe-inspiring, does have occasions of numinosity. But the heart of the Theravada is to do with meditation and peaceful insight, with no sense of a wrathful Other. So there are consequences for our model of religious experience, or rather types of experience, when we take the Theravada seriously. Briefly, as I have argued elsewhere often enough, there are at least two major categories of religious experience, one numinous and the other mystical or contemplative. Actually, one can add other forms, too. But that implies that insofar as modern philosophy of religion makes appeal to religious experience, the appeal has to be very complex and sophisticated in terms of the history of religion. This is the main deep challenge of the Theravada: it is mysticism without God.[9] It may be asked how this affects the future of natural theology.

8. John Hick, *An Interpretation of Religion* (London: Collins, 1989).
9. Ninian Smart, *Buddhism and the Death of God* (Southampton, England: Southamp-

First, it ties in with a Wittgensteinian motif, namely that we need to see religious belief-statements as embedded in forms or ways of life. Or, more concretely: the history of religions is a necessary context for the philosophy of religion, and so we must note how doctrines and stories realize themselves through the actual rituals and behaviors of a religious community. These, in turn, relate to and reflect types of religious experience.

Second, more particularly natural theology can be seen as having an affective or experiential side to it.[10] The cosmological arguments have a connection with the numinous, in that they help to induce a kind of vertigo: the thought "What if nothing existed at all?" or "What if the cosmos did not exist?" The teleological argument has often been tied to the elaboration of examples of the marvels of the cunning construction of the universe, especially of the living forms within the world. I suppose the necessity of God's existence and properties, which is something allegedly brought out in the ontological argument, has an emotionally satisfying aspect. Thus, Findlay seemed to think that a merely contingent God would not be worthy of worship, and of course Malcolm made much of the emotionally compelling side of the ontological argument.[11]

But in the wider context of world religions, one would have to ask what we are to make of systems such as the Theravada and of the Madhyamika, which have no deep affection for these feelings. By rejecting the concept of substance and by being skeptical about a God they do not cultivate numinous feelings.

We can note that the radical philosophical questioning in the Madhyamika is itself perceived as being part of the process of training in meditation. Philosophy is here practical. It is to induce a different sense of vertigo. It is designed to break down ideas of substance in a way that opens up a kind of emptiness: a mental void that helps to promote the contemplative experience of the Light of Enlightenment, uncluttered by the ordinary concepts that overlay and encrust our experiential world. So here, too, as perhaps in religious natural theology (as contrasted with the merely cerebral arguments about the technical problems exhibited, for instance, in the ontological argument), philosophy is part of spiritual practice. In short, both in East and West there is a religious function of philosophizing, and for that

ton University, 1970), and K. N. Jayatilleke, *The Message of the Buddha* (London: Allen and Unwin, 1975).

10. As argued recently by John P. Clayton, *Theologische Realencyclopädie* (Berlin: de Gruyter, 1982), xiii, 5, "Gottesbeweise II," 724–82.

11. Ninian Smart, *The Concept of Worship* (London: Macmillan, 1972).

reason we need to pay attention to the relevant ways in which such reasoning is embedded in communities and traditions.

One way of interpreting the "form of life" idea is to think of a form of life as expressed in a specified community. It is true that theology and natural theology have occurred typically within communities. The theologian is a sort of spokesperson for a group: and thus should strictly speaking never be used without an adjectival prefix to indicate the community for which he or she speaks (Christian, Catholic, Scottish Presbyterian, Reform Jewish, and so on). We find some trouble with a case like Hans Küng: is he still a Catholic theologian, despite being disowned by the Vatican?[12] Recently, William Christian[13] wrote an important analysis of the relations between doctrines and communities. Nevertheless, various factors have tended to erode the authority and insularity of communities. Ecumenical dialogue, inter-religious dialogue, the formation, incipiently, of a world community, metropolitan living, and various other developments mean that a more questioning and a more fluid atmosphere prevails. One may still keep the "form of life" idea, but it would be folly to look on communities as sealed from one another. Moreover, the individual makes up her own mind, often, and as such forms a community of just one.

Let us now draw together some of the threads of the discussion. First, we may note that because of the diverse history of different intellectual histories there is nothing necessary about the development of Western philosophy, and therefore of the tradition of natural theology. Any pretensions to rigor dissolve, even where argumentation may appear rigorous: because the cultural and conceptual assumptions of a given philosophical milieu are automatically challenged by alternative systems. In particular, the Theravada and Madhyamika systems challenge the Western tradition. In a sense they ally themselves with such dissolvers as Foucault, Derrida, and Rorty (though these figures do not know it yet). Second, this does not mean that natural theology is altogether without force—partly because it has a spiritual function. And the question "Why is there anything at all?" for instance does not go away even if there is no particular answer to it that is mandatory. Third, the process of arguing about natural theology merges imperceptibly into more general arguments about religious experience and practice. In the multireligious situation apparent to us in the modern world, this means that natural theology, and so

12. Though, interestingly, his status as an ecumenical Christian teacher is not in doubt.

13. William Christian, Sr., *Doctrines of Religious Communities* (Princeton: Princeton University Press, 1987).

on, has a very wide purview. It becomes the deployment of arguments about religious experience and practice East and West, North and South.

Apart from this, it is worth noting that the very distinction between religious and nonreligious worldviews is a Western, and culture-bound, one. It is useful legally in relation to tax laws and separation of church and state. It is useful as a form of self-deception for secular intellectuals, who can start from, say, a Marxist perspective and assume that this is a cleaner way of dealing with the world than flaunting Catholic assumptions or whatever. But it has rather little substance as a distinction, unless one places very strong emphasis (which not all religions do) on the transcendental reference of religion as its defining characteristic. As we shall see, the idea of transcendent-directed experiences is important, but not necessarily as a defining characteristic of religions per se. Had the comparative study of religion begun in China rather than in Northern Europe and America, it would be doubtful whether a strong distinction between religions and secular ideologies would have been made. For this reason I prefer to use the term "world view analysis" rather than "comparative religion" and the like. In terms of world view analysis, the arguments of natural theology and its periphery stretch out even wider. We can ask questions such as "Is it reasonable to trust the transcendentally oriented experiences of prophets and/or mystics?" or "Is it reasonable to think of any tradition as authoritative as to revelation?" Such questions are vital ones, but they consciously incorporate the possibilities of various atheistic and agnostic world views as alternatives to religious ones. In short, the theologies are not insulated from the real world.

The reflective intellectual's task is no doubt to think about the criteria by which we might attempt to settle questions about religious choices. Consider the choice seemingly presented as between the prophetic tradition of Israel and of early Christianity and the contemplative tradition of Buddhism. Each ignores, for the most part, the main experiential values of the other. But in the wide world of human history, we find that both types of experience have been important. There seems plausibility in accepting either both types as telling us something about the ultimate, or neither—rather than discriminating between them. It is true that tensions, which can be amply demonstrated in the history of religions, exist between them, since the one sort tends to stress the gap between the human being and the ultimate, whereas the other tends to emphasize identity. The turbulence of the numinous and the passions of devotional religion on the one hand contrast with the serenity of the contemplative life on the other. But such tensions need not be contradictions.

It appears to me that such reflections do not themselves depend upon revealed ideas or images. It is true that revelations may reflect differing kinds of religious experience plus diverse cultural and other circumstances. But the above reflections raise general issues about human nature and the possibilities of access to the ultimate and, as such, belong in a general way to natural theology. Thus one way in which natural theology may develop is in the direction of general reflections upon the history of religions.

Another way of regarding this is from the inside of various religious traditions.[14] It is obvious that every tradition needs to have a sensitive view of every other, and to engage in questions that get posed from the outside, whether by other religious traditions or by nonreligious world views. The task of engaging in debate with other world views corresponds, in the modern world, to what once was known as natural theology.

Philosophically, this means a cross-cultural engagement with the arguments of other traditions: the Christian theologian of the future, for example, will need to engage dialectically with the Madhyamika critique of all positions.

Now I think it will become obvious that all argumentation and attempted proofs of one position over another, or of one element over another, will not yield clinching results. It is not merely that natural theology in the old sense is, to say the least, controversial and doubtful: but this wider interreligious and inter-world-view discussion is necessarily soft as to conclusions. While it is unreasonable to become a relativist, the non-relativism which we will retain will have to be soft. No proofs, except rather trivial ones, could be offered as to world views. It seems therefore to me that the directions of natural theology lie towards a world-wide discussion issuing in a soft non-relativism. This is for some people rather unsatisfying, to say the least. Many yearn for certainty of faith, authority, and clearcut directives. These seem to me to be impossible to attain, for in the plural world of today everyone has only one foot in her own tradition. The Pope may teach *this*, but we know that others teach *that*. We are called upon, by our education and circumstances, to call all authority into question. We may feel strongly that our own position is the truth, but we cannot produce proofs, only reasons. Perhaps that itself is the nature of faith or trust. We may trust the Buddha or have faith in Christ: but we are irrational if we think there is any proof of the authority of either leader.

14. See such publications as Hans Küng and Jürgen Moltmann, eds., *Concilium* 183, *Christianity Among World Religions* (Edinburgh: T and T Clark, 1986).

Such a softly non-relativistic world encourages blends and adoptions.[15] It encourages, too, personal experimentations. No longer will traditions themselves have a traditional traditionalism. People will affirm them because they have a choice, or reject them. An affirmed, consciously chosen tradition has a different character from a traditional tradition.

There are still questions as to what remains for the older natural theology: for the attempts to frame a cosmological or teleological or ontological argument. One thing is that we need to absorb into that perspective parallel concerns in India with arguments for God's existence, for rebirth, and so on. In my view, there remain some elements of force in the cosmological and teleological arguments, and a hypothetical ontological argument may have force, that is, if God exists her existence will be necessary. But none of these reasonings are probative, of course. The gap between the Cosmos-Explaining Being suggested by a version of the cosmological argument and the fleshed-out God that the Christian, Jew, or Hindu encounters in her tradition is still there: bare theism has little purchase on human feelings or commitments. Thus traditional natural theology turns out to be an indication of possible supporting reasons for a fleshed-out belief that itself is what might be described as a kind of live and living hypothesis. It might be a hypothesis held with certitude, as, too, with certain political commitments, but not with public certainty, for none can exist in the plural domain of religions.

University of California at Santa Barbara

15. Ninian Smart, *Beyond Ideology* (San Francisco: Harper and Row, 1981).

10   Experience and Natural Theology

EUGENE THOMAS LONG

Since the nineteenth century, philosophical discussions of religious metaphysics and attempts to prove the existence of God have often taken second place to discussions of religious experience. In some cases, efforts to argue for the existence of God have been understood to be in opposition to religious faith. In *On Religion: Speeches to Its Cultured Despisers,* published in 1799, Schleiermacher argued that religion is distinct from all systematic forms of knowledge. Religion, according to Schleiermacher, is rooted in pious feeling, in what he called in *The Christian Faith* the feeling of dependence or a feeling of absolute dependence on God. "Piety," he wrote, "cannot be an instinct craving for a mess of metaphysical and ethical crumbs."[1] Although Schleiermacher made a place for knowledge and morality and thought religion to be inseparable from them, he nevertheless located religion in pious feeling and understood it to be the natural counterpart to knowledge and morality. Pious feeling was not merely subjective on Schleiermacher's account. The feeling of absolute dependence included an intentional reference to God as the whence of the feeling of absolute dependence, and this feeling was understood in the context of the community of faith. But his view does depend on the universality of this pious feeling, and efforts to prove the existence of God were thought to be superfluous.

Whatever one thinks of the adequacy or inadequacy of Schleiermacher's description and interpretation of religious experience, it is clear that his work touched a nerve center in religious thinkers. For many, Schleiermacher introduced new life and energy into the discussions of religion. In his Introduction to a reprint of the first edition of *On Religion,* Rudolf Otto spoke for many when he wrote that "one is time and again enthralled by his original and daring attempt to lead

1. Friedrich Schleiermacher, *On Religion: Speeches to Its Cultured Despisers* (New York: Harper and Row, 1958), 31.

an age weary and alien to religion back to its mainsprings; and to reweave religion, threatened with oblivion, into the incomparably rich fabric of the burgeoning intellectual life of modern times."[2] And in 1928, John Baillie, although critical of Schleiermacher's neglect of the intellectual dimension of religion, spoke with warm gratitude of the great service Schleiermacher rendered to theology in providing a reasoned alternative to rationalism at one of the most crucial moments of history.[3]

Yet four decades after the publication of *On Religion,* Ludwig Feuerbach provided an alternative reading of religious experience that some would argue is the logical outcome of basing religion on feeling. According to Feuerbach, the feeling of self and feeling are inseparable, and the feeling of God is nothing but man's highest feeling of self. "The last refuge of theology," wrote Feuerbach, "is feeling. God is renounced by the understanding; he has no longer the dignity of a real object, of a reality which imposes itself on the understanding; hence he is transferred to feeling; in feeling his existence is thought to be secure. And doubtless this is the safest refuge; for to make feeling the essence of religion is nothing else than to make feeling the essence of God."[4]

The efforts of Feuerbach and others to explain away religion may not provide proof that God does not exist, but they do raise the question whether the difference between the religious and nonreligious person is merely a matter of how we look at the world of experience. Experience of the divine is not recognized universally by all human beings, and if one eschews understanding and argument in favor of religious experience, there is the risk that religion can be defended only by authoritative appeals to self-authenticating experience or revelation and faith. This is, of course, what some of the so-called encounter theologians of the twentieth century argued. For Karl Barth, religion was a matter of revelation and faith and there was no place for natural theology. Speaking of natural theology in his Gifford Lectures, Barth wrote, "I certainly see with astonishment that such a science as Lord Gifford had in mind exists, but I do not see how it is possible for it to exist. I am convinced that so far as it has existed and still exists, it owes its existence to a radical error."[5]

---

2. Ibid., vii.

3. John Baillie, *The Interpretation of Religion* (Nashville: Abingdon Press, 1956), 208.

4. Ludwig Feuerbach, *The Essence of Christianity* (New York: Harper Torchbooks, 1957), 283.

5. Karl Barth, *The Knowledge of God and the Service of God* (London: Hodder and Stoughton, 1938), 5. Cited in John Macquarrie, *Thinking about God* (New York: Harper and Row, 1975), 134.

There seems to be something correct in the appeal to experience in religion. The roots of religion lie deeper in the being of persons than speculative efforts to explain the nature of reality. Arguments may point to or help open one up to the religious dimensions of experience, but religion itself seems to have to do primarily with a sense of divine presence within the believer's experience of self and world. Even if one were to develop convincing arguments for the existence of God, many have argued that there would remain a significant gap between the object of the arguments and the experienced reality that is reported to be at the heart of the religious life.

Does this mean, however, that the experiential approach to religion is ultimately destined to appeal to self-authenticating experience, and that any hope for natural theology has to be surrendered? Perhaps this would be the case if we restricted natural theology to classical formulations. Suppose, however, that natural theology is a product of the age in which it is developed? Suppose that we no longer, except in very limited spheres, expect to find the kind of rational certainty in knowledge that some sought in the arguments for the existence of God? There seems to be no reason why natural theology has to be limited to a particular historical form. Presumably, natural theology has the aim of providing some connection between one's religious faith and one's general knowledge and experience. Indeed, on closer inspection, natural theology often, if not always, appears to presuppose religious faith or at least a religious interest. It is not a completely neutral or disinterested activity, if there ever is such, but an effort to show that religious knowledge is not limited to appeals to the authority of particular historical claims of revelation and faith, that religious faith makes sense within the context of the general wisdom of humankind. We could say, writes John Macquarrie, "that the function of natural theology was to provide a connection between our ordinary everyday discourse about the world or even our scientific discourse on the one side, and theological discourse on the other."[6]

Looked at from this perspective, the question of the possibility of natural theology has less to do with the question of the origins of religious knowledge, whether or not all knowledge of God is in some way dependent on God, and more to do with whether ultimate reality or God can be understood within the range of ordinary human experience. If there are not some "evidences" of God in general human experience, it would seem that one could only appeal to special in-

---

6. John Macquarrie, *Thinking about God*, 137. My position in this essay is much influenced by Macquarrie's approach to natural theology.

sights or particular revelations of the divine, in which case there would be a radical divorce between secular and religious experience and no way to bridge the gap between religious experience and ordinary experience and knowledge. The possibility of a natural theology based on experience, then, appears to depend on the presence of the divine in ordinary human experience.

The term "experience," however, is filled with difficulties. Experience is often understood to refer to a private and subjective phenomenon. This view of experience is rooted in the tendency of some empiricists to begin with a subject set apart from and over against the reality of the world. On this account, the subject having or undergoing the experience has the difficulty of getting from her subjective experience to the reality that she claims to experience. This subjective view of experience, however, is hardly adequate to the complex situations in which we find ourselves as beings in the world.

To borrow the language of Heidegger, we might say that human existence as it becomes aware of itself is already thrown into a world, is already related to persons and things in the world, including the past and anticipated future, which make up what it means to be an existing person. It might be said that experience takes place in a context in which one relates to other persons and things and that experience includes one's history and tradition. It is the understanding of experience in terms of interaction between self and world that enables us to evaluate experiences as rational or irrational, adequate or inadequate to reality. As John Smith says, the one who experiences may be said on the one hand to *reflect* what is given, what is there to be encountered. But we do not merely provide a mirror image of what is given. The being who experiences may also be said to have a structure and to belong to reality. We take or interpret what is given in different contexts of meaning and in this sense we may be said to *refract* as well as reflect what is encountered in the world.[7]

On this account of experience, there is a reciprocal relation between me and what is given, requiring an interpretive act on my part, and it is in this that my efforts to understand and explain are rooted. Interpreting, understanding, and explaining, then, are not activities contrary to experience but are part and parcel of my efforts to articulate my encounters with persons and things in the world. In this sense, experience has a social dimension, for it is in interpreting that I encounter others, interact with them, and compare judgements. This means that I cannot make of experience what I will, and that expe-

7. John Smith, *Experience and God* (New York: Oxford University Press, 1968), 25.

rience is not self-authenticating. It is always subject to error and mis-understanding, and one must try to give an account of the data of experience that neither ignores nor distorts the data.

If experience is understood in this way, I doubt that one can attain the kind of intuitive certainty which for H. D. Lewis provides the foundation for religious experience. Experiences, as Lewis says, are always someone's experiences, but just because of this it would seem experience is never completely free from what one brings with one to experience, and hence never free of interpretive disagreements. Some philosophers and theologians, however, have argued that there are dimensions of ordinary experience that point us beyond our frag-mentary nature and toward a fuller understanding of self and world in a wider range of reality than can be grasped in ordinary empirical terms. We might call these religious or, perhaps better, transcendent dimensions of experience, and natural theology might be understood as an effort to describe and interpret these transcendent dimensions of experience. In describing and interpreting these transcendent di-mensions of experience, we may never be completely free of what we bring with us that gives shape to such experiences. But we may be able to provide descriptions and interpretations without reference to any specifically religious interpretation. Such an effort might enable us to establish contact points between different religions as well as between religious and nonreligous views of reality.

If God is totally transcendent to the world, then perhaps one would not expect to find "evidences" of God in our experience as beings-in-the-world, and perhaps then natural theology based on experience would not be a live option. If, however, as Macquarrie says, man is "a creature of God and dependent on him, then this should show itself in a study of man. It should be possible to see man as fragmentary and incomplete in himself so that we are pointed to God and if we can see man in this way, then we can go on to a fuller understanding of him in his relation to God."[8] Putting this in a slightly different way, we might say that if knowledge of God is rooted in our experience as beings-in-the-world, then experience should direct us beyond self and world to a broader range of reality, in which we find our completion or fulfillment. The role of natural theology, in this case, would be that of describing and interpreting the general dimensions of human ex-perience, showing to what extent experience points to a transcendent or ultimate ground of reality, and answering the question, what sense can be made of it.

8. John Macquarrie, *Studies in Christian Existentialism* (London: SCM Press, 1966), 5.

This task cannot, of course, be fully undertaken in this essay. However, I do want to take a few examples to illustrate what I have referred to above as the transcendent dimensions of human experience. First, there is what might be called the experience of contingency, that sense of mystery or wonder that is often associated with the question why there are beings rather than nothing. Even in cases where the cosmological argument for the existence of God is rejected, some philosophers continue to give testimony to the experience of contingency which appears to lie at the root of the argument. The experience of contingency may not be universal and there may not be a consensus concerning what to make of it. But the experience itself appears to be recognized by persons from very different philosophical perspectives.

At the end of an essay in which J. J. C. Smart has provided a critical assessment of the cosmological argument, showing that it is illegitimate to infer from the experience of contingency the idea of a necessary being, he writes:

> Nevertheless, though I know how any answer on the lines of the cosmological argument can be pulled to pieces by a correct logic, I still feel that I want to go on asking the question . . . . That anything should exist at all does seem to me a matter for the deepest awe. But whether people feel this sort of awe, and whether they or I ought to is another question. I think we ought to. If so, the question arises: If "Why should anything exist at all?" cannot be interpreted after the manner of the cosmological argument, that is, as an absurd request for the nonsensical postulation of a necessary being, what sort of question is it?[9]

Karl Jaspers, at the end of a critical discussion of the cosmological argument, reports a similar experience of the mystery of the contingency of the world, although he appears to point more affirmatively to what he calls the experience of the Comprehensive. Speaking of the cosmological argument, Jaspers writes:

> But this notion takes on a new meaning when it is no longer regarded as a proof. Then metaphorically, in the form of an inference, it expresses awareness of the mystery inherent in the existence of the world and of ourselves in it. If we venture the thought that there might be nothing, and ask Schelling: Why is there something and not nothing? we find that our certainty of existence is such that though we cannot determine the reason for it we are led by it to the Comprehensive, which by this very essence is and cannot not be, and through which everything else is.[10]

---

9. J. J. C. Smart, "The Existence of God," Antony Flew and Alisdair MacIntyre, eds., *New Essays in Philosophical Theology* (New York: Macmillan, 1970), 46.

10. Karl Jaspers, *Way to Wisdom* (New Haven: Yale University Press, 1954), 43.

Both Smart and Jaspers may be said to be pointing to or describing an element of irreducible mystery that arises in our experience of the world. Neither is willing to define the mystery in terms of a transcendent being. Smart refers only to a sense of awe in the face of mystery. Jaspers points towards a ground of the mystery in the Comprehensive, but the Comprehensive is neither a subject nor an object but that which is manifest in the phenomenon as a background that boundlessly illumines the phenomenon.

The experience of contingency focuses on our experience of the world. However, there are also experiences more directly related to what it means to be a self in the world. Here, again, in descriptions of what it means to be a self, there appears to be an element of mystery that points us beyond our fragmentary nature and toward what we are calling transcendent dimensions of human experience. The experience of freedom is one such experience.

The experience of freedom, according to some writers, is more than an awareness of choices between alternatives. Freedom is associated by the existentialists with what it means for me to be human, with what it means for me to give shape to my existence. Jean-Paul Sartre gives us one of the more radical descriptions of the experience of freedom. According to Sartre, I begin as nothing. There are no determinations of my existence. In answering the question, What do we mean in saying existence precedes essence? Sartre writes, "We mean that man first of all exists, encounters himself, surges up in the world—and defines himself afterwards. If man as the existentialist sees him is not definable, it is because to begin with he is nothing. He will not be anything until later, and then he will be what he makes of himself."[11] On this account, there is a clear break between man as an autonomous being and man as a social and natural being, and in Sartre's more extreme statements there would seem to be little recognition of obvious constraints on human freedom and little basis for human community.

This, it would seem, however, is not the whole story for Sartre. Later in the same essay, where he is again explaining the meaning of the claim that existence precedes essence, Sartre writes, "Thus we have neither behind us, nor before us in a luminous realm of values, any means of justification or excuse. We are left alone, without excuse. That is what I mean when I say that man is condemned to be free.

11. Jean Paul Sartre, "Existentialism Is a Humanism," in Walter Kaufmann, ed., *Existentialism from Dostoevsky to Sartre* (New York: New American Library, 1975), 349. See an extended discussion of this and related issues in Schubert Ogden, *The Reality of God* (New York: Harper and Row, 1966), 120ff.

Condemned, because he did not create himself, yet is nevertheless at liberty, and from the moment that he is thrown into this world he is responsible for everything he does."[12] Sartre does not appear to have escaped essentialism in every sense. Freedom appears to be some kind of necessity. Presumably this could not be a necessity of nature. Freedom would seem to be part of that greater reality of which human existence is a part. Implicit in the experience of freedom would seem to be a recognition that reality itself has the character of enabling or perhaps determining us to be free.

Jaspers presents us with a somewhat different description of the experience of freedom, but he, too, points beyond the self to some ground of freedom. Jaspers is more sensitive than Sartre to the constraints on freedom. However, like Sartre, the experience of freedom transcends efforts to fully comprehend the whole of human existence within the natural and social order. To say that I am free is in some sense to say that what I do with myself in the world makes me what I am. But according to Jaspers, "I can will, but I cannot will myself to will . . . . In my freedom, in being free and in fulfilling it, I am given to myself."[13] Or, as Jaspers says elsewhere, "Existenz can grasp itself in its own freedom only if at the same time, and in the same act, it will perceive something other than itself . . . . For my self-realization I depend on a fulfillment that comes to me . . . . The test of the possibility of my Existenz is the knowledge that it rests upon transcendence."[14] Freedom for Jaspers is not something capable of being proved. It is what one realizes only in creative activity when one chooses oneself from beyond the limits of empirical or theoretical certainty. It is a choosing or being responsible for choosing one's way of being. This action is not independent of my being in the world but ultimately it is bound up with Transcendence in that I experience my freedom as a gift from beyond myself. Freedom and Existenz are never directly known, according to Jaspers, but are encountered in the act of existing. Yet neither is real apart from Transcendence, which is disclosed to me as I leap from the dimension of immanence to that of freedom and Existenz. Existenz is grounded in Transcendence and Transcendence first becomes real to Existenz. And the life that is realized is a life of freedom.

Jaspers, more than Sartre, takes into account the constraints that

12. Ibid., 353.

13. Karl Jaspers, *Philosophical Faith and Revelation* (New York: Harper and Row, 1967), 234.

14. Karl Jaspers, *Philosophy* (Chicago: The University of Chicago Press, 1971), vol. 3, 5–6.

are encountered in our freedom, in our activities in giving shape and form to our life. But for both, freedom is in the final analysis not open to ordinary empirical investigation. And for both the experience of freedom ultimately appears to be grounded in a reality that transcends the world of nature. For both, perhaps for Sartre in spite of himself, my experience of freedom appears to be rooted in a wider reality that accounts for my being free.

Closely connected to the experience of freedom and its association with our creating our way of being in the world is the experience of commitment. In the absence of commitment or some focus in life, we would seem to be mere dilettantes, floating from moment to moment with no sense of direction and perhaps no self-identity. It is when I commit myself in terms of some goals or directions that my existence begins to take shape. For example I may commit myself to a vocation or to some other person in marriage. In one sense these commitments cut me off from or make secondary other commitments that I make. In committing myself to my wife, I am extending myself into the uncertainty of the future and giving myself some identity, and in committing myself to some vocation I am giving focus to my life in accordance with some interests and abilities. In both cases I may be said to be giving some focus or continuity to my existence.[15]

Commitment to another in marriage and commitment to a vocation may be understood as particular or individual commitments. In such commitments, I extend myself beyond my individual ego and beyond my present. I give shape to myself as past, present, and future. Such commitments would seem to presuppose some sense of trust or confidence in my wife and in my abilities and interests. But commitment it would seem is not merely a matter of individual commitments. The possibility of individual commitments would seem to be rooted in some more general confidence in reality as a whole. Perhaps this might be expressed in saying that, in spite of experiencing from time to time breakdowns in individual commitments and in the ground of trust and confidence that underlies these commitments, I continue to have confidence that life makes sense, that reality is ultimately meaningful or supportive, and that just because of this I can weather the challenge to individual commitments. In other words, implicit in our individual commitments would seem to be a commitment to a broader range of reality, to reality as a whole. Certainly, if reality were chaotic or absurd or threatening, it would be difficult for me to develop coherence and

15. For development of the idea of commitment, see John Macquarrie, *In Search of Humanity* (London: SCM Press, 1982), 140–157.

direction in my life. The experience of commitment seems ultimately to be based on what might be called a cosmic trust or confidence.

In an essay in which he criticizes efforts to argue from cosmic stances to God, George Naknikian speaks of the experience of cosmic gratitude or thankfulness, an experience, it would seem, closely connected to what I have called a general confidence that reality makes sense. Although he intends to show that one cannot infer God from an experience of cosmic thankfulness, Naknikian seems to allow that nontheists could have such experiences. "An atheist," he writes, "cannot (logically) be grateful if he does not believe that someone has done us a good turn, but the same atheist can have a feeling of cosmic thankfulness. The feeling of cosmic thankfulness is like the feeling of thankfulness minus the belief that someone has done him a good turn. In place of that belief there is an inclination to grant that if anything existed to bring about this (the starry heavens, my birth) in a providential way, it would be majestic enough to be the fitting recipient of my cosmic gratitude and thankfulness."[16]

Thus far, I have attempted to point to and describe what I have called ultimate or transcendent dimensions within the experiences of contingency, freedom, and commitment. Having provided descriptions of such experiences, however, we need to ask, What sense can be made of such experiences? Any effort to interpret these experiences has to accept the possibility of alternative interpretations, alternative efforts to make sense of the experiences. Perhaps no interpretations are compelling in the strict sense. We may, however, be able to identify those interpretations that make the most sense of the data without either ignoring or distorting them.

The distinction that Donald Evans draws between a cosmic and a religious conviction may be of help at this point. "A cosmic conviction," according to Evans, "is a belief that some reality pervades the whole of one's environment as a unifying constant. A religious conviction is a cosmic conviction in which this reality is further designated in ways similar to what is held in traditional religions."[17] Natural theology, we might say, is an effort to describe and interpret the transcendent dimensions of experience, showing the cosmic convictions that are implicit in experience.

Both J. J. C. Smart and Karl Jaspers point to an experience of

---

16. George Naknikian, "On the Cognitive Import of Certain Conscious States," in Sidney Hook, ed., *Religious Experience and Truth* (London: Oliver and Boyd, 1962), 159. Cited in Donald Evans, *Faith, Authenticity and Morality* (Toronto: University of Toronto Press, 1980), 253.

17. Donald Evans, *Faith, Authenticity and Morality*, 92.

mystery inherent in our experience of the world as it is for us. The mystery of which they speak is not mere ignorance. Smart speaks of the deepest sense of awe, and Jaspers speaks of this mystery pointing beyond the merely finite to the Comprehensive. Neither Smart nor Jaspers is attempting to draw logical inferences from this experience of mystery. It is rather that the experience itself appears to bring them up against the wider range of Being or Reality in which things have their being. The experience of mystery can be interpreted to testify to the incompleteness of finite existence, to its not being self-supporting, and to its grounding in Being that transcends finite reality but is immanent in it in pointing beyond it.

With regard to the experience of freedom, both Jaspers and Sartre appear to understand that there is an act of will that pulls things together, that gives shape to our being in the world. At first glance, Sartre would seem to understand that man is an autonomous being dependent on nothing that transcends itself. Yet Sartre does not seem to be consistent here. To say that man is condemned to be free would seem to say that freedom is in some way dependent on Being or Reality having the character that enables or perhaps even requires this act of will. Jaspers, in analyzing the experience, goes further in saying that I realize my freedom only in recognizing Transcendence. In both cases, however, the experience of freedom appears to refer beyond self and world to a greater reality and to what might be called a natural grace at the heart of Reality. Reality, we might say, must be such as to enable or even demand an act of will in our giving shape to our being in the world.

And again, with regard to the experience of commitment, we appear to be pointed beyond our individual commitments and beliefs about others to a belief that Reality is supportive in our efforts to give shape to our being in the world. Erik Erikson spoke of the necessity of a basic trust for a healthy personality. At the root of this committed form of existence that gives shape to human existence and continuity over time is a basic trust, and ultimately the ground of that trust would seem to be Being or Reality itself. The issue here is not whether or not a transcendent being exists but whether Reality is supportive and gracious, threatening and absurd, or merely neutral.

If these experiences can be interpreted in somewhat the way suggested it would seem that we have evidence of something like what Evans calls a cosmic commitment. Reality is understood to be greater than can be conceived in ordinary empirical terms. Reality has the character of freedom, and Reality is supportive or gracious. An adequate natural theology would have to go much further than this in describing and interpreting the various transcendent dimensions of our experience as beings in the world. The aim would be to provide an interpretive scheme that could give an account of the various dimensions of human experience.

An interpretive scheme as envisioned here would be limited and fragmentary by comparison with more traditional schemes of metaphysics. If the existentialists have taught us nothing else, they have taught us of our finiteness and historicity, which set limits to our efforts to develop a universal picture of reality. Further, an interpretive scheme as envisioned here would not lend itself to strict demonstration. If all experience is in some sense interpreted experience, then the possibility of misinterpretation is always present. And if all interpretations of experience are both made possible and limited by our historical being in the world, then limits are imposed on the universality of our claims. This need not result, however, in pure relativism. The evaluation of interpretative schemes depends on others looking with us in the same direction. But we can also evaluate them in terms of their ability to account for the data of experience without ignoring or distorting them, and in terms of their ability to illuminate related ideas. The aim of such interpretive schemes would be to answer the question, How else can you account for the data of experience?

Thus far we have been focusing on what has been called the transcendent dimensions of experience. Some authors might want to speak here of religious dimensions of experience. But, in any case, we would still seem to be a step removed from more distinctive religious experience, the kind of experience that takes place within a specifically religious context and which includes a more definite referent, whether of a theistic or nontheistic kind. Schleiermacher's description and interpretation of religious experience is an example of what I have in mind, but presumably we would want to include all religious experiences that are associated with particular religious traditions and that give more definite shape to what has been referred to as the wider range of Reality.

Of specific religious experiences, it is often said that they provide *prima facie* evidence for Reality having the kind of character assigned to it in such experiences. In theistic cases, it is often said that such experiences provide *prima facie* evidence for the existence of God. Given the widespread reports of such experiences, and the integrity and critical acumen of many who report such experiences, there would seem to be some justification for such claims. At a minimum, we could say that various efforts to explain away such experiences have fallen short of proof. This is not to say, however, that such experiences can stand alone in efforts to provide justification for religious belief.

Perhaps for some it makes no more sense to question the existence of God than it does to question the existence of the person sitting across the desk from me. However, even in the case of the person sitting across the desk from me, I can distinguish between the experience I am having and the claim that this experience represents reality as it is. And this distinction would appear to be even more important in the case of religious experience, where I do not have the checking procedures that are normally available in cases of sense experience. Distinctive religious experience may provide *prima facie* evidence for the referent of that experience, but we will need first to provide a detailed description and interpretation of that experience and then look for corroborating evidence elsewhere. It is in this context that we can see the importance of natural theology. A natural theology based on experience could not, on its own, establish a distinctive religious faith or prove the truth of its claims. It might, however, provide the basis for connecting distinctively religious experience with the kinds of experience that make up our more ordinary existence in the world.

Here, I believe, we can begin to see more clearly the relation between so-called natural and revealed theology. The difference here may have less to do with whether or not knowledge of God is revealed and more to do with our ability to understand what God means in the context of the general dimensions of human experience. Natural theology, as represented in this essay, is an effort to describe and interpret what I have called the transcendent dimensions of human experience. This effort would lead eventually to what might be called an ontological map of the Being of self and world, an interpretive scheme intended to make sense of the experience of ourselves in the world of persons and things.

However, even if one says that all knowledge of divine reality is in some sense revealed, and that no hard and fast distinction between natural and revealed theology can be maintained, there would still be a distinction between a general and a particular knowledge of transcendent reality corresponding to the distinction between the transcendent dimensions of experience and distinctive religious experience. Distinctive religious experience as suggested above cannot stand on its own. However, one may attempt to provide an interpretation of distinctively religious experience with the intent of showing, in the words of James Richmond, "whether a religious or a nonreligious interpretation of the world is the most satisfying, the most rational and the most illuminating."[18]

18. James Richmond, *Theology and Metaphysics* (London: SCM Press, 1970), 89.

Here we may find the contact point between natural and revealed theology or, better perhaps, between philosophical interpretations of the general dimensions of human experience and theological interpretations of the experience of a particular historical community. The particular experiences within a religious community may be taken as contributing to an understanding of one's being in the world, but they depend for their fuller understanding and corroboration on their being systematically related to interpretations of the general dimensions of experience. It is in this sense that the theologian may look to the various interpretative schemes that purport to give accounts of the various dimensions of experience. In this activity, the theologian, if she is a theist, moves from the more immediate experiences of the historical community of faith in an effort to fill out and correct what is implicit in her speaking about God and in an effort to find confirmation for religious faith in an independent realm of understanding. In this way the theist recognizes that God is both Being in whom one finds fulfillment and that which accounts for things being the way they are.

It is not my intent here to make religious faith and theology dependent on any particular philosophical interpretation of the general dimensions of human experience. Distinctive religious experience has evidence of its own to bring to its effort to make sense of the human experience of existence and Being, and any interpretive scheme will have to be judged adequate to religious faith where the emphasis is often more practical than theoretical. But it is in the dialogue between theological and philosophical efforts to provide interpretive schemes that one may judge whether or not a religious interpretation is the most satisfying, the most rational, and the most illuminating of human experience.

University of South Carolina

11   Theodicy: The Case for a Theologically
Inclusive Model of Philosophy

LOUIS DUPRÉ

I

Despite vigorous attempts to free itself from its tainted rationalist heritage, modern philosophy still remains the legatee of the Enlightenment. Its epistemic problems were formulated during the seventeenth and eighteenth centuries and, for the most part, it has not abandoned the criteria of rationality that were then forged.

Nowhere is this more evident than in the philosophy of religion. The very idea of studying religion independently of any theological content emerged from rationalist premises. In his essay "What Is Enlightenment?" Kant distinguished what he called "private reason," that is, reason serving religious or civil institutions, from "public reason," which is critical and analytic. Only the latter is truly enlightened, and one of its tasks consists of rethinking and revamping those institutions.

Philosophers came to feel that they were in charge of the subject matter of their speculation as well as of the reflection upon it. Thus philosophical theology, or "theodicy" as it was mostly called, defined itself as standing outside religion (*about* religion) rather than consisting of faith's own inner dynamic outreach. Modern philosophers have kept themselves at a methodic distance from the religion they philosophized about, accepting neither its experience nor its object as genuine until they had it autonomously rethought. What Kolakowski writes about the academic treatment of religious myths applies equally well to faith: First it assumed that myths, as they are explicitly told and believed, have a latent meaning behind their ostensible one and that . . . this latent meaning, accessible only to the outsider-anthropologist, is the meaning *par excellence*, whereas the ostensible one, i.e., the myth as understood by the believers, has the function of concealing the former.[1] The problem is not necessarily remedied by believing

1. Leszek Kolakowski, *Religion* (New York: Oxford University Press, 1982), 15. Rob-

philosophers who attempt to defend the validity of their faith in the light of reason alone. Strange as it may appear, philosophical rationalism may easily survive in a religious and even in a fundamentalist environment. The guiding assumption thereby appears to be that the entire created order, including revelation itself, is one rationally coherent expression of an intrinsically "rational" God. Precisely this rationalist presumption conveys to such arguments the spare and bare look that renders them rarely convincing to other believers and never to unbelievers.

How strongly our earlier philosophical tradition differed from this abstract rationalism can be seen in Plato and the Presocratics. In key passages of *Republic, Symposium, Phaedrus,* and *Phaedo,* myths determine the scope and the very meaning of the philosophical project. Plato, our first master in logical argument and methodic reasoning, fully continues to accept the older reflection expressed in mythical narratives as the sole avenue leading to the deeper and darker recesses of existence. Cautioning us not to trust the myth uncritically, he nevertheless considers it indispensable in the pursuit of wisdom. Even Aristotle felt increasingly that the language of the myth was irreducible to purely rational discourse. For the early Christian writers, the very words of faith defined the measure of adoptability of the ancient pagan philosophy. Philosophy, to them, obeyed faith's intrinsic call to reflection. Thus the principle *fides quaerens intellectum* remained for a millennium the heart and inspiration of philosophical reflection on faith.

In this paper, I intend to return to the approach that prevailed before philosophy cut the umbilical cord from religious wisdom. In doing so, I do not revert to a precritical past, but merely follow the example of philosophers in their recent attitude to the physical sciences as well as that of sociologists and anthropologists with respect to religion itself. In matters concerning the meaning and purpose of life, one can philosophize only from within the subject. To study religion as a complete outsider is to reduce faith to the carriers of its meaning—historical events, social behavior, psychological symbols—while neglecting the meaning itself they carry. I do not mean to reduce philosophy to theology, as I would by requiring that the philosopher fully accept the principles, dogmas, and narratives of the faith he studies. But I consider it a minimal condition for the understanding of that faith. To grasp the meaning of the religious act, one must be

---

ert Wilken, who quotes this text in his presidential address for the American Academy of Religion ("Who Will Speak *For* the Religious Traditions?") convinces me that the academic attitude toward religion extends far beyond philosophy.

able to share, at least ideally, in the believer's faith. This means not, as Scheler once argued, that a living faith is a necessary condition for a philosophical study of religion, but that some inner experience that is more than a purely extrinsic acquaintance with the religious act is required.[2]

Theodicy today enjoys the dubious reputation of a failed experiment. Few outside the small circle of persistent believers in it would grant that it has succeeded in accomplishing what it set out to do. That failure has become more painfully apparent as our sensitivity to, and the increased visibility of, evil, both moral and physical, have intensified our questioning. The sheer magnitude of evil that our age has witnessed in death camps, nuclear warfare, internecine tribal or racial conflicts has lowered our tolerance level for what once was accepted as a necessary part of life. Indeed, the presence of evil has impressed itself more powerfully than the presence of God upon the minds of many of our contemporaries, for whom the primary question is no longer how God can tolerate so much evil, but rather how the more tangible reality of evil still allows the possibility of God's existence. Beyond religious and ideological differences, our contemporaries have attained a remarkable agreement that evil "was not meant to be," that it constitutes an alien invasion into our lives. To an unprecedented degree we feel the need to "justify" the presence of evil in our world. Yet we have lowered or abandoned our expectations to receive an adequate answer to the question *Unde malum?* from philosophy. Indeed, speculative attempts to reduce the question to a theoretical issue tend to render the reality of evil less rather than more acceptable.

Evil invites philosophical speculation, yet it is the cliff on which philosophy suffers shipwreck. By a paradox unique to our time, we remain simultaneously aware of both terms of the opposition. Schopenhauer anticipated the paradox when he wrote: "Without doubt it is the knowledge of death, and along with this the consideration of the suffering and misery of life, which gives the strongest impulse to philosophical reflection and metaphysical explanation of the world. If our life were endless and painless, it would perhaps occur to no one to ask why the world exists, and is just this kind of world it is."[3] Two distinct philosophical reactions have emerged. Some contemporary thinkers attempt to repair by one philosophy the damage wrought by

2. Louis Dupré, *The Other Dimension* (New York: Doubleday, 1972), 109–11.
3. Arthur Schopenhauer, *The World as Will and Representation*, Supplemental chap. XVII (added to sec. 15), trans. in *Schopenhauer Selections*, ed. H. DeWitt Parker (New York: Charles Scribner's Sons, 1928), 283.

another, believing that what has been philosophically misstated can be philosophically corrected. Logicians have endeavored to point out the many *non sequiturs* that lead to the conclusion—"Hence an omnipotent, omniscient, good God cannot exist." Rightly. A remedial strategy alone does not suffice, however, particularly when its authors fail to question the premises that inspired the objections.

An essential factor to account for theodicy's failure is that it uses a concept of religion in which the believer will hardly recognize his or her own. As Kant defined it, theodicy consists in "the defense of the supreme wisdom of the Creator (*Urheber*) of the world against the charges raised by reason on the basis of what conflicts with a meaningful order (*Zweckwidrig*) in the world."[4] The God whom this theodicy attempts to defend is a God who has not revealed himself and has never been personally involved in human history. It is, in fact, the God of Deism, whom only the tenuous thread of a vague concept of causality (in creation) connects with the Christian, Jewish, or Moslem one. Theodicy thereby takes its place within the kind of purely autonomous philosophical theology that, independently of any intrinsically religious support, proclaims itself adequate to provide the idea of God both with a content and a full proof of its reality. Refusing to include the expressions of living faith (whether they be revealed, spiritual, or even mythical) in its attempt to reconcile the existence of evil with its concept of God, it redefines the relation between God and the world as one of rational necessity. If God is to act in accordance with the rational maxims philosophy attributes to him, then creation must with equal necessity reflect the rational nature of its Creator. The relation from God to the world becomes thereby convertible with the one from the world to God. Theodicy becomes indissolubly associated with the so-called physico-theological proof for the existence of God. After the onslaughts of Hume and Kant had shown just how vulnerable that part of philosophical theology is, the decline of theodicy as a purely rational, philosophical enterprise began. The Christian or Jew has, of course, even more fundamental reasons for feeling dissatisfied with a theodicy that deprives the idea of God from the entire revealed or spiritual content that made it religiously meaningful to their faith. Against this impoverished Deist reflection on the mystery of evil, they have persistently denied that logic alone suffices to make sense of suffering and evil. "One has actually to meet religious people, Buddhists, Hindus, Christians, Jews, Muslims, and see how they in fact confront the world's evil, if one is going to grasp something of the

---

4. Kant, *Werke* (Berlin Akademie ed.), VIII, 255.

resources of religion for coping with suffering and wrong."[5] In adopting this approach, the philosopher does not renege his philosophical method. He treats the religious sources as "hypothetical" signposts in his reflection, that is, independently of the absolute authority they enjoy within the religious community. Their function consists in providing the models and patterns that convey a concrete content to our relation with a transcendent absolute.[6] In choosing canonical texts for reflection, philosophers may well be guided by a private acceptance of their authority, as long as that authority does not become a substitute for reflection.

Here it may be appropriate to remind ourselves that not all religious traditions share the same assumptions, and hence there is no single "religious answer" to evil. Positions vary from a total dualism between two ultimate principles of good and evil in Manicheism to a denial of evil as an illusion in the more radical Buddhist and Vedantic monist schools. Between these two extremes, theist responses range from an evil inherent in the finite condition as such to evil as being the sole responsibility of the human race (through the fall and subsequent sins). Evil provokes, of course, the strongest reaction among such monotheists as Jews, Christians, and Moslems, who consider all finite being the creation of a free God. Within those faiths themselves, responses have varied as reflection developed. Judaism alone presents several models. According to the archaic retaliation model, God inflicts suffering as a punishment for human sin. But, one might wonder, why should humans, created by God, commit sin? Israel never ceased to struggle with this question, and many felt compelled to look in a different direction. One alternative model delays the overcoming of evil till a future time of history. But why should creation have to pass through evil in order to achieve final good? In the face of such major difficulties, two different models emerged. The Book of Job concludes that humans are not in a position to question God's inscrutable decrees, whereas Deutero-Isaiah, in his description of the suffering servant, equally desists seeking the origin of suffering or its future goal, but reveals suffering itself as intrinsically redemptive.

Christianity adopted all four of these models, but connected the idea of punishment primarily to Adam's fall, while grounding the idea of redemptive suffering in the passion and death of Christ. Yet as

5. Brian Hebblethwaite, *Evil, Suffering and Religion* (London: Sheldon Press, 1976), 10.

6. For a justification of such a "hypothetical" use of intrinsically religious sources in philosophy, the reader may consult my "Blondel's Reflection on Experience" in *A Dubious Heritage: Philosophy of Religion After Kant* (New York: The Paulist Press, 1977).

Christian thinkers began to incorporate these insights within ancient philosophies that were not fully compatible with them, problems developed. Thus St. Augustine accepted the Neo-Platonic idea that evil consists in a lack of being—a *privatio boni*. As John Hick has shown, this solution, suitable for an order of being in which necessary emanations move down from the One, causes serious difficulties in a universe *freely* created by God. While the Neo-Platonic One is not responsible for all the ills inherent in the lower realm that necessarily emanates from it, a free, omnipotent Creator chooses what is to exist. Augustine, who was chiefly responsible for establishing this privative conception of evil in the West, attempted to counter the objection by means of a Greek aesthetics of form. Creation would be less formally perfect without contrasts, including the one between good and evil. Needless to say, such an aesthetic principle of perfection, that requires the presence of moral evil and that results in the final damnation of most moral agents, hardly suits the Christian ideas of God's goodness and of the individual's responsibility for evil. The God of love preached in the Gospel of salvation here has made room for an Olympian Artist of dramatic form. Nor does one soften that grim picture much by declaring that the Creator merely allows moral evil, as long as God remains capable of freely creating a world that contains less suffering and less moral evil. "One cannot say both that God is blameless in respect of the natural evil in our world, because He alone allows it as something inseparable from the world's good, *and* that He could, had He wished, have created a better world in which there would have been less natural evil."[7] Augustine obviates any divine obligation to create a better world by the idea of contrast, while he uses the *privatio boni* (hardly suitable for aesthetic contrast) to acquit God from any complicity with the evil needed for that contrast.

II

From the preceding it appears how the adoption of pre-Christian philosophies originally resulted in logical incongruities. In the area of theodicy, however, the most questionable assumption thus adopted may well have been that of an idea of the good independent of, and logically prior to, God's creative act. It thereby imposed upon God the obligation to create the best possible world. Leibniz formulated the thesis most succinctly when he stated that God owed it to his

7. John Hick, *Evil and the God of Love* (San Francisco: Harper and Row, 1978), 105; see also 70–78.

goodness to create the best possible world. He thereby assumed that we *know* what divine goodness must be; next, that an omnipotent, good God must be able and willing to bestow that goodness upon creation in the highest degree compatible with contingency. But how am I, from my finite position, able to conceive what the self-expressive acting of a divine nature implies or does not imply?

Ignorant of what the divine expression in a contingent world includes or excludes, we know even less what the *maximum* goodness would entail. Bergson dismissed the entire idea in a few lapidary sentences.

> I can, at a stretch, represent something in my mind when I hear of the sumtotal of existing things, but in the sum-total of the non-existent I can see nothing but a string of words. So that here again the objection is based on a pseudo-idea, a verbal entity. But we can go further still: the objection arises from a whole series of arguments implying a radical defect of method. A certain representation is built up *a priori,* and it is taken for granted that this is the idea of God; from thence are deduced the characteristics that the world ought to show; and if the world does not actually show them, we are told that God does not exist.[8]

One imposes no limitation upon divine perfection by declaring God unable to achieve what conflicts with the nature of the finite. But finite being is intrinsically imperfect, and any definition of the degree of perfection depends itself on finite, that is, imperfect, norms. All we can do is look at the concrete, visible result of that expression we call creation. Precisely with respect to creation, theodicy ought to follow a procedure opposite to the one it follows when it decrees that God must be good and omnipotent by standards of human rationality and that therefore the world must be good, that is, conform to the same a priori standards. A genuinely religious theodicy begins by accepting creation as it is (including its evil) as a visible expression of God's nature, rather than by dictating a priori what such an expression must be like, as the Deist does. As we shall see, such an attitude does not condemn theodicy to blind faith, for it must explore the relation between what it may learn of the divine attributes and their visible expression, and it may in the end find that expression unintelligible or even unacceptable by human standards of goodness. But it should not begin with a narrowly rationalist definition of divine goodness, nor ought it to base its judgment on the goodness of creation without

8. Henri Bergson, *The Two Sources of Morality and Religion,* trans. Ashley Andra and Cloudesly Brereton (Garden City: Doubleday, 1951), 261. See also James Felt's pertinent remarks in "God's Choice: Reflections on Evil in a Created World," *Faith and Philosophy* 1, no. 4 (1984), 370–77.

taking into account faith's entire presentation of it—which includes redemption.

In addition, we might consider that the "rational" idea of a divine choice with an antecedent moment of deliberation and a consequent moment of decision, patterned after the model of human persons deliberating about several alternatives, is itself heavily anthropomorphic.

In God Himself essence and existence converge and this implies that His will is identical with His essence. God neither obeys rules which are valid regardless of His will nor produces these rules according to His whims or as the result of deliberating various options; He is those rules. Unlike humans, God never faces alternative possibilities and then freely decides which of them He ought to choose; His decisions are necessary aspects of His Being—and therefore they could not have been different from what they are; yet they are free in the sense that no superior powers, no norms of validity independent of God, bind Him. He *is* what He does, decides, orders. Consequently we may say neither that the definitions of what is good and true precede God, . . . nor that He precedes them.[9]

At this point in the discussion the argument frequently takes a different turn. Could at least moral evil—and with it, all the physical pain it trails in its wake—not have been avoided? Both adversaries and advocates of the traditional brand of theodicy tend to agree that it could have been. Thus Antony Flew argues that for an action to be free it suffices that it not be compelled—which entails not that it is unpredictable, but that the person nevertheless could have acted differently had he chosen to do so. From these premises he concludes that an omnipotent Creator could have created persons who would always (or more often) have acted rightly.[10] J. L. Mackie concurs. Human beings could have been so constituted as freely to choose the good. The idea of a God who could not control men's actions leads to what he calls the "paradox of omnipotence."[11] But how the idea of a will determined always to choose the good remains compatible with freedom escapes me. A freedom created with a greater resistance to evil appears a most questionable concept. Freedom is far more than the power to say "yes" or "no" to divinely preestablished values with or without a divine impulse toward one or the other. Its signal characteristic consists not in the power to ratify preestablished values but in the ability to create them. Freedom can tolerate contingency and

9. Leszek Kolakowski, *Religion,* cited above, 25.

10. Antony Flew, "Divine Omnipotence and Human Freedom," in *New Essays in Philosophical Theology,* eds. Flew and MacIntyre (London: SCM Press, 1965), 152.

11. J. L. Mackie, "Evil and Omnipotence," *Mind,* LXIV, no. 254 (1955), 200–12. Reprinted in *God and Evil,* ed. Nelson Pike (Englewood Cliffs, N.J.: Prentice-Hall, 1964), 46–60. Reference to p. 57.

an extremely restricted field of operation. But to interfere with its creative source is to replace freedom by causality. Creativity constitutes its very essence. Both theists and atheists admit freedom to be "given," but it is not given in the way of causal determination. Even a wholly preestablished order of values reduces its scope. Most of us agree on that point when it comes to humanly induced unconscious conditioning (including hypnosis), such as B. F. Skinner proposes for the improvement of society as a whole. But the same objection holds true for any divine "conditioning." Even a divinely preestablished order leaves man none but a negative creativity, as Sartre perceived. Yet, strangely enough, this inauthentic, reduced freedom of choice, the very same one they reject in predestinationist theologies, is the one secular critics of theodicy propose as the only viable alternative to man's unlimited capacity for committing evil.

God creates neither values nor strong or weak inclinations to choose them: he creates creators who depend on a divine source for the exercise of their creative spontaneity, but not for its determination. Now, a freedom responsible for creating its own values remains intrinsically and irrevocably able to erect false absolutes and even to invert creative impulse into annihilating power. It is endowed with a capacity unlimited for evil as well as for good. In creating free agents, God has released a power that may turn against himself. In Berdyaev's words: "Evil presupposes freedom and there is no freedom without the freedom of evil, that is to say, there is no freedom in the state of compulsory good."[12]

Another questionable assumption that entered theodicy from the Aristotelian-Neo-Platonic philosophical tradition is that God and creation remain totally separate. What concerns the creature does not affect God and neither does the creature have any impact on God. A philosophy that denies any real relation between God and the world is not in a good position to defend God against the charge of indifference to the suffering of his creatures. But if philosophy were capable of accepting that the sufferings of creation, including the suffering caused by human evil, affect the Creator himself, evil would cease to be the creature's lone burden in the face of an omnipotent, impassible Creator. A number of philosophical systems broadly comprehended under the general name of "process philosophy" have attempted to justify such a divine participation in finite processes. Despite essential disagreements concerning the relation between the

12. Nicholas Berdyaev, *The Divine and the Human*, trans. R. M. French (London: Geoffrey Bles, 1948), 92.

finite and the infinite, divine personhood, the role and ultimate destiny of human individuals, all these systems share Whitehead's overall vision of the real as a creative process, whereby God comes to be with his creation rather than above it. In Whitehead's terms: "He shares with every new creation its actual world."[13] Indeed, only through the creative process does God attain that full actuality to which Whitehead refers as God's "consequent" nature. Rather than being an unchanging, transcendent Prime Mover, God is the actual entity from which each creative development in time "receives that initial aim from which its self-causation starts."[14] Various philosophers have interpreted this divine participation in various ways, ranging from an impersonal "creative event," the source of all human good (Wieman), to a creative personalism (Brightman). But only when the idea of a personal God is preserved can process philosophy contribute toward making the monotheist position with respect to evil more acceptable.

Peter Bertocci in *The Goodness of God* shares this concern and first establishes that a creative force resulting in human persons must itself be personal. But such a Creator-Person need not be conceived as self-sufficient, uninhibited by restraints other than those he imposes upon himself. If personhood reaches its highest realization in interpersonal communication, then the perfection of the divine Creator would likewise culminate, rather than weaken, in responding to persons. Furthermore, such a divine Person exposes himself to risks analogous to those run by humans in their attempts to create good—what Bertocci calls "creative insecurity." "Insecurity inheres in the very nature of being a person whose actual freedom of personal choice is involved in the pursuit of truth and goodness. Intrinsic to the good for persons is the insecurity that can become creative, because values are compenetrating, and because persons themselves can choose orchestration-within-pattern as they change and grow."[15] Bertocci surpasses this bold application of the personalist principle to the Absolute by an even more daring one. For he reads in the insecurity of the creative act the expression of a fundamental uncertainty, one that affects the very nature of the Creator-Person. A refractory element, not a "flaw" in the divine or an impediment imposed upon the divine, but the essential passivity inherent in the very act whereby the Absolute gives birth

13. Alfred North Whitehead, *Process and Reality* (New York: Macmillan, 1929), 521.
14. Ibid., 374.
15. Peter Bertocci, *The Goodness of God* (Washington, D.C.: University Press of America, 1981), 267. John Dewey made the point in a general way when writing: "No mode of action can . . . give anything approaching absolute certitude; it provides insurance but no assurance." *The Quest for Certainty* (1929) (New York: G. P. Putnam's Sons, Capricorn Books, 1960), 33.

to the relative, prevents the Creator from achieving his goals without at the same time having to allow the possible intrusion of suffering and evil.

With this conclusion, an admirably consistent philosopher joins the very axiom from which all gnostic, theosophical systems start and that many spiritual theologies assume, namely, that for finite being to be possible, infinite Being must create an emptiness (Maurice Blondel called it an "annihilation") within itself. "Created" being is by definition dependent being. The Creator must sustain, support, and nurture it *from within*. If the creature cannot subsist without the divine act to which it owes its existence, then the creature continues to inhere in that divine act as its "otherness," for outside that act nothing could support the dependent being of the finite. In the very act of creation, then, a God immanent in the finite introduces a passive factor within *himself*. Christians and Jews insist on calling God "the Creator of all that is," but they appear less anxious to accept the consequences of this principle. Following Aristotle's definition of God as pure act they tend to take it more or less for granted that passivity must be excluded from God. Yet if pure act is translated as pure activity, it is no less anthropomorphic than passivity. To "act," as we know it, means to react effectively upon events and circumstances. It estranges the acting subject from itself in order to enable it to return to itself in a different way. The agent loses himself in order to find himself anew. But, independently of creation, this kind of acting does not apply to God, who is no more "active" than passive, but rests within himself. In order to "act" as Creator, however, the Infinite must in some way render itself passive.

III

At this point the question may rise whether the concept of creation as it was presented in the preceding section, far from supporting theodicy, does not dispense with the need for it altogether. If we assume that God, in the act of creation, acquires a kind of passivity with respect to his creatures, especially the free ones, what warrants our attributing the predicate "good" to him? How could we continue to call "good" a Creator who must decline all responsibility once his work exists? If we accept the Deist thesis (still present in most modern theodicies) that whatever we know of God's relation to the world must be restricted to what reason can attain on the basis of a "common," that is, not specifically religious, experience, the only alternative consists in the total silence about God of negative theology.

Precisely on this point, our project differs from a purely rational theodicy. For in addition to a common, religiously neutral experience, it takes account of the theology, and indeed the experience, of redemption. Such a broader basis, however, does not dispense the religious thinker from having to meet all the conditions required by a philosophical method. Now, one negative but basic condition for admitting specifically religious considerations (based upon particular experience or revelation) into our evaluation of the world is that they never be held to justify calling "good" a creation that may produce unqualified evil and unredeemed suffering without God "doing something" about it. Yet human beings, endowed with a freedom of causing unqualified evil and a sensitivity capable of unlimited suffering, may at any moment actualize this possibility. How can God prevent them from doing so without transforming their nature and limiting their freedom? Christian philosophy has traditionally viewed creation as a continuing divine act. But, if continuing, this act confronts ever different situations to which it must creatively respond. A divine response then may counteract existing evil by offering ever new occasions for the accomplishment of good or the redemption of evil. Without having to interfere directly with the creature's specific nature, it may provide novel opportunities for converting evil into goodness. Christian writers have consistently upheld this divine ability to restore creation to new innocence. Thus Jacques Maritain suggestively argues: "Each time that a free creature undoes for its part the work that God makes, God remakes to that extent—for the better—this work and leads it to higher ends. Because of the presence of evil on earth, everything on earth, from the beginning to the end of time, is in perpetual recasting."[16] To be sure, the ways in which God actively counteracts evil, in a creation increasingly threatened by it, remain beyond a philosophical explanation based upon a universal but abstract concept of human nature. Theology informs us that God may offer ever new occasions to convert past evil into new goodness. It may show how, in a condition antagonistic to good, such a reversal must necessarily take the form of a struggle, an *agon*. It may even claim that God himself had to provide both the means and the model of this conversion by suffering and dying under the power of evil. But in thus linking the mystery of evil in creation to the even greater mystery of redemption, it decidedly leaves the domain of philosophy and introduces considerations (based on spiritual experiences) not available to a universal, autonomous reflection on reality.

16. Jacques Maritain, *God and the Permission of Evil*, trans. Joseph Evans (Milwaukee: Bruce, 1966), 86.

To admit such a move into philosophical reflection ought to be justified more thoroughly than this essay allows.[17] Yet at least one critically significant factor ought to be mentioned: the very standards by which we measure what does and what does not count as "good" depend upon the acceptance or rejection of an intrinsically religious hierarchization of values. Any attempts to erect a system of values upon a religiously neutral basis, common to believers and unbelievers, will fail precisely in the area where theodicy matters most, namely, where evil begins and good ends. In a recent essay, Marilyn McCord Adams has shown how ontological commitments affect descriptions of values. Moral theories that omit any reference to a transcendent norm differ from value systems ruled by a relation to transcendent Being. More specifically, varying ontological commitments "widen or narrow the range of options for defeating evil with good."[18] The believer, not satisfied with exclusively immanent goods may value an intimate sense of God's presence, acquired through much pain and suffering, more highly than a satisfaction of immediate needs. But different value systems result in different judgments concerning standards of good and evil in the universe.[19] Indeed, in the entire evaluation of what constitutes unnecessary evil and what constitutes ultimate goodness, the believer often fundamentally disagrees with the nonbeliever. Diametrically opposed attitudes concerning the desirability of terminating an unwanted pregnancy appear totally irrational if we do not take this fundamental disagreement on values into account. To recognize distinctions in the understanding of what in the final analysis constitutes evil need not result in the kind of verbal equivocity on good and evil resulting in "an incomprehensible attribute of an incomprehensible substance," which J. S. Mill denounced.[20] Yet it should caution us against deciding prematurely what must count as unredeemably evil and what as unconditionally good. Once we introduce value judgments based on factors that fall beyond the range of a "common" appraisal of what benefits or harms human nature, we admit intrinsically private considerations into theodicy. I would argue that to do so is not only permissible—it is necessary.

The unbridgeable gap that separates the believer from the nonbe-

17. For a more substantial discussion, see Louis Dupré, *The Other Dimension*, chap. 3, "Religious Faith and Philosophical Reflection."

18. Marilyn McCord Adams, "Problems of Evil: More Advice to Christian Philosophers," in *Faith and Philosophy* 5 (April 1988), 129.

19. Alvin Plantinga has already argued for this position in "The Probabilistic Argument from Evil," in *Philosophical Studies* 35 (1979), 46–47.

20. John Stuart Mill, *An Examination of Sir William Hamilton's Philosophy* (London: Longmans, Green, 1872), 128.

liever does not render the project of theodicy impossible, but it changes its nature from being "purely" philosophical to one in which philosophy requires the assistance of specifically religious elements. Even if the immediate experience of evil and suffering would appear to outweigh the good of living, such a conclusion need not be final. Nor need its rejection be based upon an anticipation of future well-being. The believer may experience suffering itself as redemptive, that is, as endowed with more than a merely negative meaning. "Grace and nature not being two closed worlds, but two worlds open to one another and in mutual communication, it might happen that the greater progress (of the wheat over that of the cockle) would occur more in the order of grace than in that of nature."[21] To refer to different modes of experiencing is not to advance an exotic claim, but merely to repeat what eminent psychologists of religion, beginning with William James, have persistently asserted. Precisely this difference in experience clearly appears in spiritual theologies of various kinds, as well as in ancient myths and modern religious literature.

Before admitting such reports of a religious experience to which philosophy has no direct access, we must remind ourselves that they merely "respond," so to speak, in a nonphilosophical manner, to questions legitimately raised by philosophy. Philosophy may reflect on theological, mythical, and mystical expressions, categorize and criticize them from its own standpoint, possibly learn from them new avenues to explore, but it can never incorporate them within itself. I shall restrict my examples to Christian and Jewish sources, thus eliminating extreme dualist and monist ones from consideration. Even within that narrow compound, significant traditions deviate from canonical interpretations. Primary among those are the gnostic and theosophical ones—some as old as Christianity itself. Yet they deserve our full attention because, within the monotheist tradition, they alone among Jewish and Christian sects have pursued the mystery of evil all the way to the divine realm itself. A process of fragmentation, according to these sources, originates within the divine unity. Depending upon which stage of the process they emphasize—the confluence of the two opposite principles, or their total separation once they leave the divine realm—gnostic interpretations of evil assume a monist or a dualist quality. Yet both readings remain intrinsically connected. One focuses on the cause, the primeval unity within which the pretemporal "event" occurs that results in the expulsion of a "created," extra-divine realm. The other concentrates on the effect, the state of alienation within

21. Jacques Maritain, cited above, 89.

which good and evil stand diametrically opposed to one another as two irreducibly antagonistic powers. Most gnostic theologies trace the origin of evil to the emanation of an intra-divine multiplicity from a primeval unity—a multiplicity that in itself contains neither good nor evil but gives rise to it. Only after a mysterious fall disturbs the harmony of this multiplicity within the realm of divine unity, the possibility of conflict originates. The physical world, outcome of this intra-divine event, reflects the unrest and conflict of the primeval disturbance.[22]

We may, of course, dismiss such daring speculations as unworthy of philosophical attention. But before doing so we ought to consider that major philosophers, beginning with Plato, have persistently turned to ancient mythical and religious interpretations that trace the origin of good and evil to a single transcendent source. Even in some modern secular thinkers, we still hear an echo of this ancient concern to reduce the opposition between good and evil to a secondary development resulting from a separation of contraries complementarily united in the Absolute. Thus in Karl Jaspers's memorable treatment of "The Law of the Day and the Passion for the Night," night and day appear as two complementary elements in the Absolute.[23] Absolutizing either one of them will create the false absolute of evil. Such speculations on complementarity within the Absolute do not justify evil or suffering; they merely attempt to articulate that all finitude implies loss and separation. In metaphorical language they express what I earlier referred to as the "passivity" that accompanies the act whereby the infinite gives birth to the finite. Orthodox monotheist theologies have never accepted that creation itself is the fall, or that distinctions or separations "within" God account for the existence of evil in creation. Rightly, because the gnostic myths and their theosophical interpretations result in theological inconsistencies, as well as in morally problematic attitudes. But their radical attempt to trace the possibility of evil back to the divine act of creation continues to invite reflection.

The same holds true for those religious and mythical representa-

22. Cf. Hans Jonas, *The Gnostic Religion* (Boston: Beacon Press, 1963). Also Claude Tresmontant, *A Study of Hebrew Thought* (New York: Desclée de Brouwer, 1960), especially 13–14 for a comparison with more orthodox Christian and Jewish theologies of creation.

23. Karl Jaspers, *Philosophy* III, trans. E. B. Ashton (Chicago: The University of Chicago Press, 1971), 90. William Blake had, long before, expressed this complementarity in his *Prophetic Books*, where we read: "Without contraries is no progression. Attraction and repulsion, reason and energy, love and hate are necessary to human existence. From the contraries spring what the religious call good and evil. Good is the passive that obeys reason; evil is the active springing from energy." William Blake: *The Marriage of Heaven and Hell* (beginning).

tions that oppose good and evil as two irreducibly antagonistic powers that appear to belong to different spiritual universes. Where gnostic theologies reduce good and evil to a common origin, dualistic theologies absolutize the power of evil to a positive reality irreducible to that of the good. While traditional theology was forced to describe evil as nonbeing, thinkers impressed by the all-too-real power of evil have attributed to it a substantiality equal with that of the good. The awesome power of evil gives it a transcendence capable of attracting a diabolical worship of its own. Poets such as Rimbaud and Baudelaire, novelists such as Emily Brontë and Herman Melville, felt that, in its extreme form, evil surpasses the individual perpetrator. The shudder that came over the West when after the war the massive horror of the extermination camps stood revealed suddenly rendered those conceptions intelligible.[24] Yet precisely when conceived in its purity, evil appears to establish a dialectical link with the good, and indeed to express its subordination to it. As Sartre observed of those who commit evil simply because it is evil: "Faire le mal pour le mal, c'est faire tout exprès le contraire de ce que l'on continue d'affirmer comme le bien."[25]

Yet the principal link between good and evil, for Christian thinkers, consists, of course, in the redemptive power of suffering—the mystical transformation that takes the sting of meaninglessness out of pain and that bends moral evil back to goodness. On this theme, central to Christians as well as to many Moslems and Jews, philosophical theodicy has remained mute, unless one chooses to regard its common thesis that suffering presents an occasion for the exercise of virtue as

24. Arthur Cohen, *The Tremendum* (New York: Crossroad, 1981), passim, especially 33.

25. Jean-Paul Sartre, *Baudelaire* (Paris, 1946), 80. In Emily Brontë's *Wuthering Heights* we catch a glimpse of the negative link that joins the totally forbidden to the good. The depth of moral depravity here evoked once again confronts us with the archaic dialectic of the pure and the impure, which both share the realm of the sacred. Evil reveals itself as the other side of the good—a good pursued at the exclusion of all others and thereby acquiring an equal degree of reality. Good indiscreetly pursued turns into evil. In the fear of trespassing the boundaries of the humanly permissible lies perhaps the root of Aristotle's emphasis on the median position of virtue. In *Moby Dick*, the perversion of the good assumes the form of a demonic desire to destroy evil. Precisely by projecting all evil on the white whale and then relentlessly pursuing it, Ahab becomes what Melville describes as "the ungodly godlike man." Absolutely opposed to evil, virtue itself turns into evil. In the Manichean universe, good defines itself exclusively by its relation to evil and evil has no other object but the destruction of the good. The transcendent power of evil and its ambiguous relation to the good has remained a major theme in contemporary literature. Graham Greene, Julien Green, François Mauriac, George Bernanos all tend to view the world in starkly Jansenist contrasts between good and evil, where the saint is locked in an unceasing battle with the "prince of this world" and where the sinner in the deepest abyss encounters the face of God.

a distant echo of it. The mystery of Christ's passion and death plays a decisive role in the Christian's evaluation of good and evil. It also introduces suffering into God's own life. Needless to repeat, philosophy is incompetent to pass a final judgment on such a conversion of problem into mystery. But before dismissing the theological answer as an escape from rationality into mystification, the philosopher ought to consider whether the reference to mystery is truly an assault on reason. In the light of the preceding interpretation of the finite and the infinite, he or she may then discover that the meaning of Christ's passion and death consists not in a ransom paid to "the lord of this world," nor in a satisfaction exacted by an angry God, as primitive theologies have presented it, but in the fact that God has assumed human finitude and descended into the abyss of creaturely suffering, even the one created by the effects of moral evil.

No writer has pursued the theme of suffering redemptive through God's participation in it further into its mysterious depths than Dostoevskii. Essays on theodicy routinely refer to Ivan Karamazov's charge against a God who tolerates unredeemable suffering—the pain of innocent children, of animals, of the many who lack the capacity to learn from pain. But they leave out Alyosha's later reply. Alyosha admits the full scandal of innocent pain and, even as his brother, refuses to accept it. But he assumes this scandal into the even greater one of God's own suffering. When, dying on the cross, Christ feels abandoned by his Father, the tragic conflict enters God's own being. In this intra-divine *theologia crucis,* God is set against God, as in Goethe's dark saying: *Nemo contra Deum nisi Deus ipse* ("No one against God but God himself ").[26] In Christ, God shares all human suffering and takes upon himself the burden of all moral evil. In addition, as the legend of the Grand Inquisitor suggests, he must face the failure of a salvation that surpasses the capacity of acceptance of most of those to whom it is offered. This greater scandal does not "justify" evil, but it makes God a participant in our pain, as Christian theologies have consistently implied, and mystical and theosophical ones have explicitly asserted. Mystics, from Catherine of Siena to Teresa of Avila, from Francis of Assisi to Ignatius of Loyola, have consistently felt a desire to share in that divine suffering.

On the cross, philosophy suffers shipwreck, atheists and believers unanimously declare. But that does not dispense the believing philosopher from the task of showing that, in its concrete, theological setting,

26. Cf., Luigi Pareyson, "La sofferenza inutile in Dostoevskij" in *Giornale di metafisica* 4 (1982), 123–70.

the belief in a good God is not incompatible with the full recognition of the existence of evil. In Christianity, that concrete setting includes, beyond the order of creation, the entire course of redemption culminating in Christ's death and resurrection. The mystery of evil, then, presents itself to the Christian with a far greater complexity than to the rationalist philosopher. God himself here appears vulnerable, capable of suffering, and subject to the effects of human evil. In the end, as Hegel once remarked, only actual religious worship is able to overcome evil. Religion alone finds the proper attitude for what emerged as a mystery within religion itself. To admit this, far from abandoning the rational method of philosophy, is, in fact, the only way to prevent that method from reducing a transcendent mystery to a logical problem.

Yale University

Index

~~INVOICE~~ RECEIPT   № 6820

C. K. Broadhurst & Co. Ltd.

BOOKSELLERS
5 & 7 MARKET STREET
SOUTHPORT
MERSEYSIDE, PR8 1HD

Tel: (01704) 532064/534110
Fax: (01704) 542009

28th February 1995

JOHN PERRY

1 × PROSPECTS FOR NATURAL		
THEOLOGY	£51	50
	V.A.T.	

Receipts not posted unless requested.
V.A.T. Reg. No. 164 2880 54

Prospects for Natural Theology
was composed in 10/12
Baskerville by Brevis Press
and printed and bound by
Thomson-Shore, Inc.